1 — The Fall of Icarus
2 — Beyond the boundaries of human sight
3 — Between Earth & Moon
4 — In that dark house
5 — Their backyard
6 — Riddle
7 — Something quite startling
8 — The blind musician
9 — Reaching out
10 — He won't bite
11 — They lived there a long time ago
12 — The wanderers
13 — A barren place
14 — Woodgatherers
15 — Carrying water
16 — Burning grass
17 — Food for thought
18 — Give us this day
19 — Our daily bread
20 — Misunderstood
21 — Thirst conquers all
22 — Tryst
23 — Life goes on
24 — Sick humour
25 — We are the Roman soldiers
26 — Confidences
27 — Spitting flames
28 — Mending nets
29 — A simple meal
30 — Mask
31 — We're not afraid
32 — But why don't we get married?
33 — The eavesdropper
34 — I didn't mean it that way
35 — Lovers' quarrel
36 — Mine is the silent face
37 — A handful of thorns
38 — Nocturne
39 — Night flight
40 — The moon, passing, sees nothing
41 — Dij alweer tyd om op te staan
42 — The sun also rises
43 — Walking between reeds
44 — A small backyard
45 — Lines of flight
46 — The other side of the wall
47 — Today
48 — The window is open
49 — Ambition
50 — Someday I'm going to try to fly high
51 — Hold fast to dreams

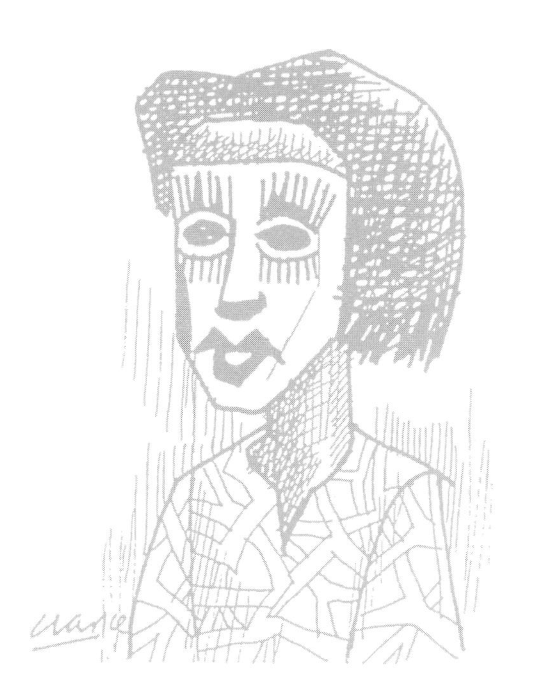

It's funny — in a way — how immediately behind a mask you've become transformed into another person. You are no longer who you used to be. For a moment you ask yourself who you are if you aren't who you are. The whole world, of which you were a part, now exists only on the outside of the mask. You, on the inside, behind the mask, have taken on the external face of another character.

You could play games with people & with yourself. You can go on questioning yourself about your true existence disguised as someone else — until in the end the whole thing becomes so complicated that you find yourself wondering why a stranger's mind & thoughts inhabit the face behind the mask.

MORE THAN BROTHERS

Peter Clarke &
James Matthews
at Seventy

Compiled and Edited by Hein Willemse

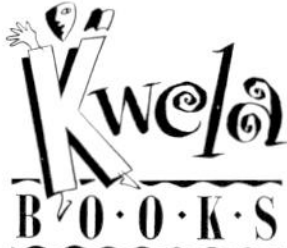

Kwela
BOOKS

The publishers gratefully acknowledge the generous financial support of the
Arts & Culture Trust of the President and the National Arts Council
which made the publication of this book possible

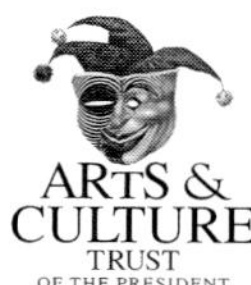
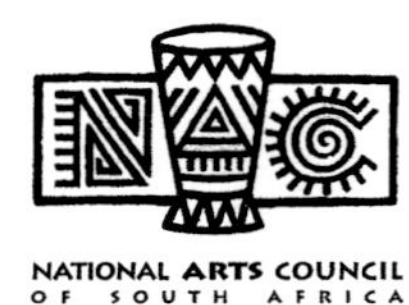

Photographs on front cover and left back cover © George Hallett
Photograph right back cover reproduced with permission of Terry Matthews-Grove
Cover design and typography by Nazli Jacobs
Set in New Century Schoolbook
Printed and bound by CTP Book Printers (Pty) Ltd,
Caxton Street, Parow 7500, Cape Town

First edition, first printing 2000

ISBN 0-7957-0095-4

TAF7211-2

Contents

PART ONE

Background

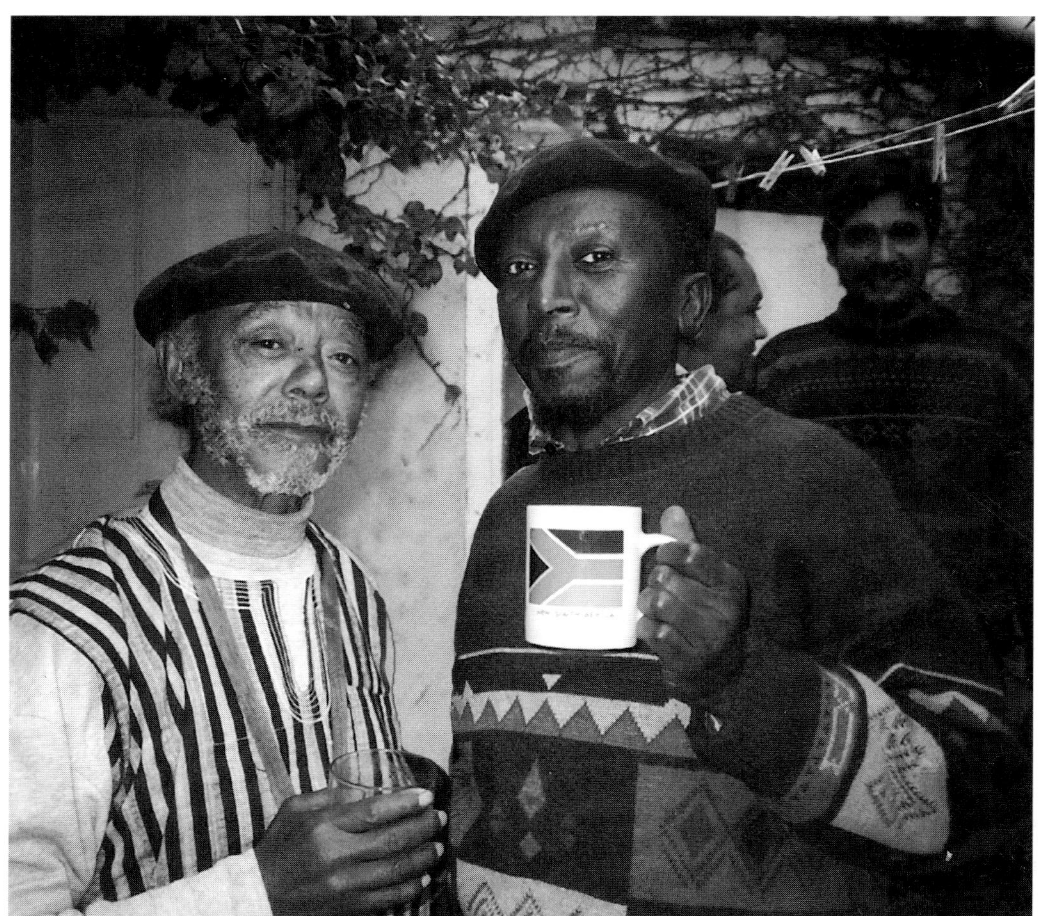

Old friends in the new South Africa: James Matthews and Peter Clarke. 1999.

More than brothers:
Peter Clarke and James Matthews
at seventy

HEIN WILLEMSE

You're certainly not the first writer to emerge from a slum.
Think of Genet. Stop fretting about your past, use it.
Put it into writing.[1]

1

Peter Clarke and James Matthews were born within days of each other. On 2 June 1929, in their stone cottage perched against the mountain, overlooking False Bay, Peter and Rose Clarke probably fussed at the arrival of the third of their six children, Peter Edward. Eight days earlier, across Table Mountain, in a Bo-Kaap tenement building facing the city bowl, Maria Matthews (commonly known as Toenkies) may have cradled the eldest of her six children in her arms, showing him off to her husband, James. These two boys would grow into young men before they would meet.

Clarke came to know about James Matthews junior through his stories published in the Cape Town newspapers. They formed a friendship that would last a lifetime. Yet they are complete opposites: Clarke is characterised by his dignified reserve and meticulous order, Matthews by his forthrightness and bohemian disorder. In his younger, wilder days Matthews was often a dreaded party guest, who would, as he himself said in a different context, '[knock] all the pretentiousness out of a man [to make] him realise that a human being shouldn't be bolstered by pomposity and false pride'.[2] Clarke's self-control could never have been more complete.

Over a period of more than forty years a rewarding friendship developed between these contrasting personalities. At seventy Matthews confesses, elsewhere in this book, that he and Clarke were 'almost more than brothers'.[3] In a comparatively small city like Cape Town, with its tiny group of artists, perhaps this friendship was destined to happen, for creative people often seek each other out.

Clarke and Matthews share similar backgrounds. They grew up in the city's shabby working-class neighbourhoods, left school prematurely and laboured in menial jobs before establishing themselves as artists. In many respects this is the story of black artists in this country. Clarke became a poet, short story writer and primarily a painter. Matthews started out writing short stories and novels, before establishing himself as the dispatcher of raging Black Consciousness poetry. Both became well known in their respective disciplines. As always in such cases, they may perhaps be better known outside South Africa than within. As the saying goes: 'A prophet is not without honour, save in his own country.'

These are extraordinary lives lived through extraordinary times.

This book is a tribute to two fiercely independent artists, men of unquestionable integrity and unfathomable creativity, who lived through times when people of their ilk were rare in their communities; and when painting and writing were not considered professional pursuits. Through their art Peter Clarke and James Matthews mediated the experiences of the slums and the housing estates around them. If they had any direct predecessors, they were few and far between. Every generation of black Capetonian painters or writers, since then, have felt the presence of Clarke and Matthews in their own work. These two men, through their sustained efforts to secure their artistic freedom, made it possible for younger generations of South African artists to enjoy a great degree of independence today. In their own way they have contributed immeasurably to our intellectual liberation.

2

Peter Clarke was born in Simon's Town where he attended the Boys' Mission and Arsenal Road Primary schools, and later Livingstone High School in the suburb of Claremont. It was here in his place of birth, the most anglicised of environments, that Clarke as a young boy heard the lilting sounds of his grandfather from Sierra Leone, who:

Even as an old, old man [...] had presence,
a dark and marvellous dignity
and a melodious voice that embraced,
coloured as it was by
his heavily accented West African English
reaching into and holding your consciousness.[4]

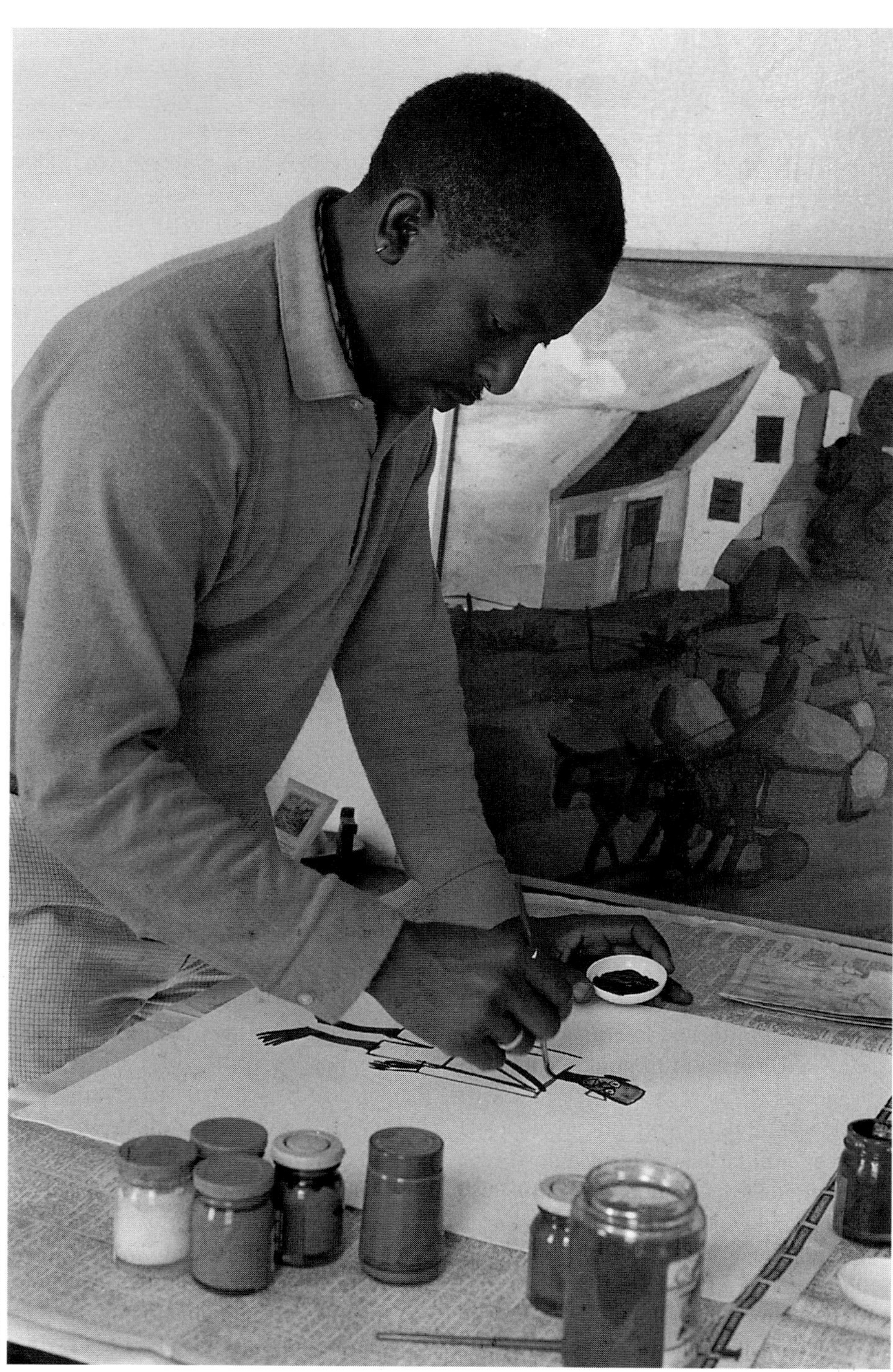

Throughout his career as an artist, Clarke worked from the confined conditions of his family home. This photograph was taken in their flat on Waterfall Road, Simon's Town, in the early 1960s.

At Arsenal Road Primary, where he attended school from standards three to six, the young Peter's interest in art was encouraged by the teachers and especially by the principal, Harold Joshua. Already at this age Clarke had a fascination with the intensities of colour. In the poem 'Observing sunlight reflected in a distant window' Clarke's narrator reveals something of the beginnings of the young painter-poet's eye for visual detail:

Watchers on a rampart
gazing fixedly at a spectacle,
in the hazy distance they would see
the late day's sun caught reflected
momentarily in a window
of a house perched on a hillrise
well into the country
beyond the blue expanse of False Bay.[5]

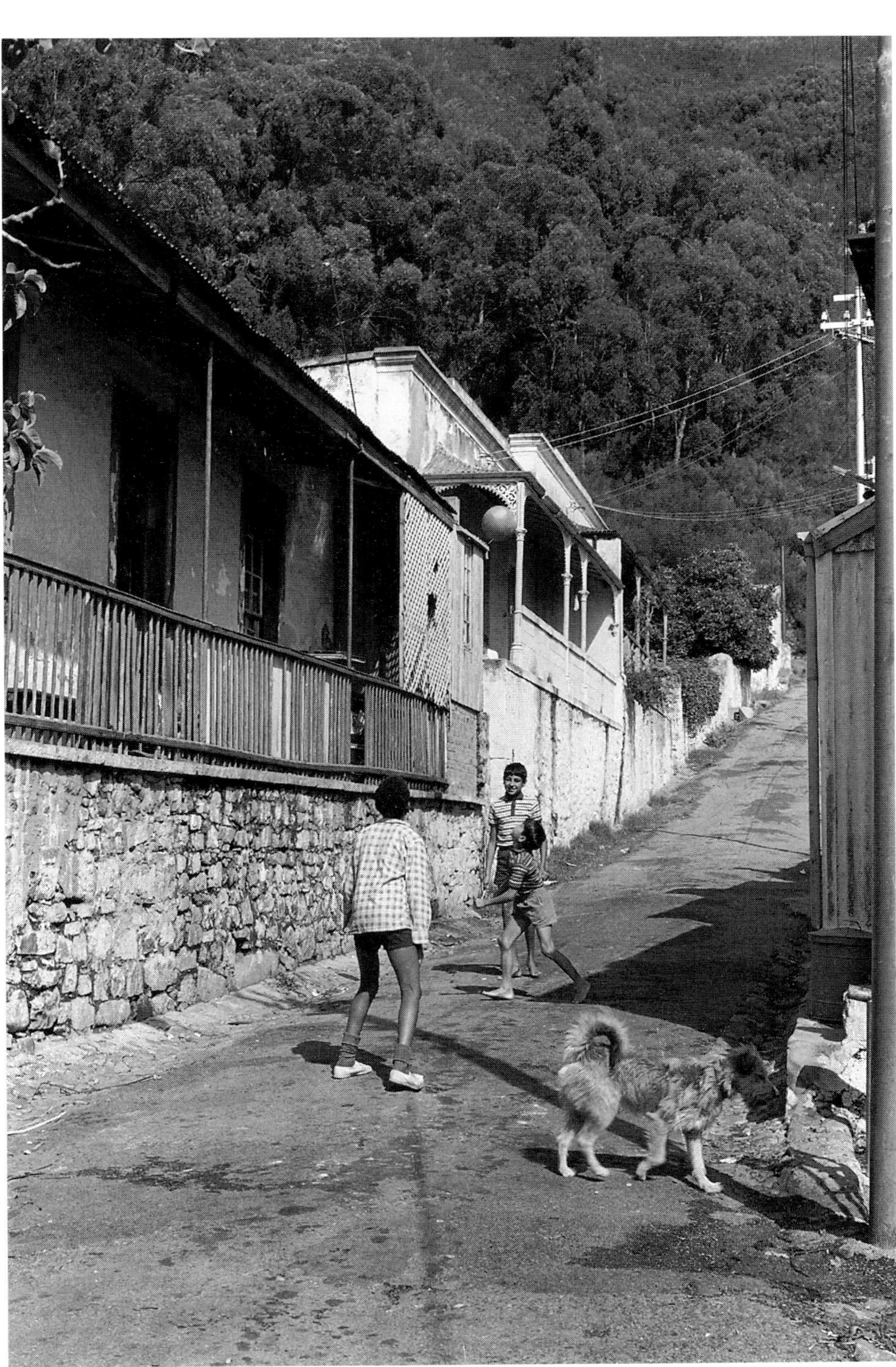

The house of Albert and Gladys Thomas on Cardiff Road, Simon's Town. In the background are the Thomas's sons, Adrian and André, with John Kindo in the front. In 1969, under the Group Areas Act, they were forced to move to Ocean View, designated as a new Coloured township.

Clarke arrived at Livingstone High School where Hendrik Esterhuizen taught art in 1944. To this day Clarke recognises his art teacher as his most immediate influence. Paging through his teacher's pile of *Studio* magazines his interest in lino- and woodcuts was aroused – and entrenched. At the end of that year, aged fifteen, Clarke left school to work at the naval dry dockyard, where his father was a plumber's mate. Initially he worked as a ship painter, stripping warships of old paint and repainting them with red lead paint.[6] After the war he was laid off, re-employed as an office messenger and later promoted to the monotony of naval-yard stores assistance.

From 1947 onwards he attended John Coplans's art classes where he studied life drawing and still lifes. The interest sparked by his high-school art teacher presented him with alternatives to his soul-destroying job. He remembers the eleven years at the Simon's Town dockyard as the 'agonies of dock yard labour'.[7]

In 1956 Clarke left his job for a three-month vacation in the farm village of Tesselaarsdal near Caledon. Tesselaarsdal, colloquially known as Teslaarsdal, holds a special place on his palette. In 'Winter shepherding', a selection from his diary, he writes,

My heart is in this place and I love it. That is so true and so definite. There is always a place, a kind of extra-special one, that a man sees and is attracted to and loves intensely, in the same way that he sees and admires and loves one particular woman above every other woman, with everything that is in him because that particular place, like that one woman, holds everything that his soul seeks.[8]

Clarke shared his special place with his fellow writers, James Matthews and Richard Rive, as well as the photographer George Hallett. Clarke and Matthews often spent their leisure times together, whether at the beach in Simon's Town or Kalk Bay, with – among others – the poet Gladys Thomas and her husband, Albert, the painter, Kenny Baker, or Hallett. In the late seventies Clarke spent time with Hallett, then exiled, at his home in the south of France. Matthews would follow in 1981.

Rive once took Clarke on his scooter to Tesselaarsdal, cruising along the dirt roads through the Solitaire Valley, near the coastal town of Hermanus. Clarke's notes in his neatly organised photo album testify to the pleasant times they shared. Under the date 1 July 1959, he entered:

We had gone through the Solitaire Valley to Hermanus. The road was terrible in places, at times as rough as a mountain track. Richard wanted to see Hawston & the road as far as Bot Rivier (sic), along which he had once hiked. [...] It was a glorious day, lovely & warm. Afterwards we went on via Onrustrivier to Bot Rivier (sic), then to Caledon, then home via Dunghye Park [...] where we stopped long enough for me to do a landscape sketch & to take [a] photo.[9]

Rive did not share his enthusiasm for Tesselaarsdal and returned to Cape Town earlier than expected,[10] but the trip made enough of an impression on Rive to spark his short story, 'No Room at Solitaire'.[11]

Following his vacation on the farm village in 1956, and an unsuccessful attempt to obtain employment as a graphic artist at an advertising agency, Clarke became a full-time artist. Though he is mostly self-trained, from September to December 1961 he spent time with Katrine Harries at the University of Cape Town's Michaelis School of Art. At about the same time his work was included in exhibitions of South African graphic art in Munich and New York.[12] In September 1962 he and a fellow South African, Amos Langdown, arrived in the Netherlands aboard the cruise liner Edinburgh Castle to commence their studies at the Royal Academy for Graphic Art in Amsterdam. Here he concentrated on etching, lithography, lino- and woodcut print-making.[13] In the years that followed Clarke would participate in many solo or group exhibitions, nationally and internationally.

Most of his work is done on a small scale, a consequence of working in confined conditions, mostly in his bedroom in a small flat in the township of Ocean View, close to Simon's Town. His earlier work is described as 'primitively drawn and formalised in treatment [while] later graphics display more assured draughtsmanship'.[14] He employs pencil, watercolours and oils, and often uses gouache, pen and ink, wood- and linocuts. He has broadened his scope to include printed fabric, bookbinding, leather-worked containers, belts, decorated glass bottles and printed plates.[15]

Painting has not always provided Clarke with a sustainable income, but he has been able to augment his earnings with his crafts and book illustrations. His pictorial style is well suited to book illustration and he has won several awards. Among his notable awards are the C.P. Hoogenhout Award for *Snoet-*

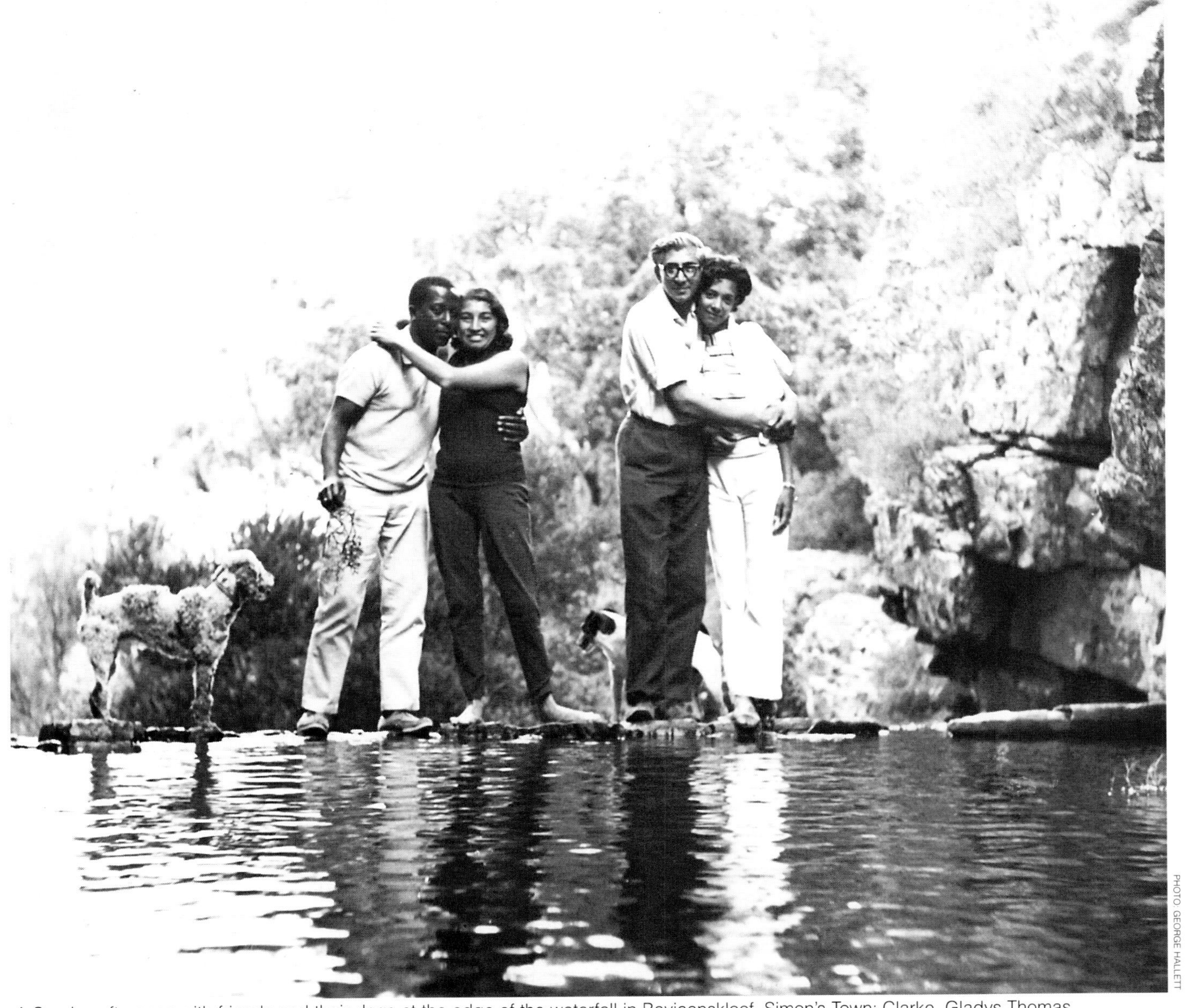

A Sunday afternoon with friends and their dogs at the edge of the waterfall in Baviaanskloof, Simon's Town: Clarke, Gladys Thomas, Albert Thomas and Charlotte Hallett. 1966.

alleen (Freda Linde, 1964) and the Adventure Africa Award for *A Message in the Wind* (Chris van Wyk, 1982). He also designed the covers for D.D.T. Jabavu's *Izidungulwana* (1958), Alan Paton's *Aber das Word sagte Ich nicht* (*Too late for the Phalarope*, 1960), Ezekiel Mphahlele's *The Living and Dead and Other Stories* (1961), and (with George Hallett) Amilcar Cabral's *Unity and Struggle* (1980). When James Matthews's short story manuscript, *Azikwelwa* (1962), was about to be published he turned to Clarke to design the cover, as he would do later with *The Park and Other Stories* (1983).

Clarke's style is descriptive and he explores a range of motifs in his paintings, quite often depicting life in poor, urban Cape Town, its rural hinterland or the foreign places he has visited. His work is characterised by strong lines often displaying an emotional distance between viewer and object. Patricia Hardy, the curator of a retrospective exhibition of his work held in 1992 under the auspices of the South African National Gallery, insists that the emotional distance in some of his paintings is balanced by his writing, which displays a 'riveting immediacy'.[16] She argues that 'this underlines the

11

importance of seeing Clarke as both a poet and a painter, with one form continually balancing, drawing from and sustaining the other'.[17] In fact, writing often accompanies and complements his drawings.

Throughout his career Clarke has shown a remarkable self-reliance, an ability to make do with what he has around him. This attitude also extends to his craft. One of his most striking and recurrent images is that of a stylised bird. In an interview he attributes his fascination with birds to the time of the death of an uncle, who was a pigeon owner. At the uncle's funeral his pigeons were placed in baskets around the grave and released at the end of the burial. When the family arrived home, all the pigeons had returned, 'liberated but [coming] home to roost'. Clarke says that he 'thought about it a lot as an adult [...] and about the bondage of indoctrination'.[18]

Clarke, like Matthews, has been involved in many community-art endeavours, in Cape Town and nationally, from the beginning of his career until the nineties. In 1950 Clarke formed an art group with like-minded friends who worked together on Saturdays.[19] In the sixties, seventies and eighties he organised cultural events and exhibitions in local municipal libraries across the Cape Peninsula. He worked consistently on art programmes at the Cape Town Community Arts Project, the Nyanga Community Art Centre and the local library in Ocean View. Clarke, Matthews and younger painters, writers and photographers formed Vakalisa Art Associates, who during the eighties produced artwork, staged exhibitions and organised poetry readings throughout the Peninsula, Boland and West Coast areas of the Western Cape.

Peter Clarke received an honorary doctorate from the World Academy of Arts and Culture in Taipei, Taiwan in 1984, and was also recognised by the Italian Academia Fiorentina delle Arti del Disegno with the Accademico Onorario in 1965. In addition he participated, in 1975, as an Honorary Fellow in Writing in the International Writing Program (IWP) of the University of Iowa (USA).

3
James David Matthews attended Prestwich Primary in Green Point, just below Bo-Kaap and Trafalgar High School in District Six. He left school during his

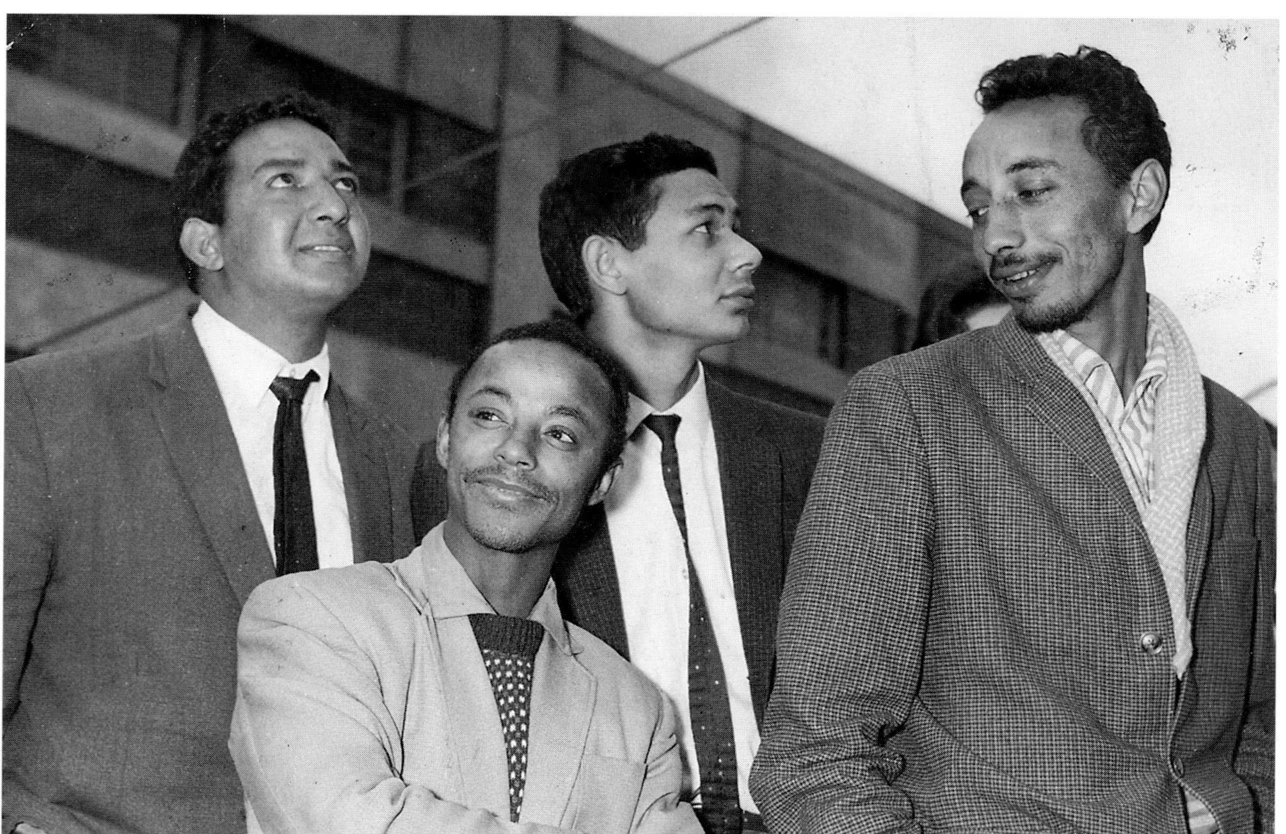

Eddie Prins, Matthews, George Hallett and Howard Lawrence photographed at Cape Town harbour in September 1962 seeing Peter Clarke off at his departure for Amsterdam.

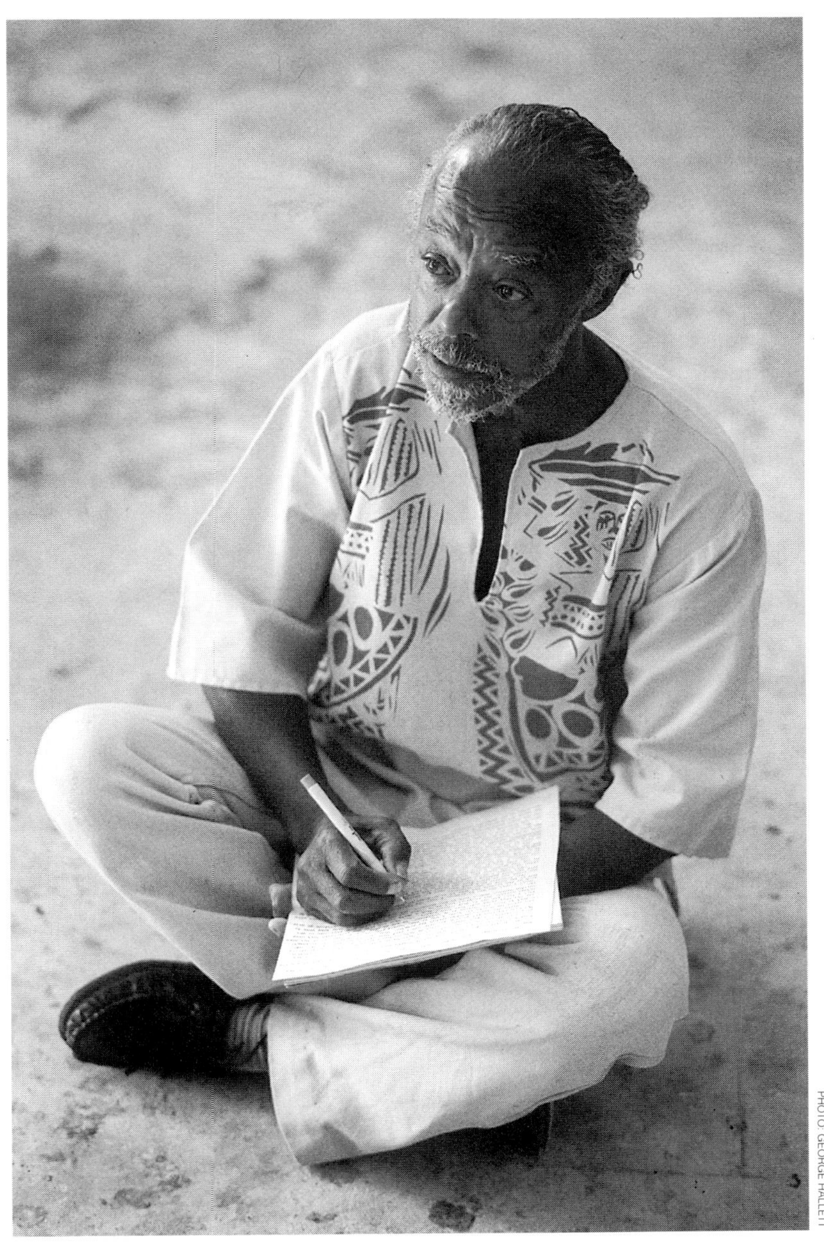

Matthews, Cape Town, 1992.

standard eight year to sell newspapers on the street corners of Cape Town. Like Clarke, he later became an 'office boy', running errands, before taking up a position as the chief editorial clerk at the *Cape Times* and later as a reporter at *Golden City Post*. After a dispute over the low salaries paid to black journalists, he left the paper and returned to the *Cape Times* to work as a night telephonist. In his spare time he started writing articles for the *Muslim News*, a newspaper serving the then largely apolitical Cape Muslim community. In the early seventies, during the editorship of imam Abdullah Haron, he was allowed to play a significant role in turning the paper into a strident anti-apartheid newspaper. Not being overtly religious, Matthews was an anomaly at the paper. After his return from his first overseas visit in 1980, he found himself 'eased out' from the newspaper.[20] He then became a full-time writer and occasionally published his books through his publishing house, BLAC, the acronym for Black Literature, Arts and Culture.

Early in his writing career Matthews met Clarke, as well as Richard Rive. Their first meeting, in the offices of a mutual acquaintance, Barney Desai, made such an impression on Rive that years later, he could still vividly recall the details of the encounter:

13

The phone rang and while Barney was on the line a small, aggressive, unshaven young man, slightly older than I was, looking ostentatiously working class, shuffled in, nodded vaguely at Barney, ignored me completely, and sat down in the opposite chair sinking his face into a magazine. For a brief moment Barney stopped the telephone conversation, clapped his hand over the receiver and said, 'Let me introduce you. Richard Rive, James Matthews.' So here was James Matthews, whose stories I had read in the Weekend Argus; the telephone operator who wrote fiction in his spare time. I knew, from the articles I had read about him, that he came from a slum area above Bree Street [...] and that he had the merest rudiments of a secondary education. I had also heard that he was a member of a powerful gang. I realised immediately that he saw in me everything he despised. I not only looked Coloured middle class, but I spoke Coloured middle class and behaved Coloured middle class. I was also a teacher with a Bachelor of Arts degree. In spite of this initial setback we overcame our mutual suspicion and our friendship cemented.[21]

Through his association with Clarke and Rive, Matthews uncovered new dimensions of creative living. With Clarke he could relax into common interests, without having to break down the subtle barriers of social class. Rive, being a teacher and decidedly upwardly mobile, was a man apart from them. As friends, however, the three had the deepest regard for one another. The value of Clark and Rive's friendship is most evident in Matthews's autobiographical novel, *The Party is Over*. His friends not only appear in different guises in the novel but also under their own names – most significantly – as artists. In a scene comparing his humdrum life with his potential, the main character defends himself:

We did have a number of serious discussions. Remember, Peter Clarke came over once. He gave us that drawing. And so did Richard Rive. He has had a collection of short stories and a novel published, and he had edited an anthology of stories. Both of them have gone to Europe. Those are the people I wish to associate with.[22]

It was on Clarke's invitation that Matthews and Rive visited Tesselaarsdal, Clarke's retreat. While Rive was less keen on pastoral poverty, Tesselaarsdal became for Matthews, as it was for Clarke, a sanctuary. Matthews recalls, in the interview published in this collection, the emotions one of the Clarke drawings evoked: 'I still get warm inside when I think of those Teslaarsdal pictures, the pictures of the raw earth, Teslaarsdal, the road. ... For me Teslaarsdal was a place of rest, with all the shit that I was in, looking at that particular picture cooled me off, made me feel calm.'[23]

Matthews and his wife, Elizabeth, divorced in 1963. *The Party is Over* draws from the well of this experience. In an exceptionally emotional scene in the novel the main character finds comfort in a similar picture: 'He bit the palm of his hand in an attempt to control his sobbing, his eyes searching the familiar walls for some kind of assurance. For a brief moment his gaze rested on the small Peter Clarke pencil sketch of a country lane. It had always filled him with a feeling of peace.'[24]

Although revised and published in South Africa in 1997 for the first time, *The Party is Over* was initially translated and published in German and Swedish, more than ten years earlier. It is set in the sixties, in the newly established township of Bridgetown where the telephonist David, his rather flirtatious wife, Yvonne, and their three daughters live. The plot revolves around the love triangle between the main character (David), his pulp-romance-reading wife and a third character, Melvyn. David's intense desire to become a recognised writer is a central concern in this tightly woven tale. This longing is jeopardised by the pressures of his personal, social and political environment. Personal and social interaction and understanding are portrayed as stunted, and eventually the marriage breaks up.

The artist in the novel remains alienated in his surroundings: nobody really understands him and this leads to utter frustration. The novel becomes a constant search for an appreciative sounding board, a compassionate ear who would comprehend his deeper emotions, and peers who would recognise his creative ability. The emerging artist is the essential outsider, not unlike the existential outsider figures of Albert Camus's *L'estranger* or Colin Wilson's *The Outsider*. But against the expressed background of apartheid the novel becomes in part an indictment of the strictures brought about by that political policy.

As a short story writer Matthews uses the surroundings he knows so well and his extraordinarily rich experiences in the inner-city neighbourhoods of

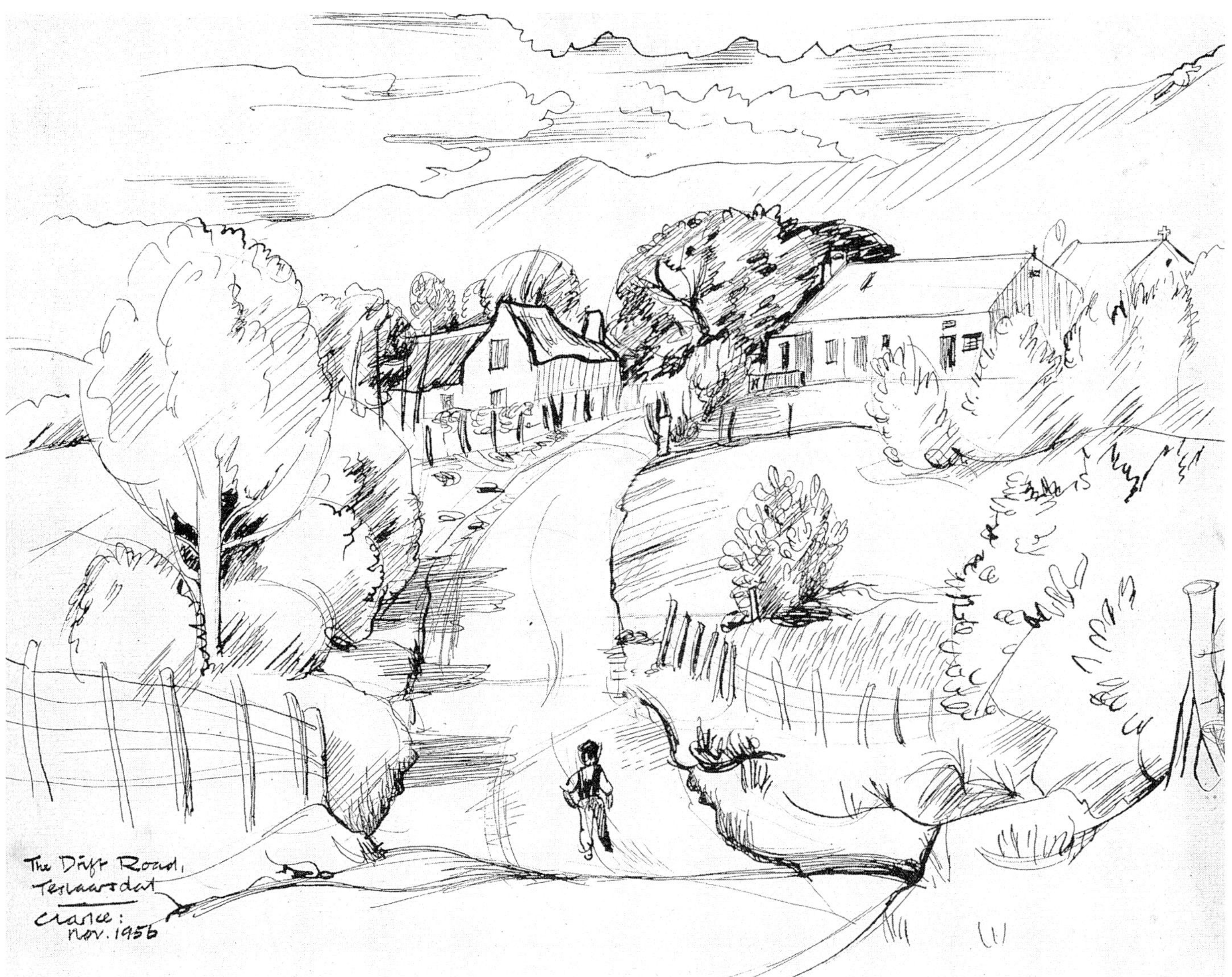

Peter Clarke, *The Drift Road*, *Teslaarsdal*, 1956. Of this and similar Tesselaarsdal sketches James Matthews says, "I still get warm inside when I think of those Teslaarsdal pictures, the pictures of the raw earth, the road."

central Cape Town, District Six and Bo-Kaap. In his youth and early adulthood he frequented shebeens, the local township watering holes, joined a street gang, practised body-building at the local YMCA Gymnasium on Chiappini Street, trained the champion body-builder, David Isaacs, and managed the flyweight boxer, Eddie Marthinus. During the sixties he became the co-owner of a Coon Carnival Troupe, the Ragtime Millionaires.

The most consistent outlets for Matthews as a writer were the local newspapers. His first short story was published in 1946, in *The Sun*, when he was just seventeen. Thereafter short stories followed in *Golden City Post*, the *Cape Times Magazine* and the *Cape Argus*. Under the pseudonym S. Matt he published Westerns in the journal *Hi-Note*. During the sixties Matthews felt that his creativity was under threat and he consciously substituted his sensibility as a prose writer for the shorthand of political poetry.

'Writing political short stories for publication in South Africa during the apartheid period was a daunting challenge.'[25] The pressures almost led to Matthews's exile from South Africa. The banning of *Quartet*, a short story collection edited by Rive which included four of Matthews's stories, forced Matthews to seek different ways of expressing himself. 'I ceased to write political short stories, fearful of what the effects of my incarceration or banning would have on my young children [the boys Jimi, Quentin, and Jason, and daughter Terry]. I turned to writing poetry with

15

political content.'[26] With the publication of *Cry Rage!* (1972), he turned to poetry or what he, with self-effacement, often calls, 'gathering(s) of feelings'.

Most of his poetry, written between the early seventies and the nineties, reflects the high intensity of political struggle and Matthews's own strident opposition to the dominant political order. Like Clarke in relation to local painters, he became a role model for emerging writers. With the establishment of the Congress of South African Writers in 1987, he was elected to the honorary position of patron, along with writers such as the exiled poet, Dennis Brutus, and the Nobel Prize-winning novelist, Nadine Gordimer. While Clarke exhibited in church halls and community art centres, and made his art available as affordable photocopied posters, Matthews took to the stage, reading at political rallies and shebeens. Like most black writers during the seventies, he took the tenets of Black Consciousness seriously. As a living embodiment of this political expression, he embraced its central tenet of self-reliance and established his own gallery and publishing house in 1974, 'for the

sheer necessity that we should have [places] of our own'.[27]

Matthews's poetry was part of 'an ideological mediation' as the South African poet, Mafika Gwala, labels Black Consciousness writing. It was writing that helped writers to 'understand the values, ideas and images that tied [them to their] social functions'.[28] After his first book of poetry Matthews edited *Black Voices Shout!*, an anthology of emerging Black Consciousness writers. It was followed by *Pass Me a Meatball, Jones* (1977), a collection written during six months of preventative detention in Victor Verster Prison in Paarl, near Cape Town. He also published *no time for dreams* (1981) and *Poisoned Wells and Other Delights* (1990). Kayzuran Jaffer, in her contribution to this book, observes that Matthews is presently producing love poetry, 'the kind of writing the South African reality has long prevented him from exploring'.[29]

For years the state refused Matthews a passport, cutting him off from his international audience and new influences. In 1980, after intervention by the

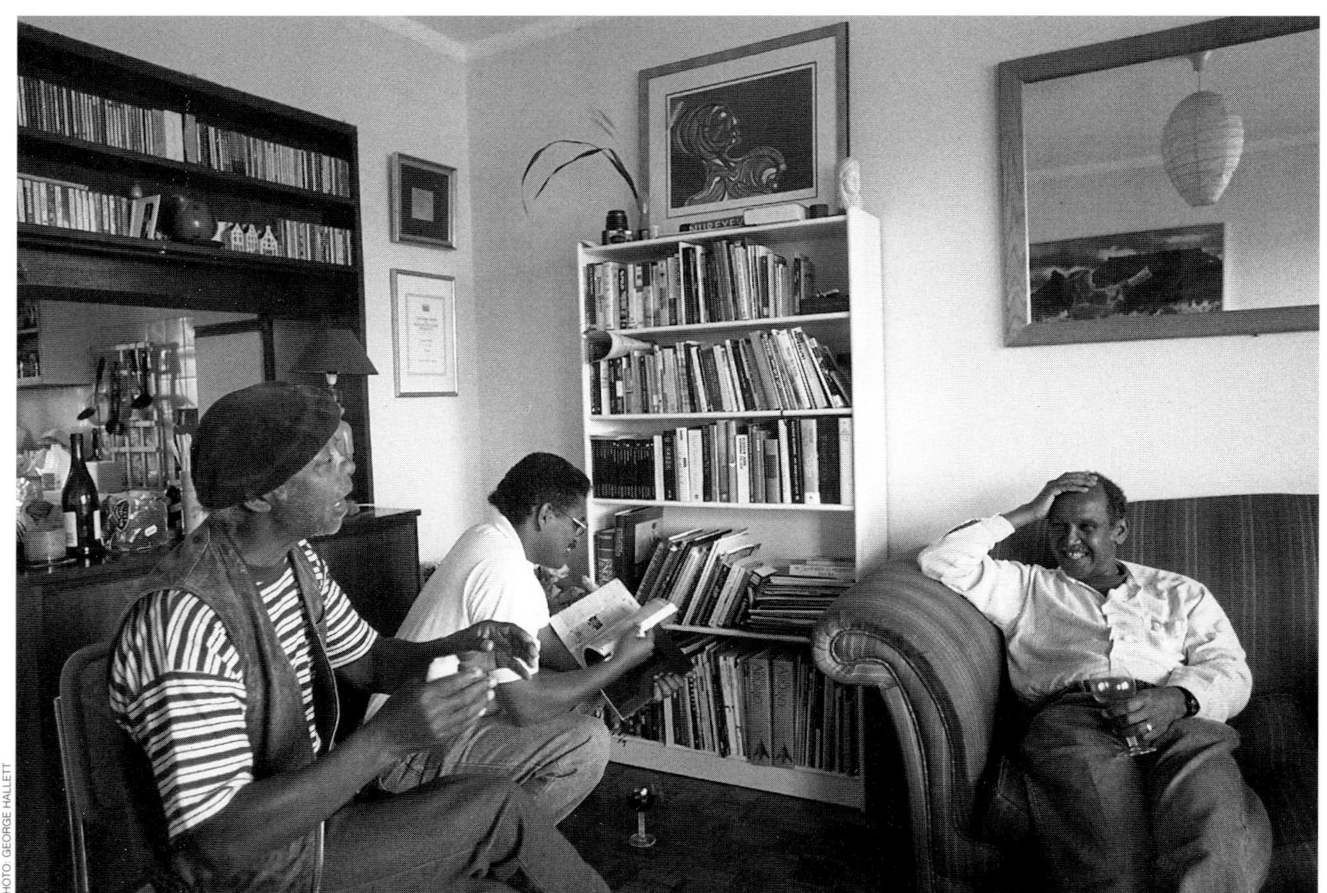

Matthews, Hein Willemse and the exiled Somalian novelist, Nuruddin Farah, being entertained at the home of George Hallett. Cape Town, 1999.

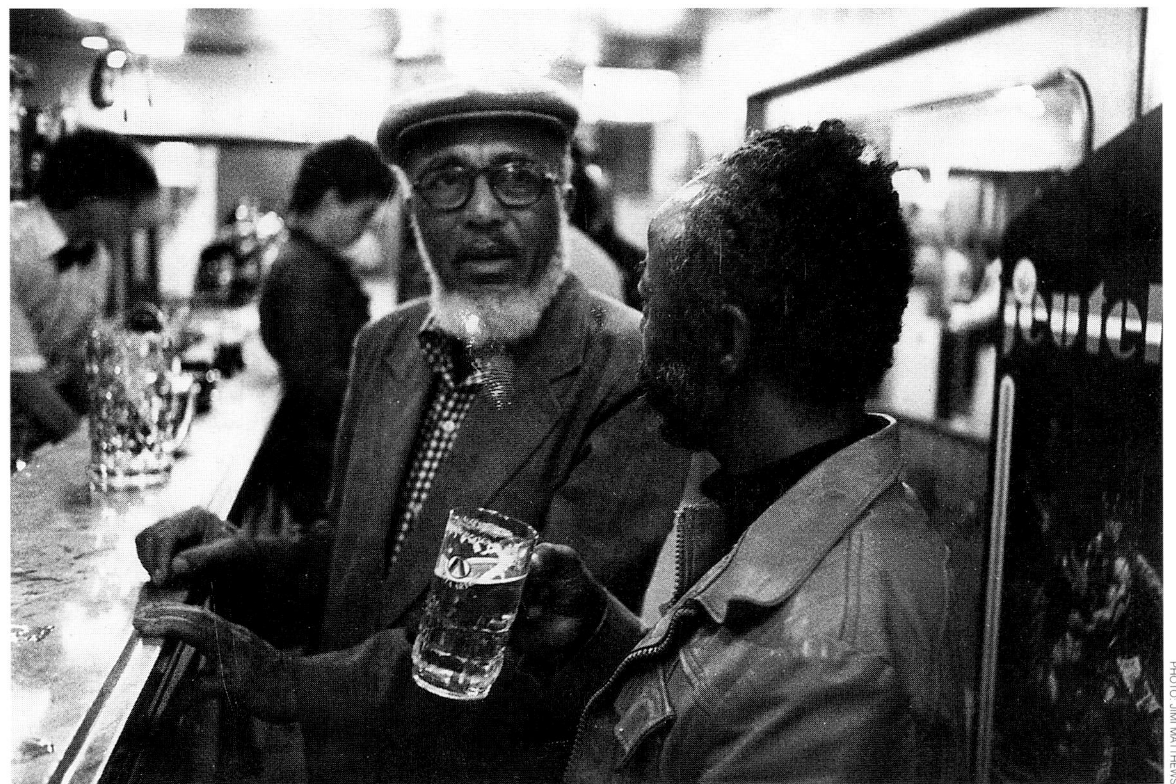

The South African painter, Gerard Sekoto, and James Matthews in Paris. 1980.

German embassy, he was allowed to attend the Frankfurt Book Fair, along with Peter Randall, the publisher of his first collection of poetry, and the Soweto writer, Sipho Sepamla. He travelled to Botswana, Germany, England and France. In Gaborone he met Wally Serote and Bessie Head. On meeting him Head, according to Matthews, promptly continued an unresolved argument they had had ten years earlier. In Paris he met the exiled South African painter, Gerard Sekoto, and spent a memorable time with him, exploring the nightlife of the French capital. In Germany he received the freedom of the city of Lehrte. The same recognition was bestowed on him in 1984 in Nürnberg, a town close to Hannover. From September to December 1984 he, like Peter Clarke nine years earlier, spent time at the International Writers Program, University of Iowa, where he was awarded an Honorary Fellowship in Writing.

3

With the upsurge of black South African English writing during the fifties, the so-called Drum-generation of writers was prominent. In Johannesburg writers such as Ezekiel (later Es'kia) Mphahlele, Peter Abrahams, Todd Matshikiza, Bloke Modisane, Casey Motsisi, Lewis Nkosi, Can Themba and Henry Nxumalo contributed to a new awareness of confident, urban writing. In Cape Town their counterparts were the foursome James Matthews, Peter Clarke, Alex La Guma and Richard Rive, and the journalist Howard Lawrence. This protest generation of writers wrote about their political and social exclusion and their ambitions as young, relatively educated people. In the Cape, as far as the black experience in the fifties is concerned, another upsurge, similar in quality and tone, was under way among black Afrikaans writers, mostly teachers such as S.V. Petersen, P.J. Philander, Adam Small, Lionel Sheldon and Paul Roubaix. Aside from the odd meeting at social gatherings, very little cross-fertilisation took place between the writers from these two nascent traditions.

This publication brings together examples of Clarke and Matthews's creative output during the fifties and early sixties, some autobiographical recollections and the writings of their immediate contemporaries, La Guma and Rive. In honouring Clarke and Matthews we also recall the broader context of these writers of the Cape. Of the four writers only Clarke and Matthews have reached the ripe old age of seventy. On 11 October 1985 La Guma died in

17

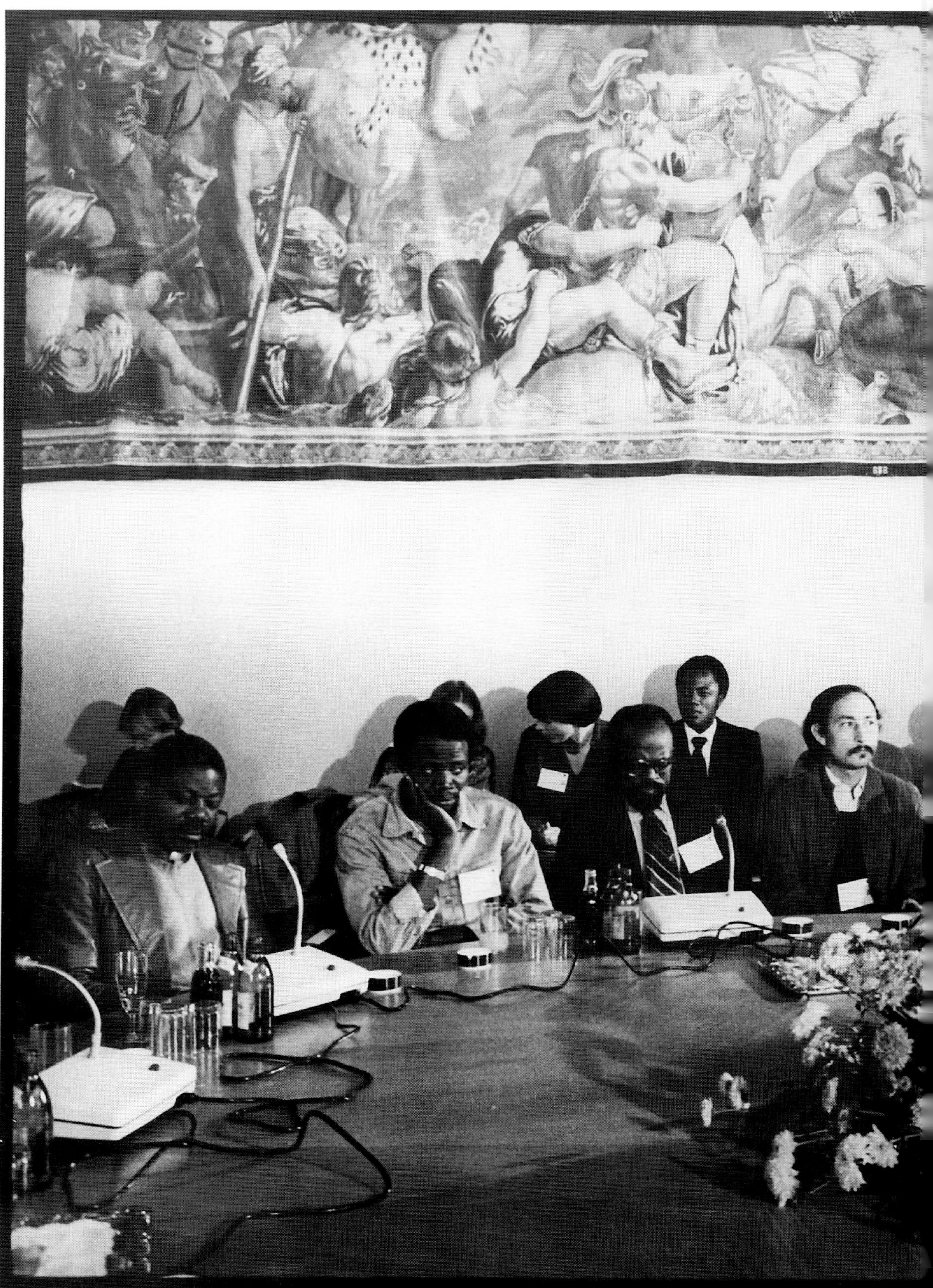

African writers at the press conference on 6 October 1980 in the City Hall, Frankfurt. During the symposium on
African literature which preceded the Book Fair with its theme: Africa – A continent asserts its identity, on this occasion
Matthews was extremely critial of the West German government's friendly relationship to the National Party government.

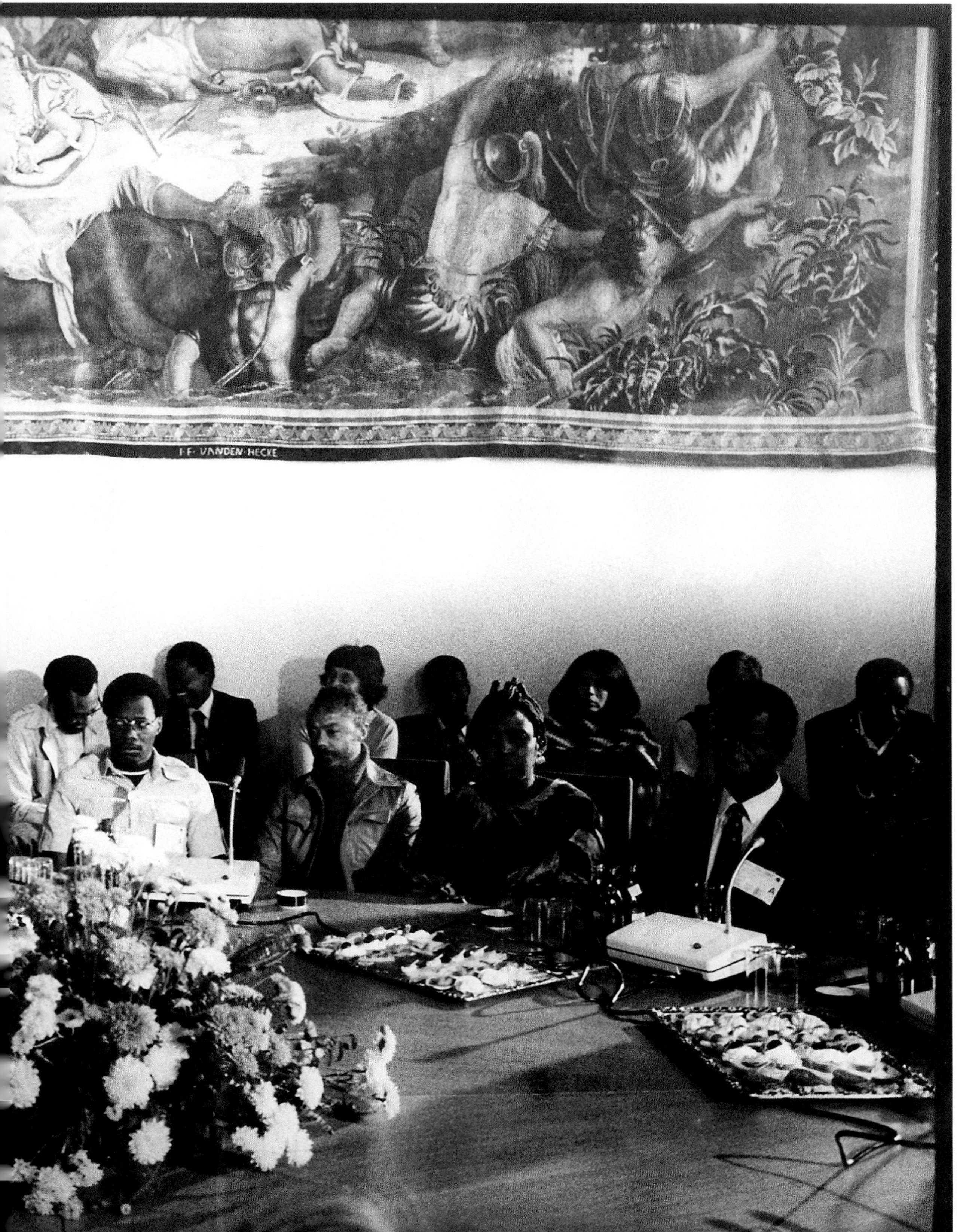

From left to right: Tchicaya 'd Tam'si (Congo), Sony Labou-Tansi (Congo), Gaston Baut-Williams (Sierra-Leone), Arlindo Barbeitos (Angola), Euphrase Kezilahabi (Tanzania), Matthews, Mariamma Bâ (Senegal) and Cyprian Ekwensi (Nigeria).

exile, in Havana, Cuba, aged sixty. Rive was murdered on 4 June 1989 at the height of his creative powers, the victim of a vicious knife attack by two youths. He was fifty-nine years old.

Richard Rive was born in District Six and grew up in what he describes as 'an atmosphere of shabby respectability' in which his family's 'hankering after respectability became obsessive. We always felt we were intended for better things.'[30] True to his vision of a better life Rive completed his school education and qualified as a teacher at Hewat Training College in 1952. He continued his studies and read for an undergraduate arts degree at the University of Cape Town, and later graduated with post-graduate degrees from the universities of Columbia (New York, USA) and Oxford.

From a young age Rive had published stories in local magazines and won prizes for his contributions.

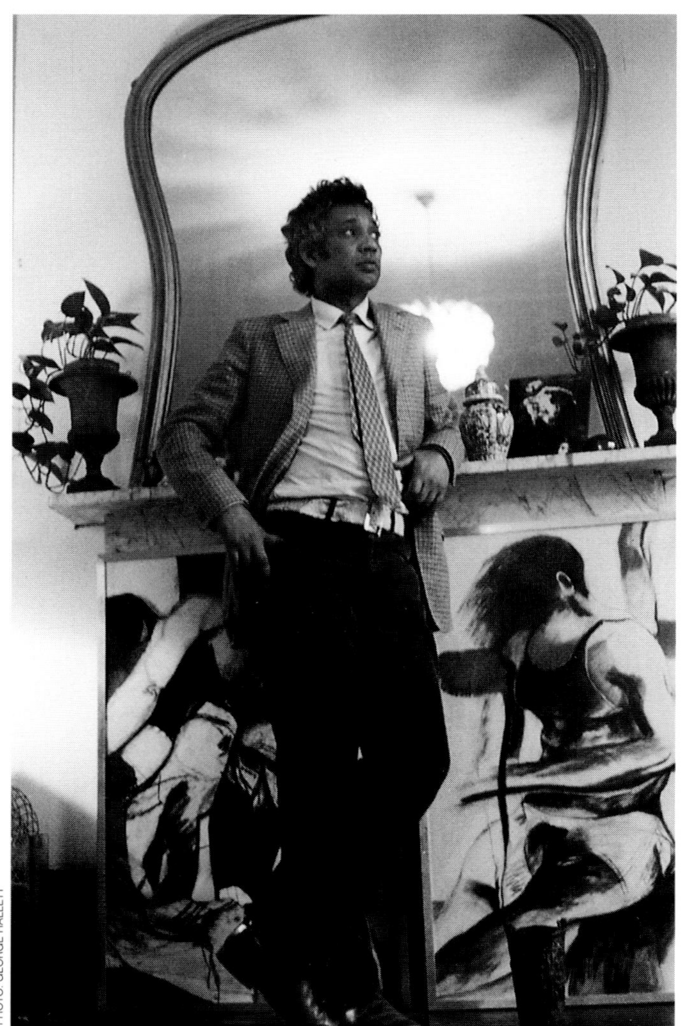

Albert Adams who, like Clarke, was taught by Hendrik Esterhuizen at Livingstone High School. Adams later emigrated to England. This photograph was taken in Camden Town, London, 1971.

In the small circle of creative people in Cape Town, he was bound to meet up with Clarke and Matthews, and other local writers such as Alex La Guma. Clarke and Rive had an enduring friendship, while Matthews and Rive had an often volatile but deeply committed relationship. Matthews introduced Rive to Gorky, Maupassant, Balzac, Flaubert and Gogol, and later took younger Black Consciousness writers regularly to meet him; Rive at times paid Matthews's house rent and introduced him to European classical music – Smetana, Beethoven and Mozart. 'Richard taught me about classical music […] it was a totally different world,' Matthews remembers.[31] They participated in the same literary discussion group, which transcended the arbitrary apartheid boundaries between black and white writers.[32] Rive introduced him and Peter Clarke to more established white writers and artists to whom he had access. These included writers like Breyten Breytenbach, Jack Cope, Ingrid Jonker, Uys Krige, Marius Schoon, Jan Rabie and Marjorie Wallace. The friendship between Matthews, Rive and Clarke went well beyond writers' circles or social gatherings. In a bold experiment they collaborated on a short story, 'Willy-Boy!', published in *African Drum* magazine in 1956.

Rive's short story, 'Riva', published in this collection, tells of the unease with which a young coloured man, Paul, reacts to the flirtations of an older Jewish woman, Riva. Underlying the story are not only the dilemmas of interaction across the colour bar or the snobbery of a well-educated dilettante, but also the sexual repression of an unsure young man. Much as this story is about one individual, it also exemplifies the tensions and insecurities of young upwardly mobile blacks in urban South Africa in the early sixties.

The same tension is evident in Alex La Guma's 'Nocturne'. The obviously working-class listener is enchanted by the unknown European classical music played on a piano in a run-down house, from across the bar where he is drinking with his pals. The listener, 'awkward as a tramp being admitted to a parish to tea', is received by the pianist in a room which 'seemed to struggle for survival with the surrounding dilapidation'. This battle for respectability is a common theme in a number of short stories written at the time by La Guma, Rive and others. Their writing served notice on especially white readers that under the veneer of the black skin of a despised working-class drunkard there were unacknowledged sensitivities. In the case of La Guma the need for an individual to examine those unknown worlds is often highlighted.

The close friendship between these writers and their influence on one another are apparent, and it may even have extended to their creative output. Some critics suggest, for instance, that the character of Willieboy in La Guma's novella, *A Walk in the Night* (1962), 'draws heavily on the style and content'[33] of the eponymously entitled story published in *African Drum* by Clarke, Matthews and Rive. Similarities in scenes and articulation may have contributed to the development of the particular character in that novella. Another example of their association is Clarke's cover design for the novella's first edition published by Mbari Publications in Ibadan, Nigeria. In 1963 La Guma, Matthews, Rive and a then unknown writer, Alf Wannenburgh, collaborated on the anthology *Quartet*, which Alan Paton, who had previously achieved world acclaim for his *Cry, The Beloved Country* (1948), proclaimed as 'a milestone in the history of South African literature'.[34]

Like Rive, La Guma was born in District Six, the son of a well-known Cape family. His father Jimmy served on the executive bodies of the Industrial and Commercial Union of Africa and the Communist Party of South Africa. Alex left school at the age of seventeen and completed his matriculation certificate through night school. He worked as a clerk at several companies, until he became a full-time party organiser for the South African Coloured People's Congress in 1954, and a journalist on the left-wing newspaper, *New Age*. Because of these activities Alex was accused of treason, but later acquitted. In 1962, shortly after the appearance of *A Walk in the Night*, he was banned from writing. In 1966 he left the country and died in exile in 1985.

4

Three contemporary scholars, Crain Soudien, Elza Miles and Kayzuran Jaffer, provide analyses and interpretations of the period, the painting and writing of Clarke and Matthews.

Crain Soudien provides a background to the changes in working-class Cape Town – the essential feeding ground of these writers. He argues that the fifties was the gestation period for apartheid and that the changing social conditions shaped 'the quality of everyday life in Cape Town'. The majority of Capetonians lived in poverty and these circumstances gave rise to 'the spirit of *kanala*', looking out for one's neighbour. He explores the effects of segregation and forced removals, as well as the emergence of violent

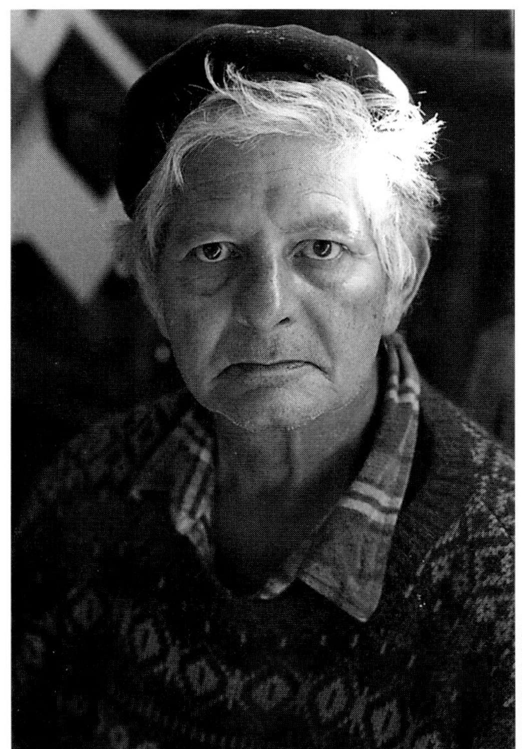

Kenny Baker, Cape Town, 1993.

crime on the Cape Flats. Amidst decaying social circumstances, numerous musicians and writers gave rise to different forms of cultural expression.

In her essay on Peter Clarke, the painter and researcher, Elza Miles, focuses on the art scene in Cape Town in the early years of Clarke's development. She traces the influences of his contemporaries and early reactions to his work. She identifies Tesselaarsdal as 'Clarke's Pont-Aven or Le Pouldu' where he could work in surroundings different to what he was used to. The last section of her chapter is a close reading of Clarke's triptych, *Haunted Landscape* (1976), a painting of 'subliminal imagery with far-reaching consequences'.

Kayzuran Jaffer examines the complexities of identity in James Matthews's writing. She provides a chronology and analyses the political and social influences brought to bear on his poetry, short stories and novel. She briefly investigates the portrayal of black women in his writing, and finds that it 'wavers between proclaiming the superior beauty of the black woman over the white woman and ridiculing some black women's attempts to adhere to white standards of beauty'. In this case, as in other matters of identity, Jaffer uncovers different and often conflicting expressions of social and political identity.

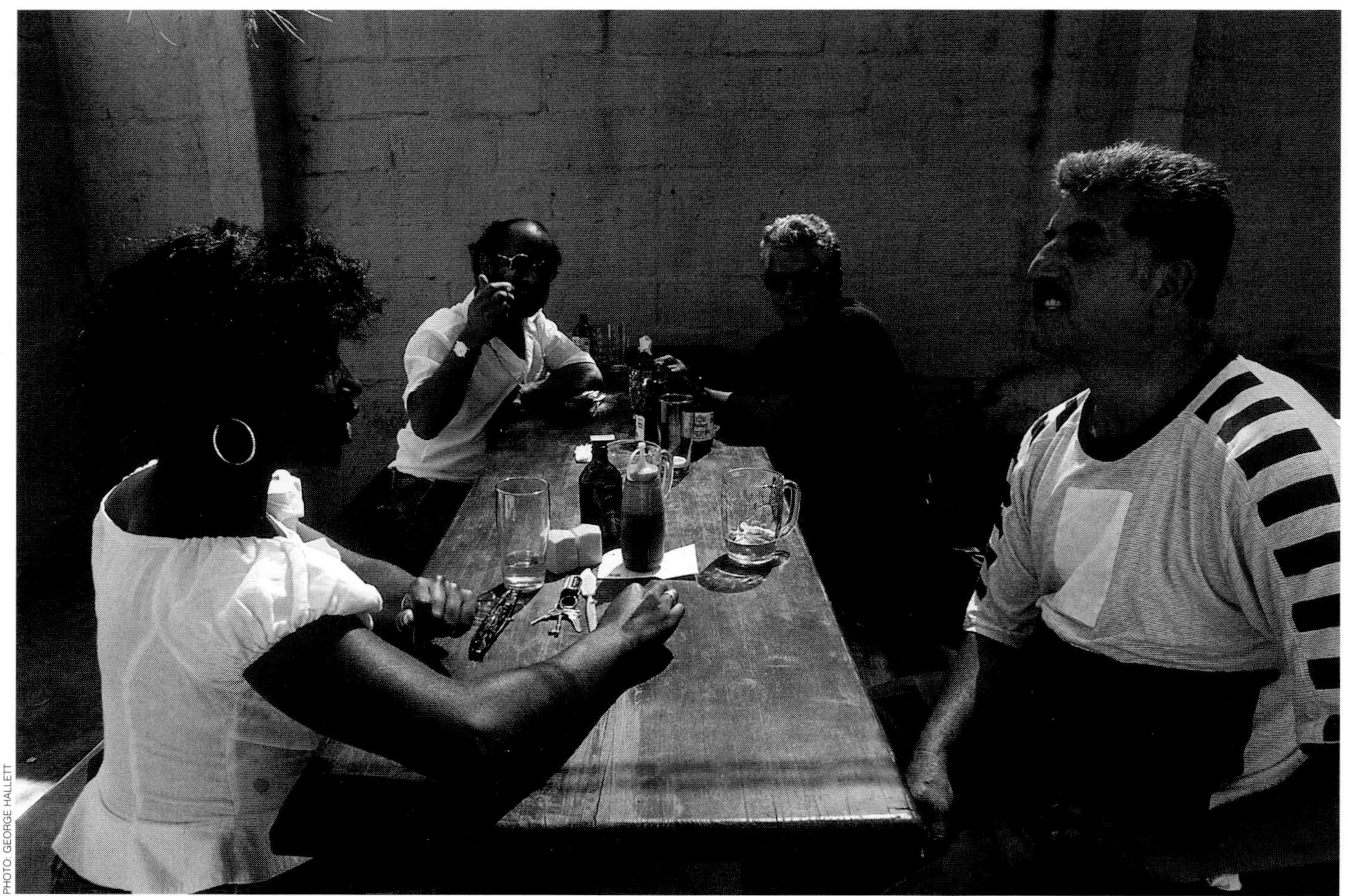

From left to right: Mēdu Hallett, Crain Soudien, Lucien le Grange and Vincent Kolbe. Cape Town, 1992.

Social conditions, cultural and political life in working-class Cape Town, 1950 to 1990

CRAIN SOUDIEN

By any measure, the defining condition of life in South Africa in the fifties, sixties, seventies and eighties, for all its various people, old and young, black and white, rich and poor, was the system of apartheid. For those who grew up and lived during this period, apartheid framed every aspect of their existence. One's working life, and the life of those who employed one, took shape according to the social and economic rules defined by apartheid. One's social life, whether it was attempting to make a home in the extensive township developments which took place in the 1960s to the 1980s, or simply managing one's rest, work and leisure, was stamped with the obtrusive markings of white supremacy and class exploitation. And inevitably apartheid succeeded in either moulding people in its desired racial image as whites, Africans, Indians or coloureds, or in stimulating in one an intense and concentrated revulsion for the race classification which decreed that some people were white and others not. The pass system dictated where and when one had the right to be at any one moment in time, and a slew of laws sought to silence even one's most private thoughts.

In appraising South Africa during the period of National Party rule, it is, as E.P. Thompson[1] said of the Industrial Revolution in England, as if the South African nation had entered a crucible and emerged shaped by the events which marked the period. First, in the early 1950s, there came a battery of legislation which outlawed political resistance, entrenched racially separate residential areas, prohibited mixed marriages, and instituted unequal education. In the 1960s, in response to a recalcitrant government, the Sharpeville uprising took place, as a consequence of which the African National Congress and the Pan African Congress were banned and the long night of political persecution marked with bannings, tortures and state violence was ushered in. In the 1970s, popular mobilisation was the order of the day, culminating in worker strikes and student uprisings, and the government outlawed the Black Consciousness movement. In the 1980s, the National Party moved to repackage its policies and developed its 'carrot and stick' strategies, and popular resistance rose to new levels with battle cries of making South Africa ungovernable.

Within this context of white domination, those who were subordinate sought to construct a life for themselves socially, culturally, politically and economically. This overview is an exploration of the social, leisure and cultural choices which the poor and disenfranchised black people in Cape Town made for themselves in relation to the economic and political structures in which they were placed.

Social conditions in the city and segregation

Two places which are emblematic of urban life for working-class South Africans during the fifties and the sixties are undoubtedly Sophiatown in Johannesburg and District Six in Cape Town. Of course, there were similar places elsewhere in the country, most notably Southend in Port Elizabeth and Marabastad in Pretoria. But District Six and Sophiatown were responsible, in their different ways, for holding up to the rest of South Africa how working-class people might *manage* their oppression and, simultaneously, groom and cultivate their talents. They constituted the hearts of their respective cities, despite the grand urban development plans of the fifties and the sixties which took shape with the expansion of the new townships on the Cape Flats and in Soweto. A comparative history of District Six and Sophiatown, which still awaits being done, will show how much they contributed to the political and cultural landscape of South Africa.[2]

While it would be an exaggeration to claim that it was the non-racial character of District Six which offended the city planners of the forties and led to its planned destruction after 1966,[3] it is true that it hastened the authorities' intentions to push through the development of the segregated city. In the lead up to segregation of the city after the proclamation of the Group Areas Act in 1950, the City Council of Cape Town was certainly ambiguous about – and on occasion did resist – provincial plans to enforce segregation in the city. It did, nevertheless, participate in the planning and building of apartheid Cape Town.[4] The Council oversaw, after the Second World War, the establishment of new working-class coloured townships such as Bridgetown, Silvertown and Gleemor, and African townships such as Nyanga and Guguletu. In this it was quietly encouraged by the white municipal electorate. While white English-speaking Capetonians were hostile to the new National Party government, they were equally hostile to the prospect of having working-class coloured and African neighbourhoods established on their doorsteps. And, as the most important political constituency in the city, they ensured that black people were placed well beyond the boundaries of their suburbs.

The first area to fall victim to the Group Areas Act was Tramway Road in Sea Point in 1957. Thereafter, a regular succession of proclamations followed. District Six, the jewel in the crown of black Cape Town, was earmarked for demolition and was proclaimed a white group area in 1966.

The Cape Town which the authorities sought to reshape was, so they said, a chaotic and disordered place. Harry Lawrence, Member of Parliament for Woodstock, argued that the replanning of the city would be to the benefit of coloured people. He said:

The method by which this will be done will be the natural and just method of encouraging people to live in areas where they will be assured, firstly, of all the amenities of decent and healthy life, and of a much fuller opportunity for employment and economic development than they have at present.[5]

The Cape Town of the fifties, sixties, seventies and eighties which Peter Clarke, James Matthews and the ordinary people knew was certainly no Nirvana. While the emerging middle class and more estab-

lished middle-class groups within the coloured community were able to derive some benefit from the implementation of apartheid, the coloured and African poor, and also the tiny African middle class, were the major victims of the National Party's new policies. For the coloured middle class, opportunities for social betterment became available as the state sought to implement and institute the system of apartheid. New jobs and elevated positions in government and business were created in an attempt to woo coloured people into the system. The provision of these new opportunities coincided with the rapid expansion of the South African economy during the late fifties and early sixties.

The central effect of these developments was to detach the fledgling middle class from the working class in places such as District Six, Claremont, Simon's Town, Parow and Goodwood, and to relocate them in smart new suburbs such as Heathfield, Fairways, Crawford and Square Hill in Cape Town, and Glenhaven and Kuils River in the northern suburbs. There, during the sixties and seventies, assisted by generous housing subsidies which they received as state employees in the teaching and health professions, and profiting from the opening up of institutions such as the University of the Western Cape in the early sixties, they were able to escape from their working-class roots and build the substantial middle-class community which today exists in Cape Peninsula.

City life and poverty
Middle-class life, however, was a distant dream for most of Cape Town's African and coloured communities during the entire period of National Party rule. As many commentators have remarked,[6] life for ordinary people was played out against a backdrop of intense poverty and squalor. Of the almost half million people who lived in Cape Town in the fifties, 280 413 were coloured,[7] and the majority[8] of these accounted for the city's large poor population. Of every ten households which lived below the poverty datum line in the city, eight were coloured, one was African and one was white. Between 1939 and 1952 the number of coloured women in industry rose from approximately 11 200 to about 34 000.[9] Most women, however, were unemployed and managed the impecunious households they and the rest of their families were able to put together.

In the late forties it was estimated that of 25 000

coloured households in Cape Town, three quarters were living in homes of no more than three rooms.[10] In most cases one-room households provided shelter for at least three people, and almost none of the dwellings had bathrooms. The rentals for this kind of accommodation, moreover, were exorbitant. The Reverend Sidney Lavis, a campaigner for better housing in the city, complained that rentals of up to 45 shillings a month were being paid for single-roomed dwellings by people who often earned no more than 5 shillings a day as casual labourers. An article in the *Cape Times* in 1924 carried the following comment: '[The] slums are crowded with little children whose chief fare is plain bread and coffee day in, day out – and this is so because so large a part of the meagre wages of their parents is extorted in rentals for slum tenements.'

Health conditions, predictably, were atrocious. In 1946, the infant mortality rate for whites was 33,84 per thousand; for coloureds it was 119,9 per thousand. 51% of coloured children and 71,4% of African children were suffering from malnutrition.[11]

By the fifties, conditions had not improved significantly. If anything, they had deteriorated, and some parts of the city were certainly worse than others.

John Valentine, a resident of Protea Village (a settlement which today forms part of the Kirstenbosch complex) from the time of his birth in the late forties until he was resettled in Grassy Park in the seventies, remarked that:

We were very poor in the fifties and even in the sixties. We didn't have taps, no running water. We used to come home from school in the afternoon in our gelapte broeke [tattered pants] and had to go to the spring first with our paraffin tins [to collect water]. We used to carry these tins on poles and filled them up for drinking and washing. And then after we washed we would be ready to eat. Sugar on bread.[12]

The ubiquity of poverty had already shaped the character of Cape Town in the early part of the century. It continued to do so in the latter half. In the seventies, eighties and nineties, despite the further expansion of new housing estates in areas such as Blue Downs and Delft, working-class Capetonians continued to struggle. It was estimated that the official housing backlog in Cape Town in 1980 was 46 000 units.[13] A 1992 survey showed that over 440 000 people continued to live in 88 664

shacks spread throughout the city.[14] It was, despite the nostalgia which many Capetonians have for old Cape Town, profoundly grim and decidedly unromantic.[15] Communities struggled to make good against almost unbearable odds. Not unexpectedly, as in poor places elsewhere in the world, poverty was the mother of invention of stratagems both honourable and dishonourable.

Places such as District Six, Harfield, Kalk Bay and Windermere were undoubtedly complex in their composition and in the ways and habits of their people. Crime was certainly not absent from the old areas such as District Six.[16] What is unmistakably clear, however, is that there were long-standing traditions of caring and mutual co-operation present in the old working-class neighbourhoods before the era of forced removals.[17] The spirit of *kanala*, of looking out for one's neighbour, ran deep in these communities. In District Six, for example, people battled the challenge of poverty, buoyed by memories of a hard-borne slave past. While many narratives of the area emphasise the horror of blocked sewerage pipes, rat-infested corridors, incessant noise and absentee landlords, those of insiders speak of an intense will to survive.

Richard Rive,[18] a contemporary and friend of Peter Clarke and James Matthews, made the point that the District had a mind and a soul of its own. In a recent memoir, Linda Fortune illustrates this argument by telling of people in District Six being unable to keep perishable goods. When her father bought fish or crayfish, he would ask the shopkeeper to keep it fresh for him in his refrigerator – 'the shopkeeper would never refuse and dad always saw to it that the man got a fair share of what he had stored'.[19] She speaks also of how, on special occasions, a shopkeeper would send a fresh loaf of bread to all the families on a street to show his appreciation for their patronage. It was often thought that this kind of generosity would bring luck to the giver.

Sharing extended too to sharing responsibility for raising children of friends and relatives, and taking in the destitute and the down and out. Images of Fortune's father with up to eight children – his own and their friends – trailing behind him as he made his way to the sea on a crayfish outing were not uncommon. When he was asked whether the children were all his, he would characteristically answer yes. Even the gangsters of District Six, it was believed, were a breed apart. Gang activity was not only a means of economic survival but also a form of external policing. 'The people, competing for scarce resources at the thin, sharp edge of a fluctuating economy, created for themselves in District Six an elaborate, alternate society; highly co-operative, often violent and tragic; and more often ringing with the laughter of a society with an identity.'[20]

Out of these descriptions, places such as District Six, Harfield and Simon's Town emerge as areas undoubtedly mired in poverty, but, in the words of Tony Grogan, a popular cartoonist of the sixties and seventies, 'there was a community spirit that the most advanced urban development will never be able to buy or replace'.[21] Gangs formed part of a social landscape which understood itself well. Crime, now rampant in the townships of the Cape, was by no means absent from the old quarters of the city and the Peninsula, but it was held in check by the social bonds which connected family, friends and acquaintances. People knew each other. Fortune, for example, tells the story of how her father, in District Six, apprehended a young man attempting to rob a passer-by in their street. Her father physically laid into the man and then, with the support of the neighbours, proceeded to take the youth back to his home.[22]

Forced removals

But there was a far less happy story. To make ends meet, it was estimated in 1961 that approximately 30 000 coloured people made a living from bootlegging, particularly, but not only, in the shack settlements dotted around the Peninsula.[23] A Dr Steyn, speaking in the Senate in 1961, said that there were between 500 and 600 shebeens in the Cape Peninsula alone.[24] Poverty and the availability of alcohol contributed to extremely high levels of convictions for drunkenness. In 1961, the ratio of convictions for whites was 1:274, 1:331 for Africans and 1:339 for Indians. For coloureds it was 1:33.

Family life suffered under conditions such as these. Community workers were aware of the effects of alcohol abuse, and took a very dim view of shebeens and taverns. In 1957, Johnson Ngwevela, the Secretary of the African Western Grand True Temple, commented in response to a suggestion that a beerhall be built in Nyanga, '[The] beerhall will disrupt the home of the people ... These establishments are in no way preventing shebeening, they only create drunkenness and add to the number of criminals and gangsters who already exist.'[25]

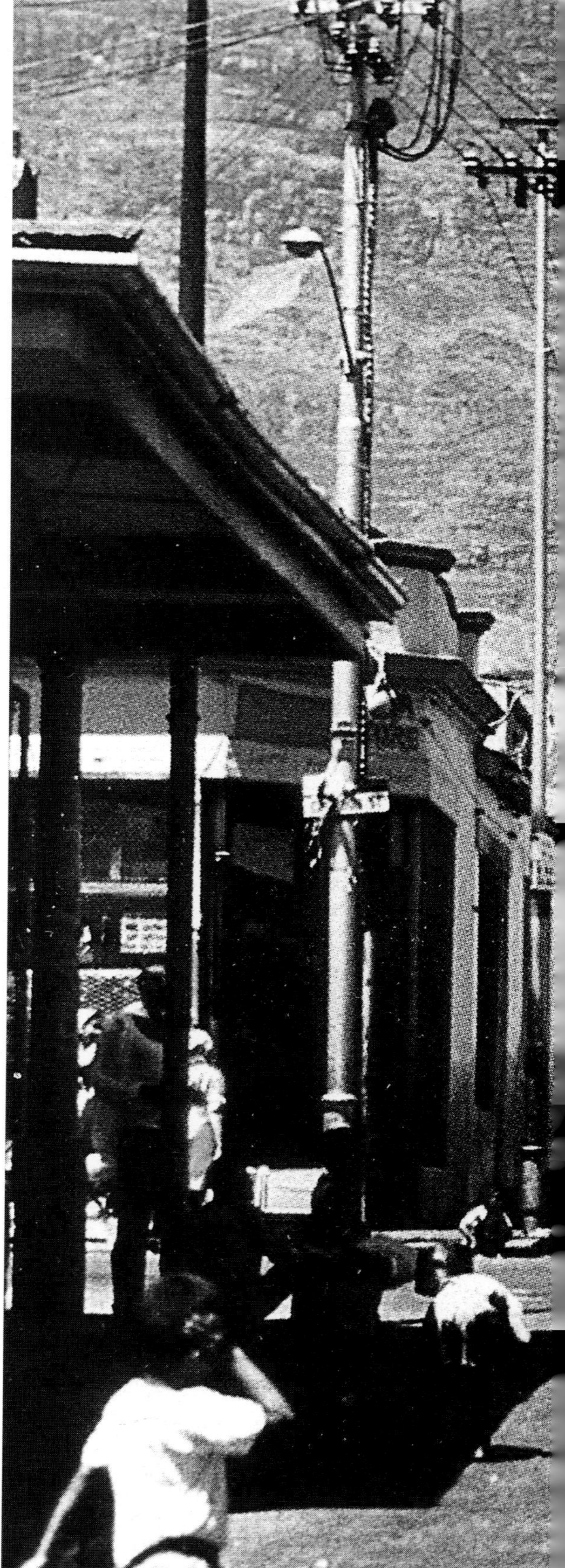

A street scene in District Six, mid-1960s.

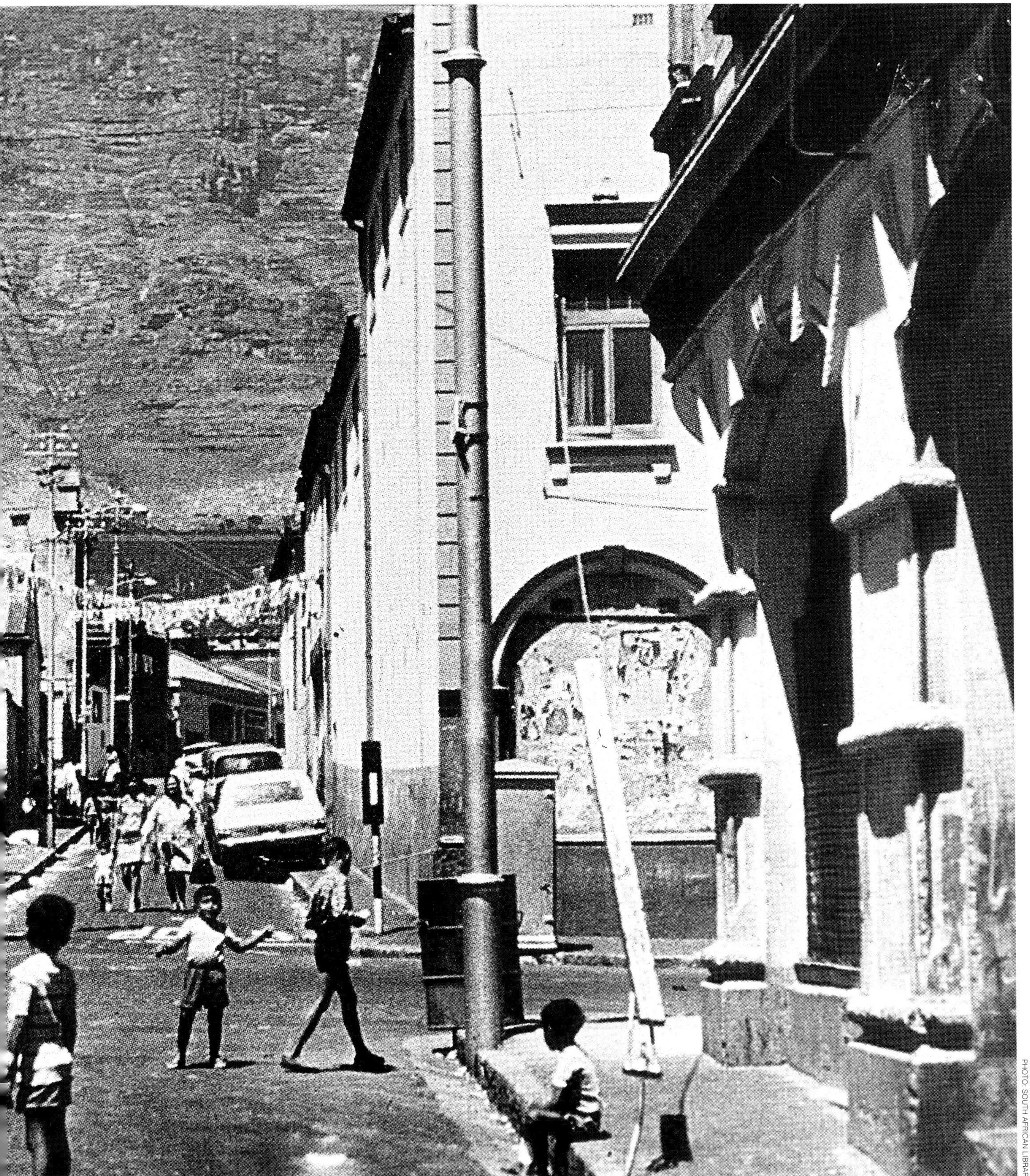

The intensification of the National Party's grip on South Africa only worsened these conditions. The National Party introduced a range of laws which segregated transport, housing, health and recreation. For African people this persecution had begun even before the arrival of the National Party. In terms of the Black (Urban Areas) Consolidation Act of 1945, African people could be in an urban area without permission for no more than 72 hours.[26] The bulk of the African community living in the Peninsula thus consisted of men – migrant labourers who were not allowed to bring their wives to the city.[27] The National Party took this a step further in the early 1960s by declaring the Western Cape a Coloured Labour Preference Area and by intensifying the controls around migration of Africans into the region. The effect of these policy developments was literally to throw a fence around the Western Cape, to declare it off-limits to African people, and from 1966, the state refused to build more homes for them.[28] These policies notwithstanding, African migration into the city continued unabated and by 1970 vast new shack settlements were coming into being at Crossroads, KTC and Modderdam.

While the state sought to turn the Western Cape into a Coloured Labour Preference Area and thereby to entrench the racial hierarchy of white, coloured and African using the Group Areas Act, it simultaneously enforced the evacuation of people of colour from the city. The Act saw to the displacement and uprooting from the city of more than 150 000 people, constituting almost a fifth of the population in the Peninsula, the immediate hinterland of the city. By 1965, more than 300 000 coloured people had been resettled on the Cape Flats,[29] miles away from their beloved mountain, to places with cynically endowed names such as Ocean View, Lavender Hill and Valhalla Park. There on the Flats, large swathes of virgin land were prepared for residential development.

While the Group Areas Act succeeded in unscrambling those parts of the city which were racially mixed, and recent observations show that by the seventies there were close to sixty such places scattered throughout the Peninsula, the more pernicious effect of the Act was to break up long-standing communities. These communities had come into being largely through the limited franchise coloured people had which allowed them to acquire properties.

More importantly, working-class African people lived relatively unobtrusively, if not always harmo-

niously, amongst their coloured counterparts throughout the Peninsula. In more destitute communities, such as the shack settlements of Windermere, Retreat and Parow, colour counted for less, as the indigent threw aside racial conceit in their common struggle to survive. The dismemberment of these communities, more especially the despatching of different members of a single family to differently defined racial townships, struck a mighty blow to social solidarities forged through years of shared hardship. In places such as District Six, extended family, friendship and religious networks were able to provide safety nets for those having to deal with prolonged periods of unemployment, unexpected illness or even death, as the graphic descriptions of Fortune and Nomvuyo Ngcelwane[30] show. Life in the new townships, however, was immensely cruel.[31] Commenting on the conditions in the new townships, a Mrs M.G. of Claremont said:[32]

Look, they [the people of Claremont] were not really poor. People never used to complain like they do today. You didn't, because everybody was happy. They might have been poor in material things, but they were rich in spiritual things and in character and so forth … If I can help you and you help me and so it went … [Claremont was] a very safe place.

Crime and the townships
The new townships to which the apartheid government sent people were anything but safe. Aside from being remote from people's places of work and recreation, townships such as Mitchell's Plain (which was established over a period of several years in the mid 1970s) initially had no facilities such as hospitals, and were literally human dumping grounds. Having been removed, people lost contact with their former neighbours, and had to cultivate friendships with strange people and build new social, recreational and religious structures. While many of the townships stabilised after twenty to thirty years, and while cohesive communities have been able to emerge from the wastes of the Flats in townships such as Bridgetown and Kewtown, the difficulties which the old inhabitants had left behind in places like District Six and Claremont were compounded as the authorities failed to keep pace with the demand for new housing. Housing estates such as Manenberg, Hanover Park, Lavender Hill, Valhalla Park, Ocean View and Bonteheuwel were characterised by unem-

ployment, overcrowding and crime. Backyard shacks sprouted wherever space permitted, leaving people in damp, poorly ventilated and cramped accommodation which promoted the spread of infectious diseases such as tuberculosis.

If ill-health was to mark people's private miseries, it was, however, crime which regulated their public lives. This was especially so in the seventies to the nineties.

In the townships the familiar gangs of the city were transformed into malevolent marauders who preyed on the people's social vulnerability. The townships bred a mendacity of spirit amongst a number of young men who found themselves drafted into one of the many brotherhoods of crime which seemed to spring up at every opportunity. Young men, often unable to find work, and aware of the nagging poverty which surrounded them, were attracted by the stability, security and prestige offered by the gang. Life as a gangster might have suited the individual and sometimes brought lucrative rewards through robbery, breaking and entering, or, less frequently, through the sale of drugs and alcohol. However, for the communities in which they were located, despite the occasional presence of Robin Hood characters who dispensed largesse and so constructed loyal followings around themselves, gangsters were an unmitigated disaster. In many places, they became street potentates holding sway over the comings and goings of the townships.

Young men were often dragooned into various orders with names such as the Ugly Americans, the Dixie Kids, the Mongrels and the Naughty Boys, in which they were subjected to bizarre coming-of-age rituals. In some gangs adolescents were required to prove their manhood by the killing of a rival gangster, or, as in recent times, by the violent gang-rape of young women.[33] Don Pinnock, a long-standing observer of the gang scene, comments that '[boys] have no model of how to be a man. They think men are violent, they carry guns and they fuck, and these are the things we have to do as men.'[34] These attitudes were cultivated over decades in the no-go zones which townships had become. Even the police retreated in the face of the gratuitous violence which came to mark gangster behaviour (see, for example, the extremely revealing account of the evolution of the gangster personality in the biography of Godfrey Moloi, a former Sophiatown and Soweto gangster).[35]

In concert with the appalling conditions of exploitation in the workplace, these circumstances played havoc with the male psyche and contributed to the sustained practices of both private and public violence. In recent years, it has become clear how much spousal abuse and domestic violence are part of the townships, created under the apartheid policy. In this context women had to find ways of managing their men in the face of considerable difficulties. Alex Tabisher, who was a young man in Kewtown township on the Cape Flats in the fifties, commented that:

It wasn't nice living in the sub-economic township. It was frightening to know that nine tenths of those whom you knew would end up badly. [...] One of the most common crimes at the time was wife battering. This was the result of drinking. When husbands were told by their wives that they didn't bring home enough money, they would beat up the family. [...] In these circumstances, it was mandatory for children to go to their father's work on a Friday afternoon and to collect his wages, otherwise he would go to the shebeen with it.[36]

Waylaying a breadwinner on his way from work on a Friday continued into the seventies and eighties. Clive McBride, an Anglican priest in the townships of Factreton and Kensington during the seventies, also spoke of the difficulties of sustaining family life and the immense pressures which were placed on men. He too used to patrol the factory gates on a Friday evening, collecting his parishioners' weekly wages to take back to their families.[37]

Opportunities for social improvement in the townships were limited. This was particularly so in the African townships of Langa, Guguletu and Nyanga where, to this day, there is not a single cinema for African people. Facilities of any kind were almost non-existent.

And yet many people survived the ravages of township life. For some, the church and the mosque offered an orientation to life and a stoicism which allowed them to see beyond the limitations which poverty and apartheid imposed on their lives. For a substantial number, it was the political organisation; for others, it was the presence of significant figures in their lives who were able to see through the hidden curriculum of apartheid and who literally tutored them into adulthood.

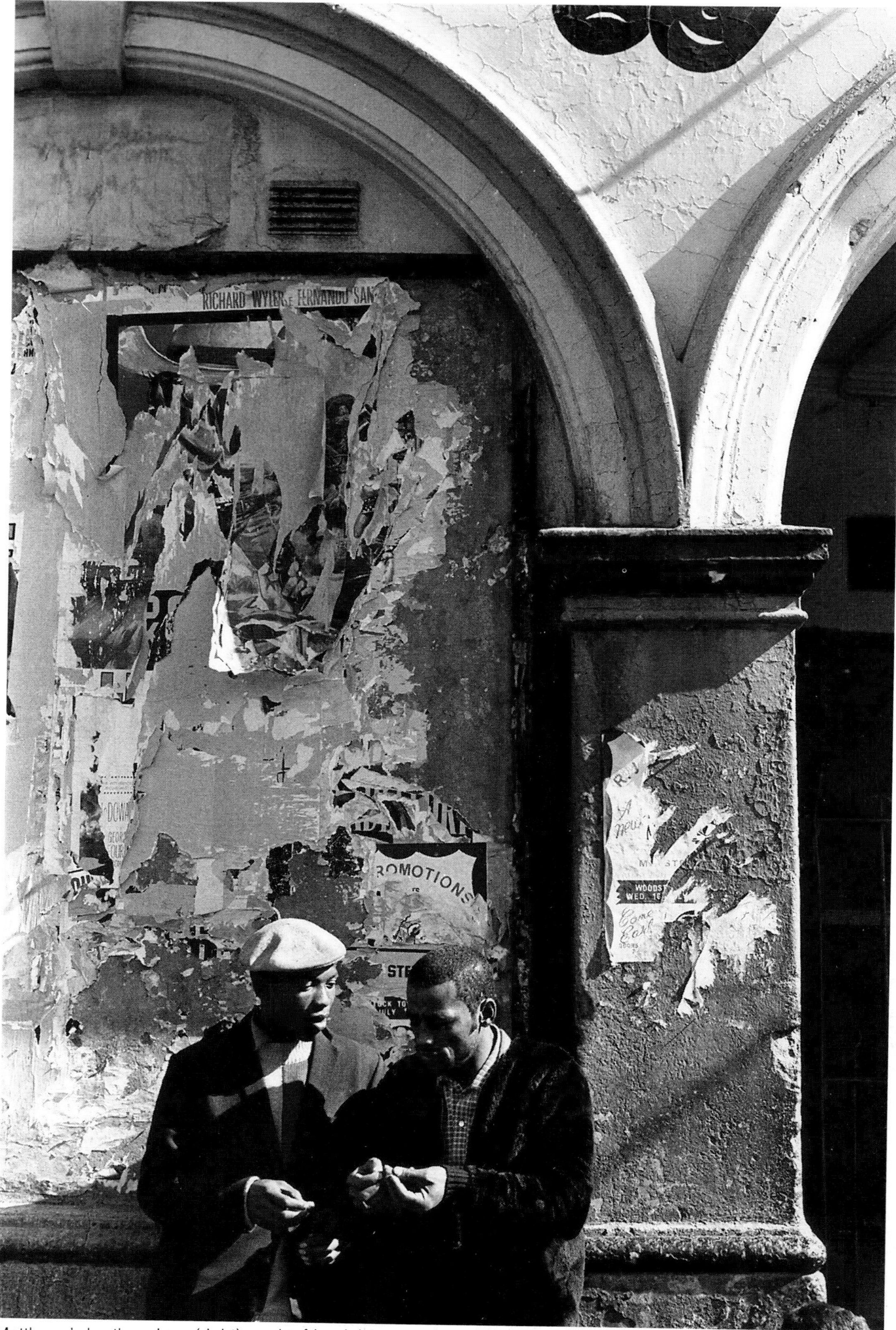

Matthews's brother, Joey (right), and a friend, known only as Manaka, in front of the British Cinema in District Six. Late sixties.

Youth and recreation

Though materially impoverished, there were, during the fifties, parts of Cape Town such as Protea Village which provided rich natural and social environments for their inhabitants. Reflecting on his youth in the fifties and the early sixties, John Valentine, who lived there, commented that 'life in that village was like heaven'.[38] He recalls being able to play to his heart's content and never knowing the kind of fear he felt when he was forced to move to Grassy Park in the seventies. For adolescents and young people it was possible to live in the bosom of apartheid and to maintain a perfectly contented life.

During the entire period of apartheid, constrained as young people were by the colour of their skins, many were able to exercise choices as to how they used their time. Music, dance and film, as opposed to more serious pursuits such as politics and the arts, flourished in the city. Attending their first dance was an immensely important milestone in young people's lives – as soon as they were allowed to, and when they began to earn some money. Stepping out required, as it still does today, intense preparation. Young coloured women placed emphasis on having their hair 'just right'. This invariably involved the subjection of one's hair to one or other elaborate hair treatment. Men went through similar rituals which included swathing one's hair in either Brylcreem, if your hair was sleek enough, or Potters and Moore, if the curl was too tight. If you could afford it, you donned a smart Vela lumber-jacket and iron-tipped shoes. The images young people sought to cultivate were those they saw in the American films screened at one of the seventeen cinemas for black people in the city. Tony Curtis, Doris Day, Marilyn Monroe, Pat Boone and Bill Hailey were all the rage in the late fifties, as were Elvis and Little Richard in the sixties. In his regular column for *New Age*, Alex La Guma wrote:

Buying cigarettes, joined conversation with boys on Hanover Street [District Six]. [...] Topic: Hollywood's latest productions. The boys like fast-shooting stuff, guys with stubbly chins and dangling cigarettes and tied-down guns. The conversation was a little blood-thirsty and I'm glad they don't allow tied-down guns in this town.[39]

Another correspondent to the same newspaper, a Mr Henry Naudé, an executive member of the South African Coloured People's Congress, described the young people of the time somewhat more generously:

[The] Coloured teenager will be found mostly at bop parties over weekends in some of the larger homes. Weeknights they gather in groups at any one of their homes where there's a gram radio and bop records. Few of them possess motorcycles or scooters, but they have completely adopted the dress of their European counterparts – jeans, sweaters, lumber-jackets and socks, all in vivid colours.

Their ages range from 13 to 30 [...] the majority are factory workers. Very few of them indulge in the smoking of dagga and hardly any of the girls partake of strong liquor. On the whole I found them to be innocent of moral vices. [...] They are generous and friendly. The girls are treated as equals. [...] On the other hand, behaviour is very free and even off-hand. If you were to apologise for stepping on a girl's foot while dancing, she would be most shocked. In order to avoid being called a 'square' and to become a real 'hep cat' one has to throw all inhibitions to the winds and just let go. Fun and gaiety is their life. They live, talk and think only of dancing, the latest bop steps, records and dress styles. Their whole life revolves around rock and roll.[40]

Across the fields in Langa, young African people were going through similar experiences. But western images were less alluring; young people, particularly in the fifties, were impatient with musical styles which called on them to be formal and correct, and demanded music which allowed them to express themselves freely.[41]

While fashions were to change dramatically between the sixties and the nineties, young people continued to retain their love-affair with American culture. When television was introduced in the mid-seventies the culture of cinema-going went into decline in working-class areas. Many popular cinemas, such as the Avalon and the Athlone in Athlone Central, and the Gem and the Palace in Salt River and Woodstock, were shut down. American images, however, continued to shape the cultural identities of all young people. Particularly popular in the late eighties and the nineties were rap music and the gangster images projected in the videos which popularised the rapping culture.

The behaviour of young people, however, remained a sore point in certain quarters throughout this period. In the pages of the political press during the fifties and sixties there was a great deal of concern expressed at the political apathy of young men and women. Commentators from across the political divide criticised the ignorance of the youth about the state of the country. In the fifties activists lamented the indifference of young people to the plight of the oppressed. Naudé, in the same article quoted above remarked,

[Most] of you teenagers are aware that Elvis Presley has sold more than a million recordings. Are you aware that more than ten million people in South Africa are living in oppression in conditions close to slavery? [...] Is it nothing to you that you are prevented by the colour bar from getting the education you want [...] that you are kept out of all the best cinemas and dance halls because of the colour of your skins?[42]

There was a great deal of discussion during the fifties about how black people should conduct themselves. Politically conscious individuals and organisations sought to make a point about youth behaviour. While these discussions were often conducted in the pages of the press, certain organisations and individuals sought to take their opinions to a wider audience. During the late forties and early fifties, for example, the Merry Macs in Langa, a western-style jazz band, deliberately played what they thought was sophisticated music in an attempt to train the ears of their listeners.[43] An organisation was established in Langa in 1952 called the Peninsula African Socialite Association which sought 'to inculcate more Western standards of civilisation in the youth of Langa'.[44] These efforts, interestingly, were resisted by young people who were interested in African styles of music and social activities.

Young people, however, were simply doing what their parents had done before them. By the beginning of the Second World War, their parents had possessed a 'well-developed repertoire of public leisure and popular cultural' activities.[45] Before households were able to afford radios, the working class engaged themselves in private pleasures such as household music-making and public past-times such as singing in choirs, going to the cinema and playing board games. Choirs and music-making were a central part of working-class culture. For this generation, and indeed for at least the next two generations into the seventies, people, young and old, made their own

music. Much of the music was generated out of the training people received in the minstrel tradition.

The minstrels, popularly known as the Coons, and the Christmas Choirs offered a way of life for aspirant young musicians. Vincent Kolbe, a legendary Cape raconteur, recalls the pervasiveness of music in District Six in the fifties: 'You walk down the street, there was always some practice [going on] – a choir practising … If you walk past the Ochberg Hall – the Eaon Group practising opera [...] daar's a Slaamse Koor.'[46] Many people were inducted into music by being part of a crowd, watching and then imitating. The many troupes offered people an opportunity to try their hand at an instrument. Imitation provided the platform for them to perform like their American heroes. It also, however, offered opportunities for working people to satirise their social 'betters'.[47] Carnival time was an occasion for the poor and the opportunity for the inversion of the social and moral order.[48] The carnival created the space in which the poor could have their say.

Serious music-making, particularly in the jazz idiom, also emerged out of this context. The fifties and sixties gave birth to two styles of jazz.[49] Emerging from the dance band traditions of the Cape, one style was influenced mainly by American jazz and particularly by Duke Ellington, Theolonious Monk and later John Coltrane; the other style took form around the fusion of sounds which were present in working-class communities, and came to be called Cape Jazz. Great jazzmen and women were produced in the latter tradition, including Dollar Brand, today known as Abdullah Ibrahim, Henry February and Jimmy Adams.[50] Playing jazz, however, was hard on the musician, because audiences wanted to hear sounds with which they were familiar, and it took a while for the kind of music developed by Ibrahim to become widely recognised. A young and talented Jimmy Adams had to forgo a regular income with the *lang-arm* dance band which he was invited to lead in the fifties, because he sought to play jazz. He faced ostracism because he dared to venture into Langa where musicians were producing the sounds he liked.

Popular music in the fifties to seventies, particularly in the coloured townships, provided a rich pastiche of sounds for the listener. Music in the township ranged from the pure sounds of the jazzmen and women to the popular funk of Pacific Express and Richard Jon Smith, musicians who commanded large followings. While individual musicians such as these

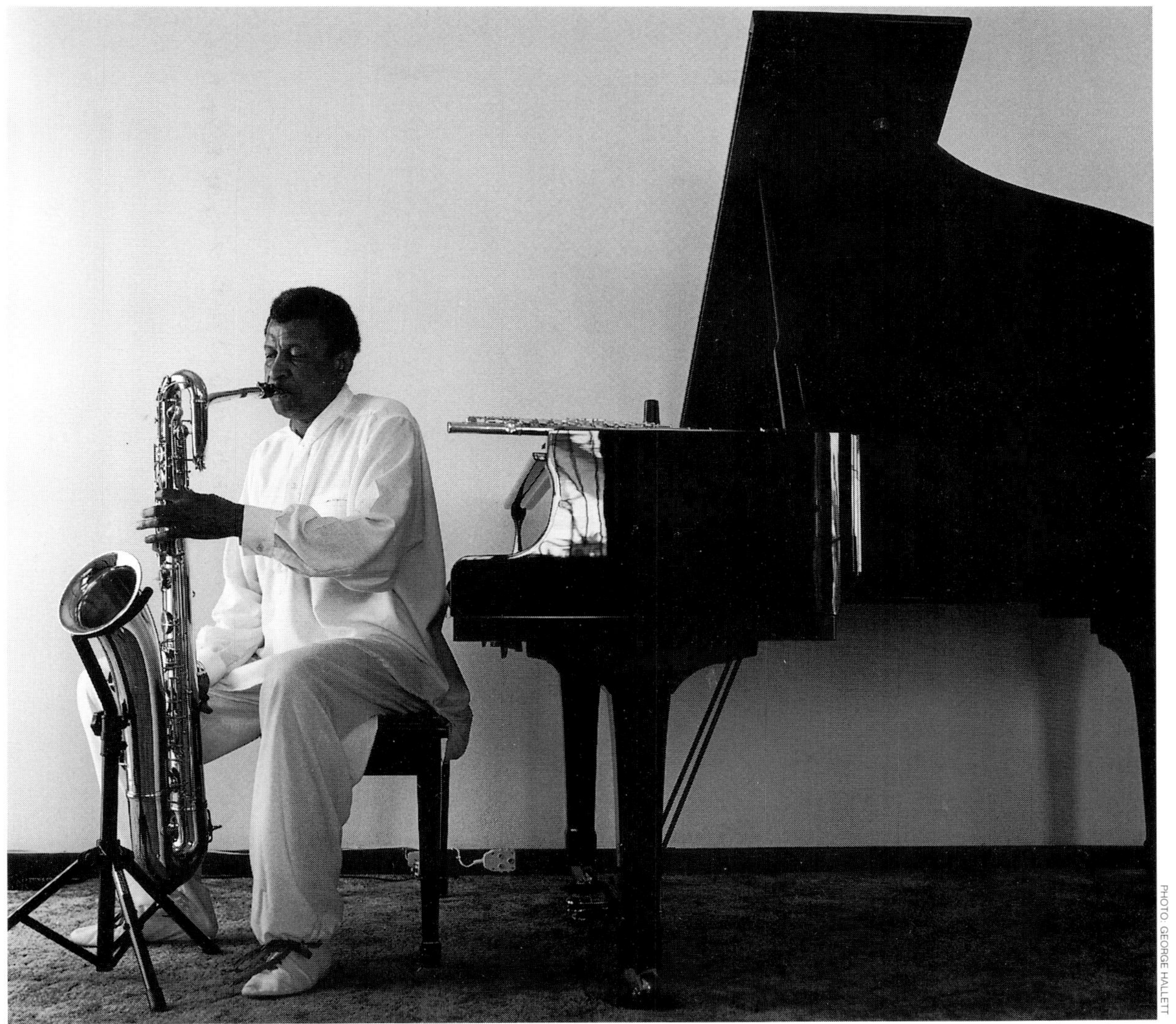

The internationally renowned jazz musician, Abdullah Ibrahim (formerly known as Dollar Brand), grew up in District Six, where he developed a distinct jazz sound. He left South Africa during the sixties and returned after the release of Nelson Mandela.

were able to hone their skills professionally, mass music continued to be performed in the colourful parades of New Year. Removed from the heart of the city, the working class took its troupes to the townships where they continued to live it up with a joyousness which not even the intensity of the pitched battles of the eighties could extinguish.

Politics and culture

But the carnival and the social practices which surrounded it were not popular amongst the politicised middle class. During the fifties organisations such as the Non-European Unity Movement poured scorn on the slave mentality they saw being acted out on the streets of the city. They actively discouraged young people from participating in and even patronising

such performances. Many commentators spoke of the tough political schooling to which they were subjected. Alex Tabisher comments: 'We were worked on by intellectuals like Hosea Jaffe who encouraged us to seek higher ground. They told us that we were not going to end up working for the City Council, where most people went. We predicated our whole thrust on saying to ourselves, "I'm not going to end up as a tattooed gangster."'[51]

Organisations such as the Teachers' League of South Africa and the Non-European Unity Movement, and the large number of civic and vigilance associations dotted around the Peninsula, were powerful voices in the communities in which they worked, and advocated a politics of what they called non-collaboration. They had established an organisation in 1943

33

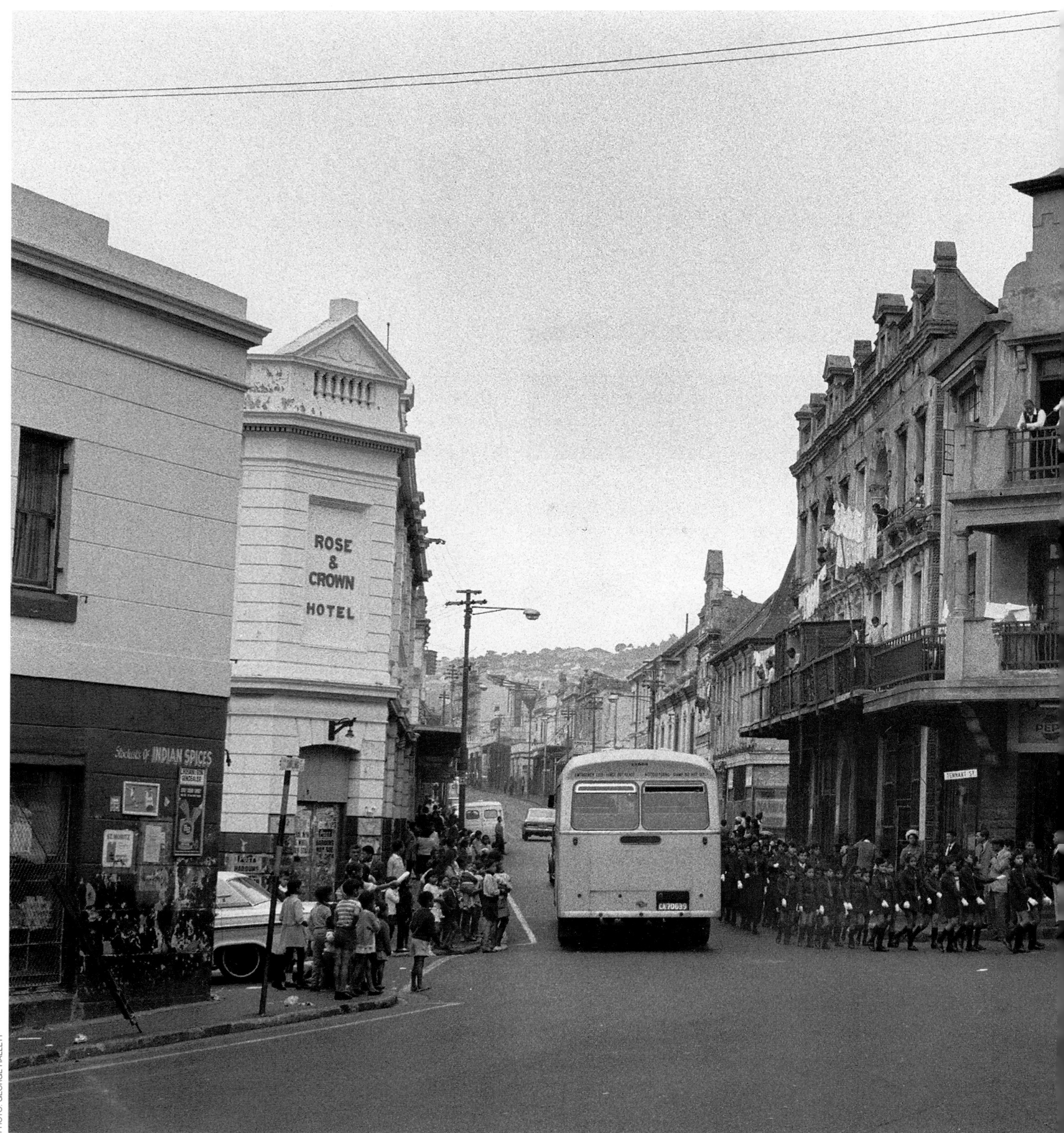

A community frozen in time. In this remarkable photograph District Six's cosmopolitan character can be seen. A church band is observed by Muslim onlookers from the balconies; a hotel is situated next to a shop for Indian spices. In the distance the typical terraced houses of the old parts of Cape Town dominate the scene.

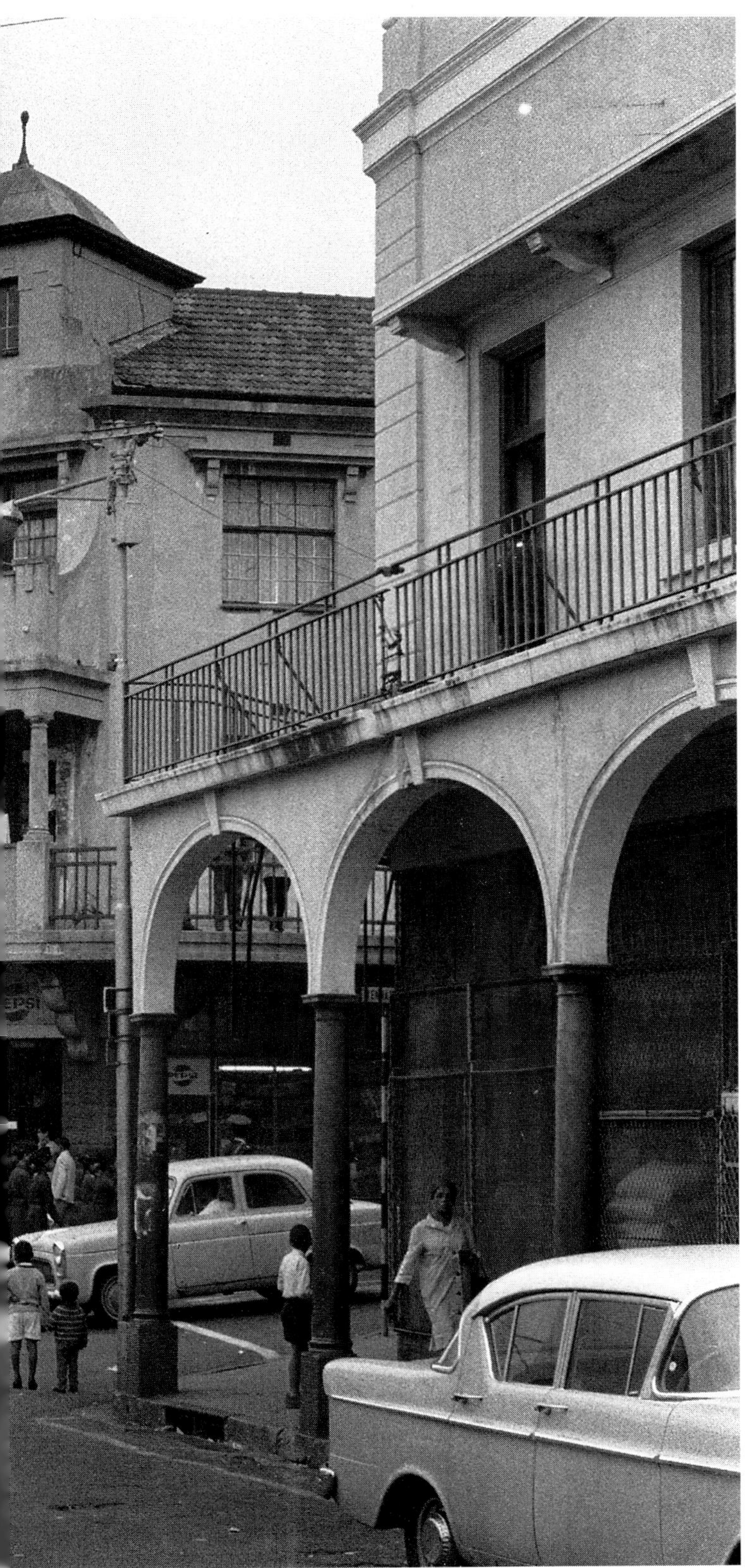

called the Anti-Coloured Affairs Department Movement (Anti-CAD) which had brought together the leading radical intellectuals in the coloured community. For the next twenty years, up to the middle of the 1960s, kindred organisations of the Anti-CAD such as the Non-European Unity Movement (NEUM) penetrated virtually every kind of organisation of the people, calling on people not to collaborate with the apartheid government or its surrogates.[52] The movement was fiercely non-racial and challenged at every opportunity the racial labelling of South Africans. Neville Alexander, a former political prisoner and academic remarks:

The vast majority of literate people in the Western Cape became politicised. The debilitating barriers of the slave mentality were gradually broken down as a new generation of young people (including artisans and clerks) left the small number of high schools in the Western Cape. Hardly any young intellectual in the Western Cape entered political life but through the portals of the NEUM. [...] At its height, the TLSA (Teachers' League of South Africa) embraced more than two fifths of all coloured teachers in the country. Because of the leverage which teachers then [1950s] had in the community, this was an inestimably important fact of political organisation.[53]

Non-collaboration became the rallying cry of the politically aware sectors in the Western Cape in the fifties and the sixties, and succeeded in staving off all attempts to institute what were called 'dummy telephones' such as advisory boards. The boycott tactic evolved and became the preferred political approach in the organisation of the people of the Western Cape. The boycott, however, also becalmed the political movement in the Western Cape during the late fifties and sixties.

The young people who were drawn into organisations such as the NEUM were largely from the incipient middle class. Most of them were teachers or ministers of religion, and a significant number were lawyers, doctors and students who, as disciples of the boycott, had, as Alexander jibes, 'an almost Calvinist fear of disporting themselves in the streets'.[54] The result was that the movement did not participate in mass political struggle after 1952 and the African National Congress-led Defiance campaign. When the social conditions for mobilisation of the masses improved in the late seventies and early

eighties, the organisation was unable to capitalise on
its earlier success and the door was opened for ANC-
aligned structures. One such organisation was the
United Democratic Front, established in 1983, to
develop politically attractive campaigns and so to
build a mass base in townships such as Mitchell's
Plain, Bonteheuwel and Elsies River. Earlier, after
the 1976 uprising in Soweto, students and workers
in the Western Cape gravitated towards ANC-aligned
organisations such as the trade union movement and
the student organisations which came into being in
the late seventies and early eighties. When the
struggle was reaching its climax in the late eighties
and the early nineties, it was the Congress movement which emerged strongly as the interpreter of
the popular will and provided the organisational
form for the establishment of the new government in
1994.

The popularity of the ANC-aligned organisations
in the Cape was made possible by the mobilisation of
the youth in the townships. The youth were responsible for taking their generally conservative communities and dragging them into action against the
apartheid state. During the eighties, with the battle
cry of 'Action, Comrade, Action', students and workers
in the UDF, the student organisations and the trade
union movement transformed the Cape into a war
zone. In Guguletu and Athlone, in Elsies River and
Grassy Park, streets were turned into no-go zones
for the police as barricades were constructed and
people took the streets. Hundreds of young people
were martyred as a new militancy swept the Cape.

Successful as the Congress movement was during
the eighties and nineties, it did not, as the NEUM had
done, focus its attention on the hard ideological work
of tutoring its membership. During the fifties, sixties, seventies and for a while in the eighties, the
NEUM continued to lecture and train those within its
fold.[55] Young people were kept abreast of developments in the international world, were trained to
read Trotsky, Lenin and Marx, and were mentored in
the arts, music and literature. They were, however, a
middle class cut off from the grime, noise and exu-
berance of the Cape Flats. The populist ANC-aligned
movement, on the other hand, mixed with the people,
drew its leadership from within the ranks of the
people and understood them in a way which the
NEUM did not. The populists, however, spurned intellectual questions, sought to focus on bread and but-
ter issues and essentially passed by the opportunity
to talk about culture and race in the communities in
which they worked.

Organic intellectuals and cultural life

The political movement was an important route of
escape from working-class subordination for people
in the fifties and sixties.[56] This was certainly so for
those young people who lived in the interstices of
working and middle-class life and who were fortunate
enough to have as their teachers towering intellectuals such as R.O. Dudley at Livingstone High School
in Claremont and Ben Kies at Trafalgar High School
in District Six. But there were other opportunities
which occasionally arose for precocious young people
in the city. These were provided by individuals who
were themselves either self-made intellectuals or
were people who had passed through the school of
the NEUM but who chose to work with ordinary
people. One such person was Cissy Gool who was in
the forefront of the anti-segregation struggles of the
fifties. She gathered around her young men and
women whom she introduced to her world of books
and music. Also influential were important figures,
as Vincent Kolbe said, 'like the writers Ziervogel and
La Guma'.[57] Young people were lucky to have these
cult figures around them. They invited young people
from the townships to their parties and lent them
books.

A key figure during the fifties was Kolbe himself,
who started out working as a librarian in the Hyman
Liberman Institute in District Six. He later worked
as a librarian in Kewtown and was angered when
the City Council began to segregate its libraries in
the fifties. Fired by the discrimination in the Library
Service, he set out to make his library as good as one
could find anywhere. It was there that he developed
his friendship with key working-class poets and
artists such as James Matthews, Peter Clarke and
George Hallett. As Kolbe said:

*The library was a place where these young people
met. They would recite poetry. I remember them as a
Bohemian set, unlike those at the Liberman [Insti-
tute, in District Six] where the discourse was very
political. The library was a cultural centre, and [...] I
was their librarian, that's why they know me – George
[Hallett] and Peter [Clarke]. They enjoyed life, went
to the Athlone Hotel and saw there the parallels, the
ingredients which they read about in the great books.
Koestler, Jean-Paul Sartre, Camus. I had to get these*

things for them. Baldwin [...] The question for these people was how to [stay] creative. [...] The public library was the poor man's (sic) university. [...] People like James [Matthews] had lots of respect for working-class life. [...] They were intelligent people who themselves came from working-class families but who defended their right to be respected.[58]

In describing the library at Kewtown, Kolbe underplayed his own significance. As Alex Tabisher said, 'Vince was ahead of his time. He was influenced by European philosophers and encouraged us to read [...] we also tapped into his love for music'.[59] Critically, moreover, people like Kolbe realised the important role of working-class culture. Tabisher explained: 'While some of us were embarrassed by coons, people like Vince said that we shouldn't ignore those guys, that it was a form of intellectual snobbery. He had a larger vision and argued that we should have a place for boeremusiek and coons.'[60] Kolbe realised that township life was not easily going to cultivate in young people a sense of discernment and an understanding of the nature of the world in which they lived, nor provide the guidance for their developing beyond its hidden prescriptions. Tabisher remarked that the rhythm of life in the townships 'was very pedestrian. Being in the company of people like Vince and James – these were high points which made the difficulty of going to a two-bedroomed house much easier [...] we admired these guys, [...] and we used these meetings with them to recharge our batteries'.[61] Kolbe continued to influence young people right up to his retirement from the library service in the late eighties.

Conclusion

In seeking to make sense of the experience of being a working-class Capetonian in the latter half of the twentieth century, it is easy to caricature the nature of that experience around the stereotypical coloured drunk. It is also easy to remain trapped in the discourse of what one might call 'victim-bashing' and to decry the propensity of working-class people to sort out their problems through the use of violence. There certainly are many references and images which one could invoke to support these representations. A violent and debauched Cape Town certainly exists. A casual perusal of the daily news over a period of years would confirm that.

It is, however, a serious mistake to read into township life the image of a homogeneous proletariat. During the period of the most intense oppression in the city, including the traumatic upheaval of forced removals, working-class Capetonians continued to cultivate a sense of community and responsibility for one another. Sociologist Elaine Salo, currently doing work in Manenberg with adolescent girls, argues strongly that forced removals and the desperation induced by apartheid did not extinguish the humanity of people in the township. She makes the point that new communities have arisen in the seventies, eighties and nineties which continue to hold fast to the spirit of *kanala* and which have been able to hold back the destructive demons of apartheid.[62] This spirit is one which is not recognised and which is rarely flighted in the news because of its very ordinariness. But it is this ordinariness which has endured and which has produced, for every gangster, several young men and women who continue to work in social and sports clubs, who take the brave step of becoming shop-stewards in their trade unions, who week-in and week-out maintain the flowers in their churches and clean their mosques, who look after the children of those who have no child-support, who dare to try their skills on the dance-floors of the dozens of ballroom clubs on the Peninsula, and who dare to be mothers and fathers to their children.

In reading this experience of the last fifty years, therefore, it is important to recognise the immense productivity of the townships and its continued ability, after the golden years of the fifties in the Peninsula, to produce writers such as James Matthews, Richard Rive, Alex La Guma and Nomvuyo Ngcelwane, painters such as Peter Clarke and Tyrone Appollis, musicians like Basil Coetzee, Abdullah Ibrahim and Winston 'Mankunku' Ngozi, and photographers such as George Hallett.

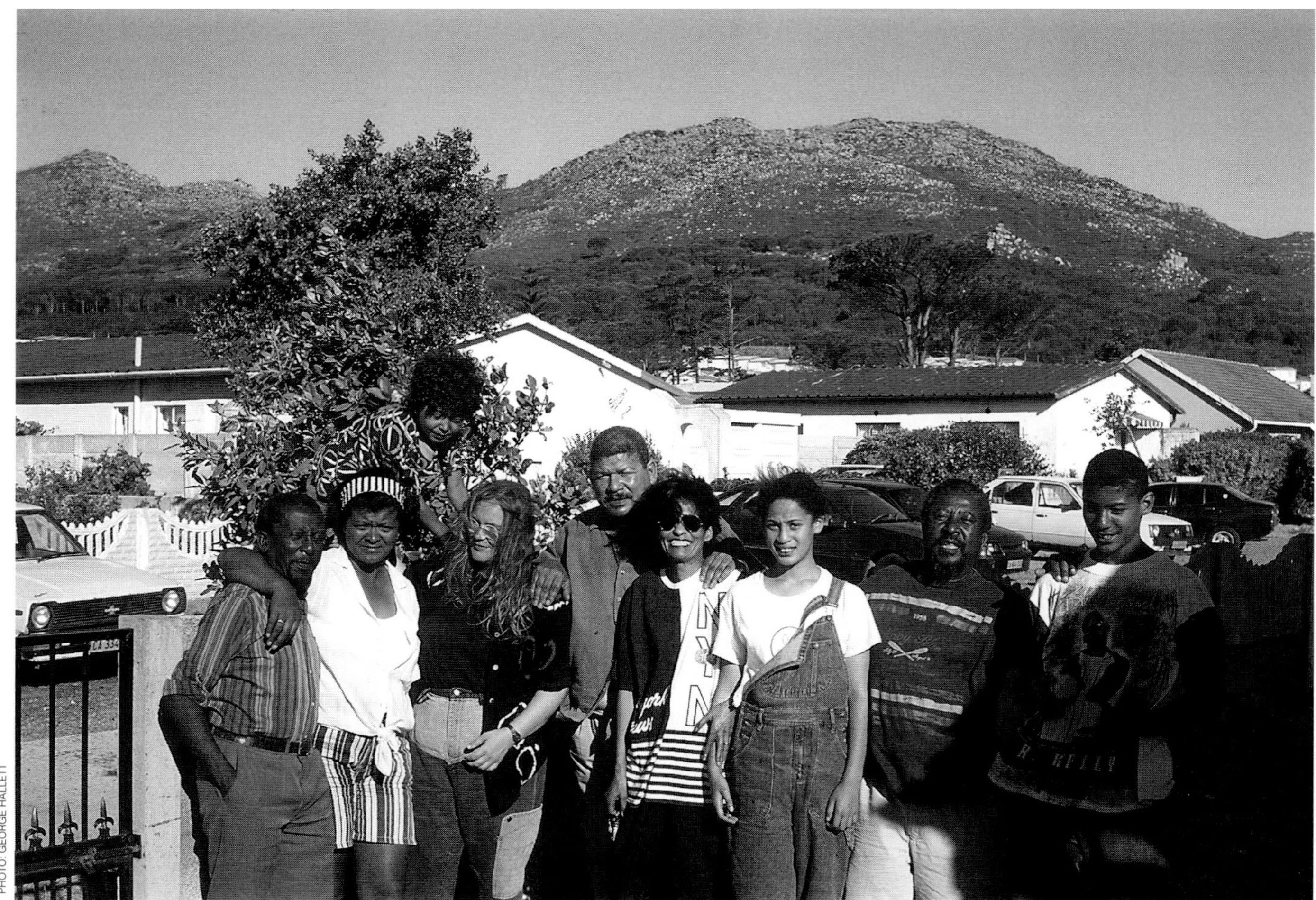

From left to right: Clarke, Lynn Warries, Leon Voss-Davis, his mother, Barbara Voss, Donald and Beverley Jansen, their daughter, Inge, Lionel Davis and the Jansen's son, Sven. Ocean View, 1997. Beverley Jansen writes short stories and Davis is a painter who served seven years on Robben Island as a political prisoner.

Living through a chunk of the century

Peter Clarke and James Matthews
in conversation with Kayzuran Jaffer and Hein Willemse

AN EXTRACT

2 May 1999, Ocean View

HW: James, you and Peter have lived through a chunk of this century in which things have changed quite dramatically, from the early thirties, through the forties, through the fifties, the upheavals of the sixties, seventies and now into the nineties. Your experiences are important for what they say about black people's lives in this part of the country. The extraordinary part for me is your presence as creative people, who have been reflective all along, for a major part of your lives. We need to record how you have experienced your environment.

JM: I, for one, would say that there's a surplus of stuff. Such an opportunity would fill a gap, provide a permanent record of the period.

KJ: There is definitely a need. What were black writers doing? What were the issues: speaking with the voices of the land?

PC: I think what you're saying is extremely important, but I feel that it is necessary to interview a range of people, getting information from them, not necessarily the egos and the stars, but many different people. Something as simple as – and this would not be considered a major art form – how to make a good samoosa. That's specialised information. And you're right that there weren't many [artists] at that time. When I think of all the writers, I ask, 'Where are they now?' The writers of the seventies, of course, weren't around in the sixties or the fifties, but their thoughts about the fifties and sixties are as valid as those of the people who have lived through it. Then one will be able to get a sense of balance. I actually wonder at times, 'Where are all the struggle writers? Did they all just evaporate?' I sometimes bump into these people, and they're not involved in writing any longer.

JM: There's no record really. Poetry was an instant form of writing; some of us suffered badly because of that. Some stopped writing because of interference by the state. Those are problems that confronted us. We lost a lot, because publishers, during that period, weren't very keen to publish our stuff. So a lot of us died in that sense.

PC: Yes, that's the same story with painters. If any painting, drawing, acrylic or whatever hinted at the political situation, it couldn't be shown in the galleries. I know in fact one person, one of my dear liberal friends, who took me up on this, because they'd got lots and lots of money and I was sure they'd buy something. And I listened to this conversation, between the two of them, and the one said to the other, 'Say, what about this one?' And the other one said, 'It is good you know, but I'm afraid I can't live with it. It is too full of *Sturm und Drang*.' That stuck with me for years. I mean, we've had to put up with this *Sturm und Drang* all our lives!

JM: We didn't bother much about it, and we brought out what we thought we should be doing. The other side, the white side, tended to determine what would be safe enough to be published, so that they wouldn't run into financial problems or be embarrassed by the system. I can only come to the conclusion that most publishing houses and galleries played a poor role in supporting the revolution.

PC: The only time they played a part in the revolution was when it was quite safe, when it was so obvious that they wouldn't lose anything in the process.

JM: Exactly, and it is so cynical, on their part, to now claim otherwise. If there was anything that would be disastrous to their financial or personal side, then they steered off. This is one of the reasons why I needed to start a publishing house. This is one of the reasons why I started a gallery, for the sheer necessity that we should have a place of our own, with no thoughts of what would be safe for oneself.

HW: What kind of support was there, at the time you established BLAC [the publishing house named after the acronym for Black Literature, Arts and Culture]?

JM: None. After Spro-cas brought out *Cry Rage!* it was banned and I started working on a project involving poetry written by black poets. I came to them [Spro-cas] with a concept of the same nature, and Peter Randall said, 'No James, I don't think we can do it, but we suggest you try and do it yourself.' I can understand that. It was expensive for them and the first one didn't work out financially. I didn't have much of an idea of doing it myself. I had to teach myself as we went along. I spoke to S & S Printers, they agreed to it, they printed it, and *Black Voices Shout!* was banned immediately. It meant that I owed the printers two years' work – money-wise – to pay them off. I made it very hard for myself with that book. I wanted the poets to work with me. The poems needed to speak about our situation. I, for instance, asked Adam Small to contribute. He sent me some stuff, lines from …

HW: *Black, Bronze and Beautiful* …

JM: … or something to that effect, lines on a horse. It was fine, but at the end this horse was castrated. That was not what we were into, we were saying, 'We are proud and we are fighters.' A poem like that would negate what we were doing. I had no fault with his writing, but I had fault with the aim.

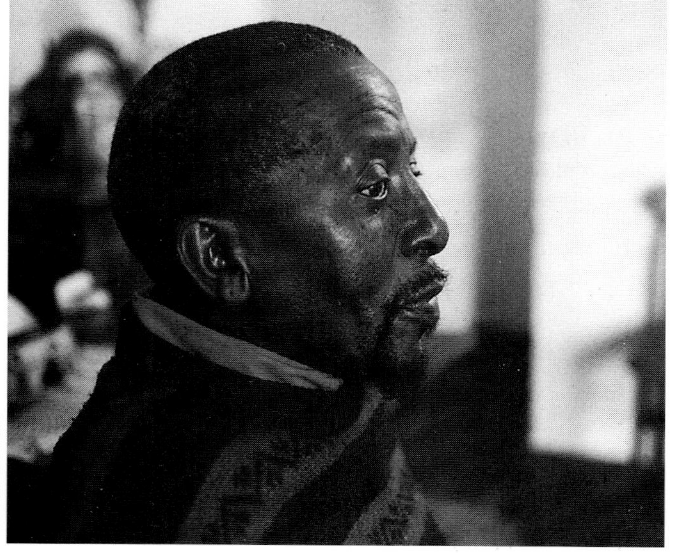

HW: So at time BLAC was driven ideologically?

JM: I couldn't see myself publishing art for art's sake. I could not allow space for a piece of work that didn't illustrate and define our stance.

HW: Peter, I was just thinking: in your paintings there's an artistic integrity, you never seem to worry too much about the whims of the time.

PC: I felt it important to express a whole lot of different things. I didn't want to stick to just one thing. I couldn't stick to just one subject.

HW: Yet, your work is also very political.

PC: I've problems with the political thing. A political poem, painting, can be for the moment, so often *is* for the moment.

JM: Yes.

PC: If I think of a political subject in pictorial terms, I think of a number of works, especially a work by Goya, which shows a group of peasants, being massacred by a bunch of French soldiers with muskets. You see all these bodies in heaps and falling in different positions. That one picture speaks for all time, there is no reference to a date. When you look at that and you compare it to Kosovo, Vietnam, even here, where I think of listening to the radio, the Truth and Reconciliation trials, somehow that painting goes beyond the moment. It speaks for all time. It speaks for anybody who was suffering anywhere.

HW: What about the *Guernica?*

PC: It's a very good painting. In a way it's related to the Goya painting.

HW: What about Diego Riviera and David Siqueiros? Riviera was a muralist and a revolutionary and they influenced you.

PC: I was very young when I came across them and they gave me something I could identify with. That's the problem with art education in the country. There were no artists on the Cape Flats, there were no artists in townships, there were no black people who were artists. I remember it was often a great surprise at those parties when you said what you were doing.

JM: When I look at Peter's early work – linocuts – it was very work-orientated, a gallery of workers as workers and not as objects.

HW: Are you're saying that it was very socialist-realist?

JM: Very much so, very much so.

PC: I think that's where the Mexicans come in, they also made paintings from their surroundings.

JM: I still get warm inside when I think of those Teslaarsdal pictures, the pictures of the raw earth,

Teslaarsdal, the road. That was one of Peter's first drawings about the place. It was published in the *Golden City Post* – beautiful! Peter didn't have money at that stage. It's printed on the inside of *The Party is Over*.

PC: That's not the correct picture [published on the inside cover of *The Party is Over*].

JM: For me Teslaarsdal was a place of rest, with all the shit that I was in, looking at that particular picture, cooled me off, made me feel calm.

PC: You know there is one other point that comes up, when I think of black painters, writers, publishers: how difficult it was to get black people to respond to art. People looked at this, but they weren't the ones who bought it. They were excited, 'Is kwaai, jy weet, jy's een van ons, ja my broe,' and so on. But they weren't the ones who were buying. It was always whitey who bought these things. I once took some books and went to friends of mine, thinking these are the ones that they would buy. There was bugger all response. They were not interested. They never gave me any reason, they paged through them. I knew that this wasn't going to work, they didn't want to. It's still a problem.

KJ: They would have bought a couple of Shakespeares. They're victims of that old education, 'What is literature? What is art?'

JM: There's nothing wrong with it, but when art signifies a sector *only*, then it's bad. Our kids are already fucked up at school as to the appreciation of what is art, poetry and literature. What's more, they are taught that only a special type of person is capable of producing it. They couldn't get into it.

PC: You know I'd given a lot of pictures to people; they'd roll it up as I gave it to them, they'd toss it onto the wardrobe and it was never seen again.

JM: I used to read in shebeens and would tear out pages as I went along. 'Maak vas!' More guys in the working-class areas, the ghetto cats, knew about my work. I was once with [the poet] Mavis Smallberg in a car and we stopped at a robot and a car drew up next to us. A guy rolled down his window and he started reciting one of the poems in *Pass Me a Meatball, Jones*. Now that was a compliment! So their mindsets had changed completely.

HW: Peter, you once sold photocopies of your work, selling pictures at 50 cents or one rand in the seventies, eighties.

PC: That went on for a long time, not only once.

JM: Yes, but Peter sometimes didn't have money to buy paper to do another drawing.

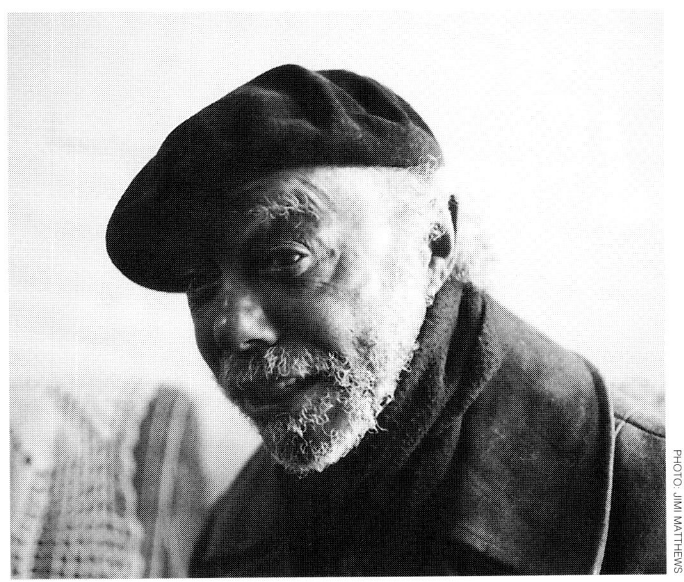

PC: That is a fact, when I think of not having backers, backers of knowledge about art or literature – we had to start from scratch.

HW: That's a very important observation, because there's no accumulated history of black literature and art in this country. On another point: the interesting thing about you, James, is the kind of technical knowledge that you've accumulated in your novels, about writing novels. In your case it's not a formally taught thing.

JM: I left school before I was fourteen years old. I don't have a Junior Certificate.

KJ: So you learnt to make books from … looking at them.

JM: Reading.

HW: I once had an interesting experience that probably illustrates James's interest in the way novels are made. James was raving coherently for half an hour about Ignacio Silone and the way he works on his characters. He was looking at the book – not as a reader, but as a writer, trying to make sense of how Silone's novel was constructed.

JM: Yes, I think most of us, even Peter, we look at a novel or a painting trying to work out how it came about. What was in the mind of the writer or the painter? I'm still particularly fond of Leo Tolstoy, Balzac, Maupassant and early Gorky. I think, both of us really, taught ourselves. I've a far broader knowledge of writing than just English writers – Dickens obviously, Meredith possibly, Thackeray possibly, Austen, Brontë, but that was it.

HW: Peter, talking about forerunners, influences.

What about Louis Maurice [a contemporary painter]? How important was he in your development?

PC: We knew each other. I think it was 1947. I was working at the docks in Simon's Town – when I found out about some art classes. Louis Maurice was one of the members. That's how I got to meet him. But I think one of my teachers at Livingstone High School, Mr Esterhuizen, was an early influence. He'd a very good collection of art books. So there was an introduction to art. He used to allow us, those who were enthusiastic, to page through the books. Direct influences came much later. As the interest started to build I started looking out for art. You know, if you see one Van Gogh you started looking out for his particular works. There was that kind of exploration and search, going to the gallery on Church Square, going to the bookshops, looking at all those luxurious books, I couldn't afford as a dock worker. I'm talking about the nineteen forties. I would go and page through those books, reading a chapter this week, coming back next week Saturday, continue, and the next, only to find out that the book has been sold. So there are several books I haven't completed reading. So I went to town to read.

JM: Peter and myself, you could say that we are almost more than brothers. Our development in this period is of a similar nature. He did the cover for *The Park and Other Stories* and inside *The Party is Over*. He did drawings of one of our most beautiful periods in Teslaarsdal.

HW: Why did you go to Teslaarsdal?

PC: I wanted to get away from the Peninsula for a little while. I'd finally made up my mind to stop being a dockyard labourer, to paint full-time for three months, before going back to look for a job. A friend of mine, who was originally from there said, 'Why don't you go there?' He spoke to his father and his father said, 'All right, he can come and stay in this house.' So I went and stayed for three months and enjoyed it tremendously. In that time I painted and forgot about the agonies of dockyard labour. I used to do this every year for the latter part of the fifties.

HW: In 'Winter shepherding' in *Plain Furniture* you write about 'getting away' from the pretence of city life, going to the 'ordinary people'. It seems to have been a wonderful experience of pastoral life.

PC: Yes, I think it was. Sometimes one forgets to be one's ordinary self. One needs humble people to make you aware of certain things. One can be caught up in

a lot of pretence, quite easily. I felt that I needed a change. I came back better equipped to cope.

HW: James, how did you reflect your experiences as a telephonist in your work?

JM: I became a telephonist after other things. My first job was selling newspapers. Then I became a messenger at the *Cape Times*, which to an extent, helped in my development, because it was writing, although not fiction, but it was a form of writing. I was always interested in writing. So being there wasn't far away from what I wanted to do. I left the *Cape Times* for *Drum* and *Post*. They had their offices in Corporation Street. The guy I was to work under was Barney Desai, but he left the same day as I was to start. Not knowing much about the editorial side of the newspapers, I learnt immediately how to do a rewrite job. They thought that I was on the ball, in the meanwhile I was stealing copy from the other papers. But I learnt, and later we were doing stuff far better than the other papers were doing, because we were where the action was. I liked Jim Bailey as a person, but we were part

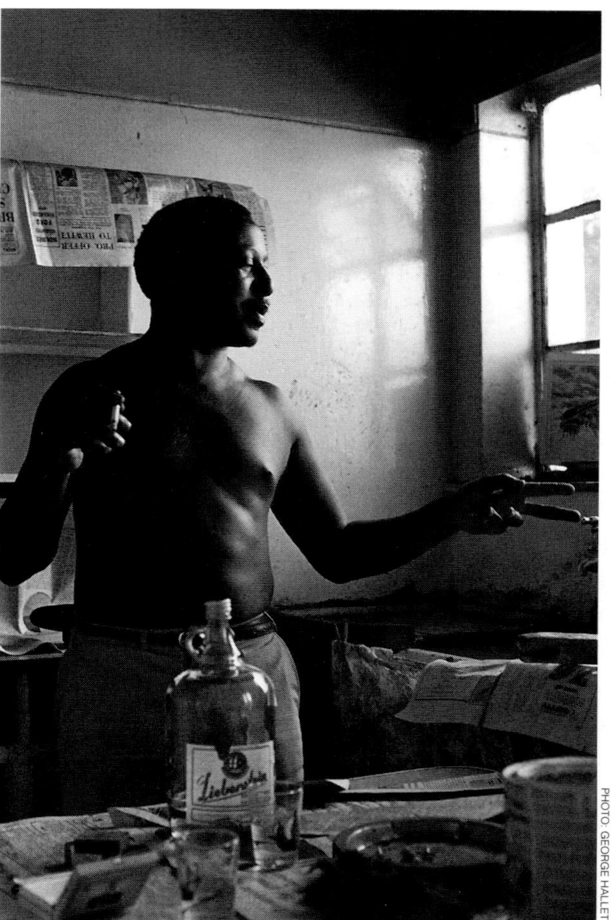

Clarke painting the house of his close friend, Bill Adams, in Silvertown. Cape Town, 1968.

of his capitalist exploitation. What pissed me off completely was a guy called Harding who worked for the *Cape Times*. He was put in charge of us, the black reporters at *Post* – coming in every morning and checking on us. A friend of mine saw Harding's cheque for coming in a few times a week. It was almost triple my salary for a month. I then initiated the first strike on a newspaper. The paper was put together in Johannesburg – by not sending up copy for a few weeks, they were in a state of panic, they had to fill the spaces. It had an effect on the paper, because it wasn't selling that well. We demanded that he immediately pay us what he paid others. Eventually I left. Then I became a night telephonist at the *Cape Times*. There, for the first and only time in my life I was fired for being drunk. It was beautiful! And the guy who fired me, his name was Judge.

PC: And then you landed up at *Muslim News*.

JM: Yes, I turned *Muslim News* into a political paper. At the time it became the most political paper in the Cape. We were the only paper that supported the struggle then. We were the only people who were allowed in Guguletu or Langa.

KJ: When was that?

JM: In the seventies. I started in 1970. When *Cry Rage!* came out I was already working for *Muslim News*. Initially the paper was only bought by Muslims, but when it was turned into a political and a religious paper then it started selling. We were banned almost every fourth issue, because of what we were doing.

HW: Were the owners of *Muslim News* instrumental in setting up BLAC as well?

JM: They were just backing me, so that I could get my books published.

KJ: That explains the connection with S & S Printers, because the Sayeds brought out *Muslim News*. Yes, the *Muslim News* was very vocal at the time, very BC [Black Consciousness].

JM: Of course we were very BC.

HW: How did you connect *Muslim News* to BC? In South Africa it's not an obvious connection.

JM: We did not put it in big bold letters. In one of my books of poetry I state clearly that I don't belong to a political party, I don't pay allegiance to any political party. I pay allegiance to freedom.

KJ: Is that connection between BC and *Muslim News* really surprising?

HW: In the United States that connection was obvious with Malcolm X and Elijah Muhammed, but locally *Muslim News* was, broadly speaking, an apolitical, religious paper and didn't want to rock the boat.

KJ: That connection was established by reasonably young people, the Young Turks. Imam Haron didn't have broad support. There were a lot of stories that it was his own community members who reported on him to the security police and the authorities.

JM: We moulded the Young Turks. It was when they started reading what we were saying that they became militant. We were careful how we represented Malcolm X; by and large their call for jihad was fucked up. Malcolm X spoke against the 'blue-eyed devils', but Islam itself or any other religion isn't meant for some people only.

KJ: 65% of Muslims in the world are living in Africa.

HW: It is very much a South African perception that Muslims have only a Malay-Asian tradition, and not an African one.

KJ: African Muslims are really getting upset with Indian Muslims in Durban and Cape Malay Muslims in South Africa, because they aren't seen to be part of the Islamic brotherhood. But of course the Arabs in North Africa also exploit their Muslim brothers of darker hue.

JM: Yet, what is the name of one of the first converts to Islam? Bilal, the African slave, and Muhammed took him as a brother.

HW: Getting back to something else: your tearful speech about apartheid and the German government at the 1980 Frankfurt Book Fair and the money you've strewn on the pavement …

JM: No, I gave it to people.

KJ: You gave it to people?!

JM: It wasn't a tearful speech, it was very emotional. I didn't know it was televised, but I would have done the same thing. I just said, 'I don't need to thank your government, because the German government is a bunch of motherfuckers.' I just could not understand the other writers saying, 'Thank you.' The German government was part and parcel of our enslavement.

KJ: What was their reaction?

JM: The Germans, because of their experience, the Holocaust and the concentration camps, have developed a different breed of thinkers. They still have atonement acts. They regret very much the pockets of racism in their country. By and large Germans are very tolerant. Just moving away from that, let's take the recent incident of the white cops here beating up

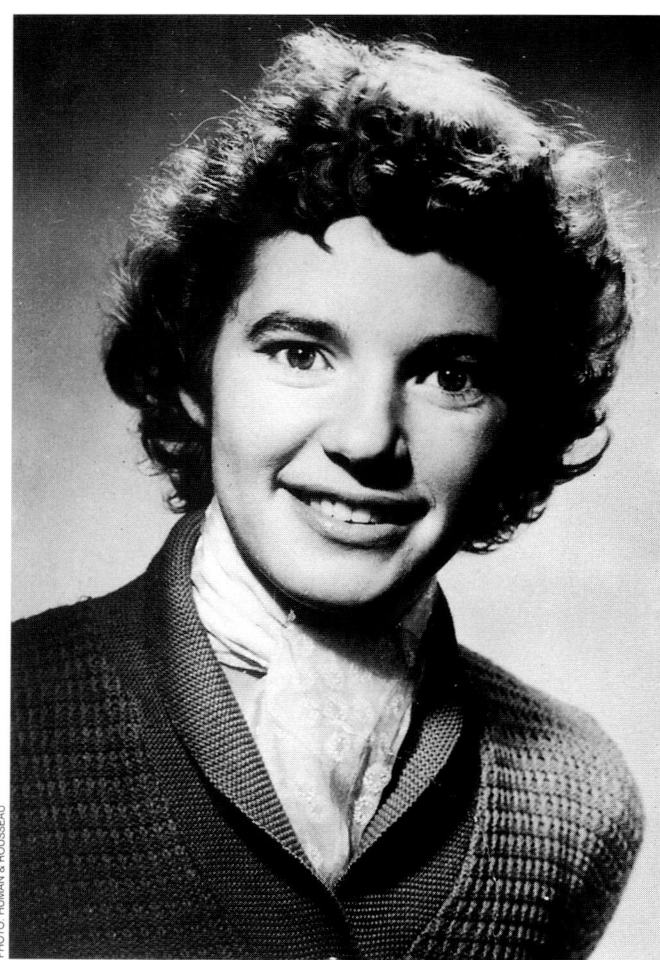

Clarke, Matthews and Rive all had a good relationship with Ingrid Jonker. They shared a common circle of friends; at times Rive would take her for a ride on his scooter. Cape Town, early fifties.

the hijackers. I was speaking to a guy and he was saying, 'Those cops were doing a bad thing, but those hijackers were *varke*, they deserved it.' I said, 'If we are talking about rights and democracy, at no cost can we allow an incident like that to happen. No matter how these cops were provoked. If we condone that, we don't deserve democracy.' That for me is important. That's what we were doing with our writing. I also had my problems with the Truth and Reconciliation process. Tutu defends it by saying that more and more things are coming into the open. We expected it, but we also need to see that the perpetrators are punished. We must safeguard freedom and justice.

KJ: So the poet still has to play that role?

JM: I wrote a poem where I end, 'has the poet now forgotten the role that he played, does he place his phrases on the political altar?' For myself I must at all times …

44

HW: … be independent.

JM: Always, always.

KJ: Take someone like Wally Serote, he has always been with the ANC. Don't you at some time have to go into areas where you can have some effect? What's the implication?

JM: Look, Wally is my younger brother. There's a real danger, the creativity has not been diminished, but what has diminished is the attitude of being the watchdog. Look, I feel a lot of books should come out, but they must be well written. A book must not just be published because we need to have it. For me this is the difference when you talk about poetry. A poem that contains four 'Amandlas' and six 'Vivas' is not a poem, it is a pamphlet – sloganeering.

PC: Isn't that also the reason why a lot of poets have disappeared?

JM: Exactly, because a lot us were not poets in the true sense. We never explored poetry fully. We thought we could use that form of expression to get across a political idea.

PC: I asked one person, 'What are you writing now?' He said, 'No, I'm not writing now, what is there to write about?' Then I thought of what Gwendoline Brooks said, 'What is there to write about, except everything.'

JM: I met her once in Chicago. She's a wonderful person, in fact, Peter, she reminds me of your mother.

PC: I only met her once.

JM: I was at a celebration of writers associated with Chicago. Then I observed Saul Bellow – that's an arrogant sonofabitch – then I saw Brooks, and I thought, Die ouens is fokken liberal, this is my mother or grandmother, who is a char lady, who is allowed to mix with …

KJ: … with Saul Bellow …

JM: … not only him but in that kind of company. I went up to her and she's a very warm person. Sometimes it is important for a writer and a painter to step back and observe, so that you can better explore. There's a difference in writing when you're writing from the outside, when you're a spectator, than when you're a participant. There's a big difference, not only creatively, but spiritually. You can be an extremely skilled writer, but cold and clinical. There is vast difference between Steinbeck's *Grapes of Wrath* and some of the writers who wrote for *The New Yorker*. They were clever cats. They were into construction and all that, but there was no soul in it.

HW: Let me explore something else: the relationship

between the small band of writers in Cape Town during the fifties and the sixties. You, Peter and Richard Rive crossed the apartheid divide to meet up with Jan Rabie, Ingrid Jonker, Jack Cope, Breyten Breytenbach and others.

JM: I would never have met those people if it were not for Peter and Richard. For me it was difficult to meet those people. By virtue of where we stayed it was virtually impossible. For Richard it was far easier, being an academic and the circles that he had chosen to be involved in.

PC: Yes, but Cape Town always had those circles, there were always those circles that overlapped. You always get to meet people in those overlaps.

JM: More so, circles of creativity …

PC: … creativity always makes things easier.

HW: So that drew people across those petty apartheid, grand apartheid lines.

JM: I feel very grateful, in that I've learned a lot of things. I also learned to retain my own respect and dignity, so that you're not swamped by all the crap. To be honest, Richard was, at times, swamped by the crap. That was the difference between Richard and myself and Peter. We were not willing to be co-opted, to be with white people just for the sake of it. We were interested to be with people who had similar needs as we had. We were not interested in upward mobility.

HW: What was the result, in terms of creativity, of that kind of association?

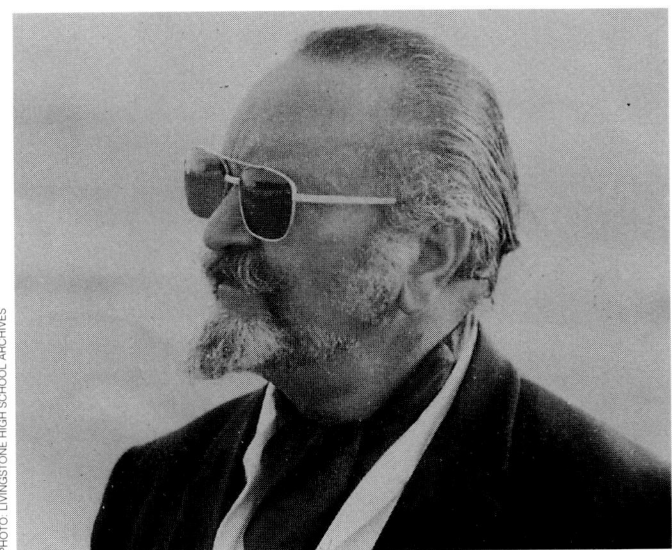

Hendrik Esterhuizen, Clarke's art teacher. He also painted under the pseudonym Henric. Most of his paintings are exhibited in the St James Hotel, St James. The photograph was taken in the late seventies.

PC: When you meet different people you're often stimulated in conversation. It presents challenges to oneself. If I think of the kinds of pictures that some of those people painted – still lifes, portraits. I sometimes felt, 'Why can't I do that, see what I can do. Perhaps I can do that, as well or better.' It was always stimulating.

JM: Creativity is an organic thing. You might be stumped at a particular moment, but then you move on to something else, a different form of writing, but you'll basically still be writing.

PC: I feel that all the art forms are related. What I feel sad about sometimes is that so many people restrict their interest to just one form. Why are they not curious about the other art forms? If you're a writer, go and have a look at paintings. Often it's a painting that can move you.

JM: Exactly.

KJ: People are always asking the artist's explanation: 'What does it mean? What is behind this painting?' How do you react to that?

PC: I feel that is a lazy way of looking at pictures. I will not give explanations for my pictures. People need to look at things and think, 'What the hell did he mean by that?'

HW: Most of your birds have the same form. The bird's a very Peter Clarke bird. It's very peculiar. How did you develop that?

PC: It's true, but I don't want to say anything about a particular kind of bird.

HW: Elza Miles somewhere says that you're very interested in 'masking'.

PC: That is something I had to get out of her head.

HW: I was surprised because I didn't see it as a consistent theme in your portfolio.

PC: I went through a little period, but it was not all that significant.

HW: James, from 'masking' to your interest in 'coloured identity'.

JM: I think each one will identify in his own way. It is not a collective thing. The creative lot amongst us will be dead set against it. I have no problem being coloured, but it is not an issue, unless it's taken in a bantustan approach. I see no necessity for a colouredstan. We shouldn't be treated differently though. I can also understand the frustrations of certain coloureds who feel that – nowadays – they are not getting a fair deal. These things breed a form of anger and lead to alienation on the part of your coloureds and Indians

HW: In Peter's work there's no emphasis on a coloured identity. There might be figures that are coloured, there may be ethnic features, but it is not the main subject matter.

PC: It will be interesting to hear what people think about the characters in my paintings. Are they coloured or what?

HW: Compare Tyrone Appollis's paintings. The subject matter is very 'coloured', ethnic specific.

JM: He's a good artist, but he makes caricatures. That's the difference. He emphasises he's a coloured *ou*: by stance, by garb. Peter paints – people. It's just incidental that they're black.

PC: No, the intention is that they are black.

KJ: In the generic sense …

PC: Yes, as opposed to white people.

HW: Like his birds, Peter's figures are very Clarkeian.

JM: Somebody else may be doing the same thing, but Peter's paintings stress the form of the bird. Their structures won't be the same. What you're saying is right. Without even checking the signature, there are the structures, your form, your landscapes, etc. You respect your identity and how you see it. The other person could see the same scene, but the aperture would be different.

HW: If we were to do a film, what would the images of your youth be?

JM: The kraal in Bo-Kaap [an open space between some houses].

PC: Paths going up a hillside, footpaths. In Simon's Town you would walk up a hill and down a hill, there would be footpaths everywhere.

HW: James, Richard says in *Writing Black* that you were reputed to be a member of a gang in your youth and that he was scared of you?

JM: Richard was a sonofabitch in many ways. He was writing for a white audience in *Writing Black*. He was always against us – as a group of black writers. He was never a BC adherent. He got late into the act when he thought there was some sense in it. When he was at Athlone High he taught his students never to read our stuff, because we weren't writing poetry.

PC: James, do you remember the period when Richard said he was born in Lower Walmer Estate? Whereas those of us who knew him said, 'Nei, daai burke is van Caledonstraat.' Only when District Six became fashionable, then he was from Caledon Street.

HW: Despite your reaction, you and Richard had a wonderful relationship.

JM: Look, it was a love-hate relationship. I had a very good relationship with Richard and we understood each other.

PC: One day Richard said to me he was going to his aunt. He explained to me where his aunt lived. I said to him, 'Good heavens, Richard, I've got relatives living just up Seven Steps. I'll go with you.' But he somehow talked me out of it.

HW: Richard never spoke about his background.

PC: No, he avoided it as far as possible.

JM: Let's look at it in this way: There is nothing wrong with upward mobility. If you're born in the ghetto, you want to get out of it. There's nothing wrong with it. But he wanted to discard his past. You've read the short story 'The party'? He's a character in that story. He recognised himself when he read it.

KJ: Isn't he called Ron?

JM: Yes, he's Ron. That was a role that Richard often played. He was a very good teacher, but not a teacher with heart enough to embrace his class. If

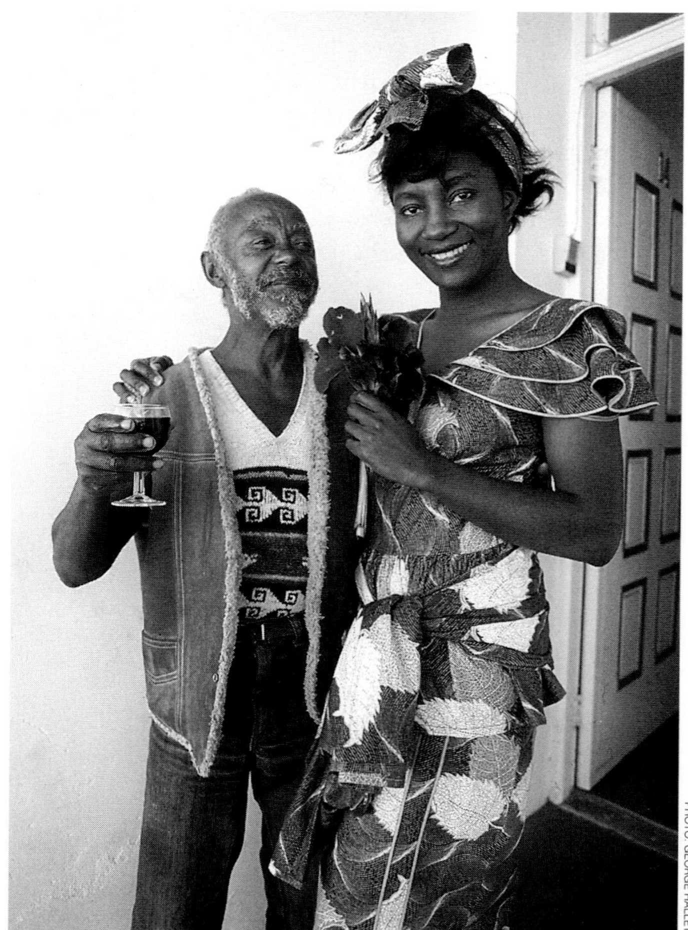

Matthews and Mēdu Hallett. Cape Town, 1992.

46

you didn't measure up to his standard then you were
not going to make it.

HW: Is Peter in *The Party is Over*? The manager,
Melvyn?

JM: We're not giving away any secrets.

HW: And David Patterson wrecking the whites'
parties?

JM: I think a lot of people are missing the point of
the book. It's a romance.

KJ: Romance in the sense of a love story. Yes, definitely.

JM: A love story that has gone awry.

HW: But it is reality disguised as fiction.

JM: That is one way of seeing it. The writing of it
was a form of catharsis.

HW: Was the cathartic process successful?

JM: I felt much freer. Not only that, this is the first
time, the year that's past, that I could write love
poems. I feel very happy about it.

HW: It has taken thirty years …

JM: … to get a lot of shit out of me. For myself to
write a love poem I must be as honest as I was or I
hope to be when I wrote political poems. It's the
same honesty. I wrote one line, 'Without love I'm as
naked as an armadillo without armour.'

HW: Isn't that in the nature of love? There is always
commitment and its drawbacks.

JM: Love has those complications and it will always
have them. My relationship with a woman now is not
to seek love in a Barbara Cartland manner or an
adolescent manner. It is to find a strong sense of
togetherness and companionship. With it comes a
strong sense of responsibility in one's relationship
with the other person. Can I ask you a question about
women?

KJ: I can't speak for all women.

JM: I'm only talking about man and woman relationships. I think that most women are not prepared
to have a physical relationship without emotional
ties.

KJ: I suppose women are brought up on this myth.
They look for the Barbara Cartland story. Women
still cling to the notion that if you enjoy sex for sex's
sake then you are somehow not such a good person …

PC: … not a nice person.

JM: Now we are coming back to love poems and
emotions.

HW: Peter, how often does that – love – occur in your
paintings?

PC: Never. It's difficult to portray that type of
emotion. If one expresses love in erotic terms it's a
different story altogether. Then it can be done.

HW: Off the top of my head I can't seem to remember whether you've done anything like that.

PC: Yes, and they are for sale by the way.

HW: But why haven't I seen those paintings? Why
haven't they been exhibited?

PC: For a long time people could not exhibit erotica.
It is only in recent times in South Africa that one
can do that.

KJ: But Peter, you can show love in a painting.

JM: The *Madonna with Child* [of Leonardo da Vinci]
is an example.

PC: That's true.

PART TWO

Peter E. Clarke

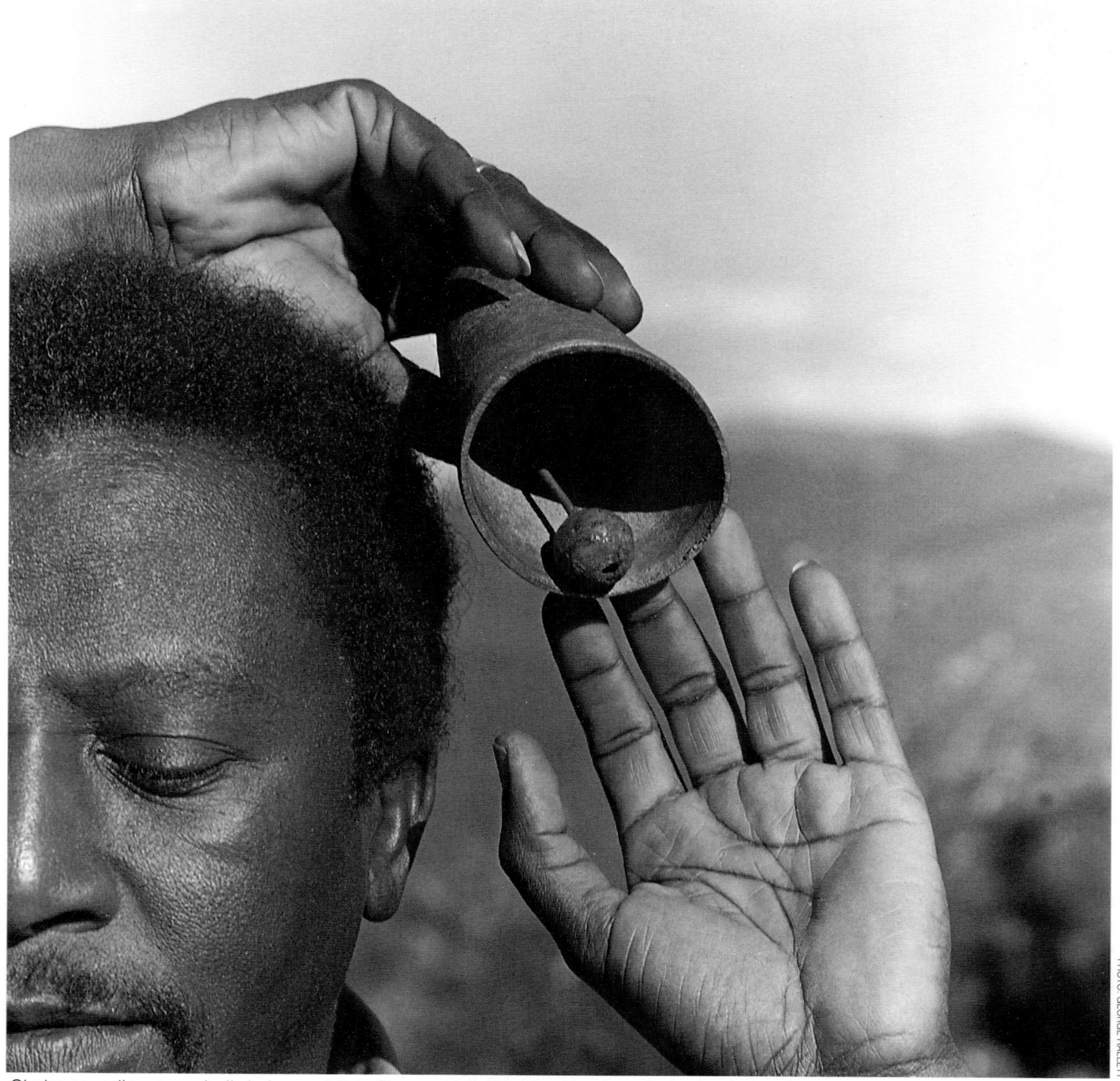

Clarke sounding a cowbell during a visit to George Hallett in Mas Domingo in the Pyrénées, in the south of France. 1979.

De man die zijn
haar kort liet knippen

PETER E. CLARKE

Sometimes one has the feeling that you are balancing on the razor-thin edge of insanity and that just a little push …

But perhaps one already is insane … Perhaps all of us living here are already insane. Imagine, some actually act at times as if the others don't exist, while the others, living in the country of their birth, feel that they are regarded as being as non-existent as the shadows of ghosts. How crazy can one get (or insist on being)?

Perhaps, as some insist, there is not a razor-edge division between sanity and insanity, but a kind of mental no-man's land buffer-strip. It seems at times that we are wandering about in this no-man's land without really knowing that we are there – or not 'all there'.

It is amusing at times to recall certain of the times when one behaved really ridiculously. A certain day comes to mind. This was years ago when I was doing art at the Rijksakademie in Amsterdam.

This particular morning, I decided I would have a haircut before going to school. I did so, having my hair cut very short. In the afternoon, after a busy day working in Loge Drie, the studio at the Akademie which I shared with Amos L. (a fellow South African artist) and a Dutch artist named Ben I. Amos and I went to Klaasen's bar. Klaasen's wasn't far from the Akademie, on the corner of Stadshouderskade and Ferdinand Bolstraat.

Klaasen's had a nice atmosphere, being snugly comfortable. One felt quite at ease. It was a popular haunt of the students during the midday break. But we usually popped in there after four when we had finished at the Akademie. We were regarded as 'regulars' and would pass the time drinking Amstels or jenevers observing the street. It was cosy and pleasant.

But this particular day – the day of the haircut – I was moody and feeling just a bit sulky, I suppose, and a little homesick, and having had my hair cut short as it was, I felt fresh and clean – and a bit aggressive. I was becoming more and more drunk because of drinking jenevers with a vengeance, instead of drinking with tact. The hours passed by. I couldn't care a damn. But at a certain stage, Amos became very worried when I announced with great feeling, 'Djy wiet, vandag lus ek om kop te slaan.'

This was so unexpected that, for a moment, Amos was uncertain about what would come up next. He told me to calm down. I did that because I could not think of any reason for banging anybody in the bar with my head and new haircut.

It was dark when Amos suggested we should go and have supper. He was hungry. I was too far-gone to care. We usually ate at Tsong Wa Low, a Chinese restaurant on De Weteringschans, because they served rice and because we both enjoyed the food tremendously. But just this time I felt, 'Oh what the hell.' We settled our accounts with the 'ober' and left Klaasen's, walking into the freshness of the night air, which made me feel more drunk and confused and heavy-limbed and aggressive.

Wanting to prove that I was sure of myself, that I was all right, I told myself that I didn't care a damn about the authorities, whoever they were. (Actually, if at that stage I had been questioned as to the identity of whomever it was I regarded as the authorities, I would not have had a very clear idea.) We walked on to Singelgracht bridge. At this point, I stepped out of myself like a third person. I looked at myself and Amos, the two of us walking.

It was after eight and we had gone directly from the Akademie to Klaasen's and I had been drinking jenevers since then. What I saw was a man, myself, his hair cut very short, walking defiantly between the tramlines and night traffic, a man who had had too much to drink, a man who was feeling a bit homesick, aggressive, melancholy. The drunk man was also thinking suddenly, vaguely, about the reclining statue on the grassy bank away on the left, now in darkness, the one that he occasionally passed by on his wanderings about Amsterdam. It was a war memorial and he had seen a wreath placed next to it, often weeks after some commemoration or other when the wreath was withered and the coloured ribbons looked a bit tatty after the onslaughts of the weather.

He felt miserable thinking about the agonies of his homeland, thousands of miles from here, and about the victims of war here, those who had suffered and those who had died in this city. He thought about Vera's mother, a person he'd never met, and about Vera saying almost hysterically, '… and then they took my mother away and I never saw her again.' He recalled Vera that night and how she looked, putting her hand to her face and sobbing and Ben consoling her, saying to her, 'Don't talk about it any more.'

He felt extremely embarrassed for starting all this merely by asking what he thought was a simple and innocent question. Unfortunately, in the process he had reopened a terrible wound.

He walked in the middle of the street, between the tracks, feeling sad about things, daring fate to make a tram, on one of its jerky metallic squeaky journeys through Amsterdam, suddenly appear out of the night and ride heavily, loudly, right over him. I looked at him and felt as sorry for him as Amos, who said, not only to break the mood, but also for safety's sake, 'Maar hoor hier, Peter, jy mag mos nie tussen die tremspore in die middel van die pad stap nie!' Amos took him by the arm, leading him carefully between the traffic and onto the curb. He obviously decided it was sheer lunacy to come all the way from South Africa to Amsterdam to have a tram ride over you.

We made it to Tsong Wa Low's and sat down. It was quiet as usual. This also served to emphasise the fact that I had a throbbing headache. 'The Rubens model', impassive as usual, took our orders. Vaguely I wondered whether she had ever been given orders by the Chinese Mafia never to be friendly with the customers, never to smile. At some stage or other, we found out what her name was, but she was always known to us as 'the Rubens model'. She had that kind of colouring, pale skin with cherry-red lips and rosy cheeks. If she took off her clothes, I supposed she would be the same colouring and as buxom as the women in Rubens' paintings. She only needed cupids floating around

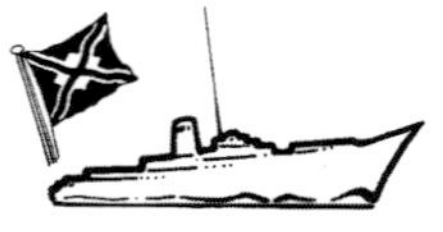

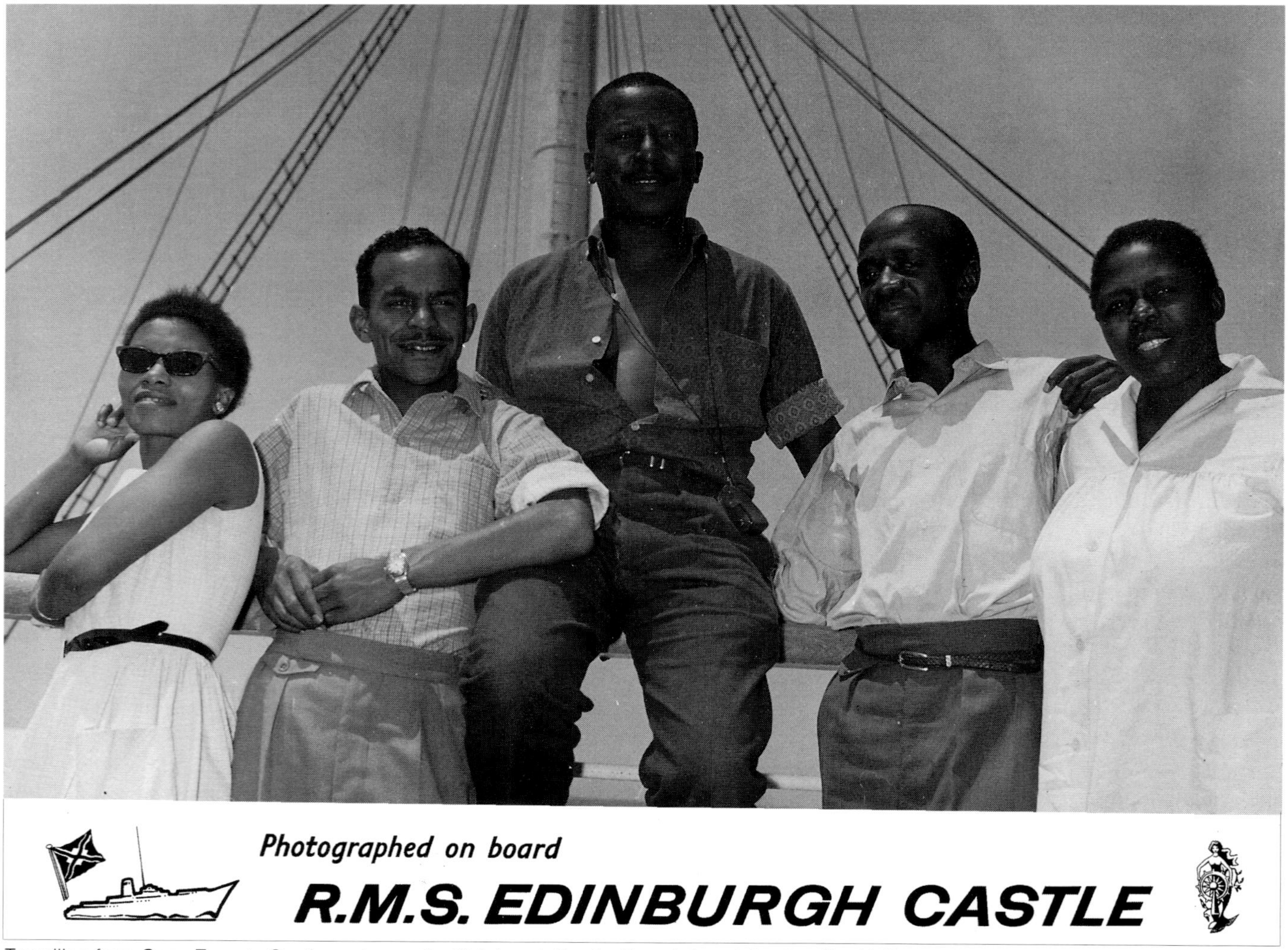

Travelling from Cape Town to Southampton on the Edinburgh Castle. From left to right: Caroline Naliseng, Amos Langdown, Clarke, Z.R. Manare and Alice Nokorosi. Langdown and Clarke were on their way to the Rijksakademie in Amsterdam; the other three, all schoolteachers from the then Basutoland, were going to study in London. September 1962.

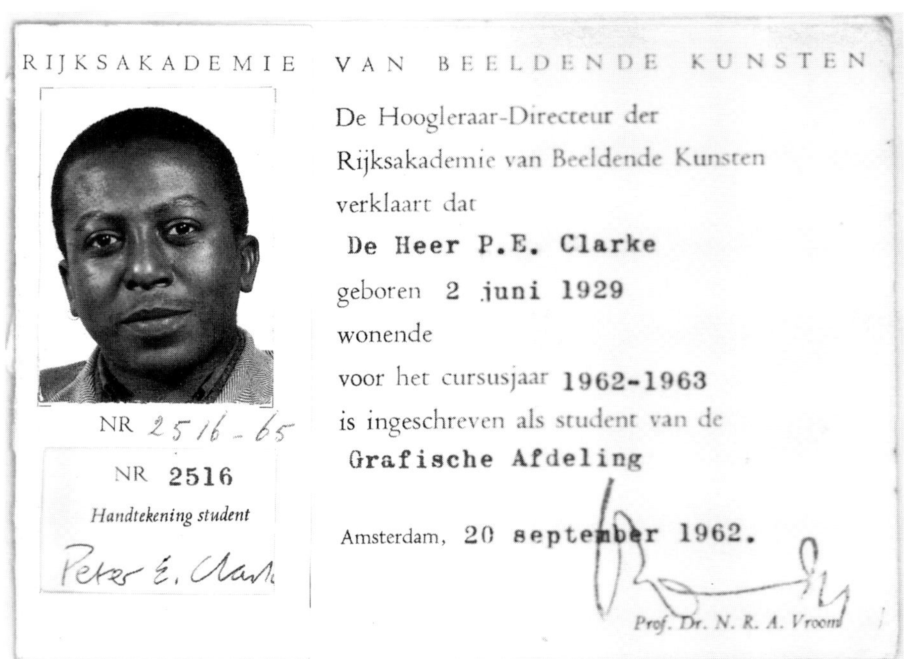

Student 2516, registered in the graphics section of the Department of Fine Arts at the Rijksakademie.

her. But cupids would have been as out of place here in this Chinese restaurant as 'the Rubens model' was out of character.

We sat and talked and listened to the traffic outside until the food came. We ate nicely prepared Nasi Goreng with its subtle flavours, one of my favourite Indonesian dishes. Only this time, with having my taste buds all screwed up and my appetite gone to hell, I had no desire for food. But I went on forcing it in because I felt I really should consume something solid for a change after drinking all afternoon, even though my conscience told me that it was too late, too late. We ate until Amos, his hunger satisfied, sat back and waited for me to finish my food. I couldn't.

Some of my earlier aggression had evaporated. Now I was merely tired and bored with eating what seemed like millions and millions of loosely cooked grains of tasteless yellow rice. I felt this rice-eating operation in which I was involved had a suggestion of disaster about it.

'Djy wiet, Amos, ek is nou net mooi gatvol van al die rys iet. Ek dink ons kan nou gaan – voordat ek alles opgooi.' I really felt that if I ate any more rice, I was going to vomit all over the place. Grains of rice would go cascading in waves on the floor, get stuck against the Mandarin red walls, the Chinese lanterns, ceiling, everything in sight. I didn't want to risk that. Amos agreed.

Maybe Amos's mind, like mine right then, was involved in fantasy too. Maybe he also felt that Tsong Wa Low would come bounding in, catlike, wearing an expression on his usually mask-like face of almost insane rage because of the ruin I had created. Not only that, in the process I'd blown the cover of what was really a drug dealing joint and exposed the opium den for what it was. It was all finished now. The police and Interpol and all manner of authorities (those authorities again!) were going to arrive and there was going to be.hell to pay.

Tsong Wa Low would come in, see the damage for which I was responsible, know what was going to happen, sit down and play a Chinese stringed instrument, a kind of mellow yellow cello, and then create some sudden catgut, bustingly plaintive strains, a signal, at which a hidden door would – TWANG-N-N-NNNNNNG! – spring open and out would come, swiftly, silently, sinisterly, the entire Oriental kitchen crew, Fu Manchu and all, all wearing black skull-caps, blue cotton clothes, white socks and sand shoes (made in Canton, but stamped 'Made in Hong Kong' because a slit-eyed red Chinese production manager decided to pull the wool over the slant eyes of a not-so-red Chinese official south of the border), all crouching Ku Fung-style and going 'sh, sh', hot breath and spittle flying from between their clenched teeth, while they crouched and then hopped about ceremoniously, chopping the air with 'wham', 'whoosh', 'shing', 'chah', before deciding just how they were going to chop me to death – with typical Oriental precision and neatness.

And as children, back home in South Africa, didn't we pass on the message to each other when we saw the odd Chinese seaman in town, which was extremely rare. 'P'sop vir hulle. Hulle vriet jou met hare en alles.' Perhaps Amos too was thinking all this as we quickly pulled ourselves together. He said, 'Okay. Voor dit begin, kom ons waai.'

We paid our food bill and fled out to De Weteringschans and into the night and safety. The air felt cool on my new haircut. Rather that, than the hot breath of Dragons.

Strangely, some of one's closest friends have absolutely no idea who the person is who lives inside the skin of the person that they believe they have known closely for years. The older one becomes, the more one acquires a kind of classic duality, becoming more worldly and therefore more puritanical.

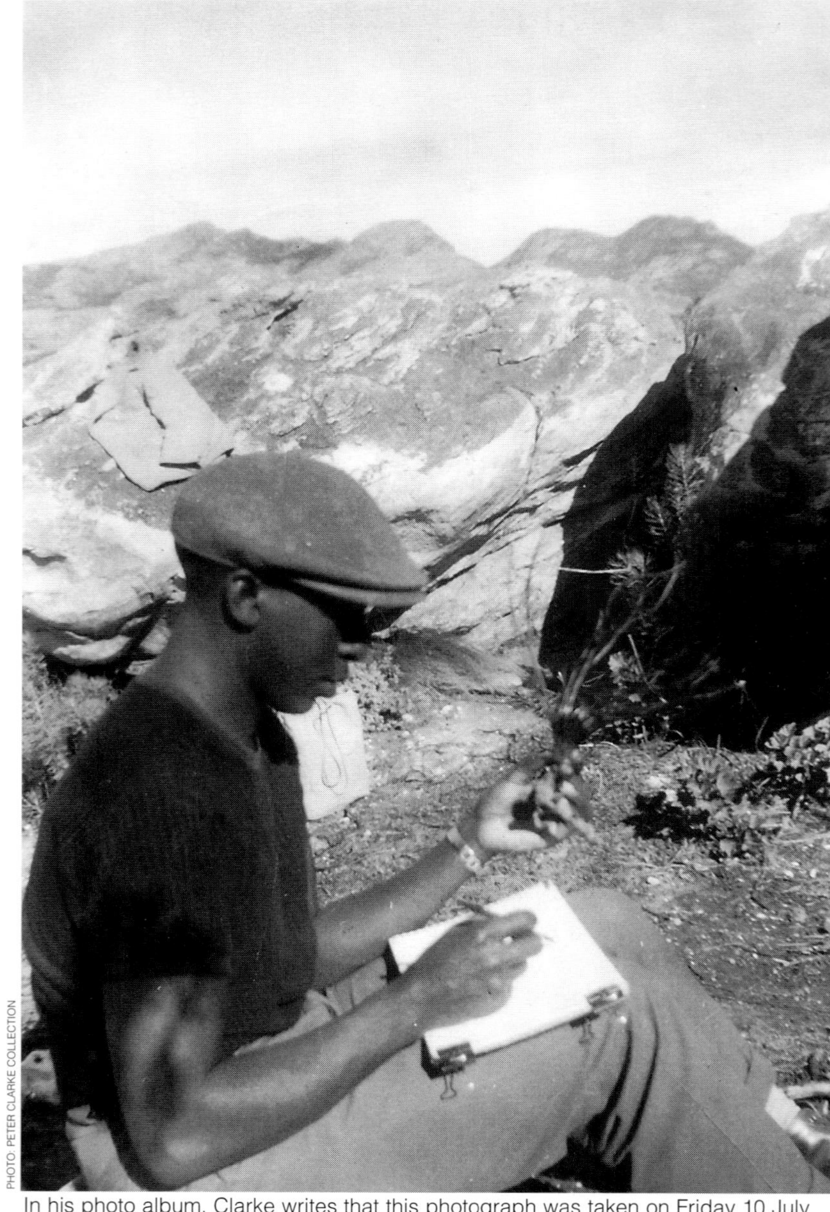

In his photo album, Clarke writes that this photograph was taken on Friday 10 July 1959, 'at the "Klipkop", that rocky outcropping on the outward fringe of Kleinberg. I do a watercolour of a "Protea Scabra"'.

Winter shepherding

PETER E. CLARKE

SATURDAY, JUNE 27

The weather was beautiful and sunny with just a hint of winter in the air. The village looked somehow different to my eye, but it was due to the change of season. I had never been to Teslaarsdal in winter so it was strange to see naked trees and untilled and untidy gardens and the lands unploughed. And it was very quiet, peacefully, soothingly quiet after the racket I left behind in the Peninsula. The stillness gave the day a kind of dream quality. Then it seemed that the stillness wasn't of a blank, dead, sterile kind. One became aware of sounds, children's voices and fragments of distant conversation and song and faraway sheep bells on the surrounding hills. This was Teslaarsdal. I felt I was back home again and it was good to be back. It made me glad.

When I first came here I did so in order to 'get away from it all'. Now it still amounts to the same thing. I want to get away from everybody and everything that is hot air, pretentious. I come to Teslaarsdal to mix with ordinary people. When I get back to Simon's Town, and after staying here, I regain my sense of balance. Everything slips back into place the way it should.

MONDAY, JUNE 29

After lunch I went to help Henna C. plough a plot of land his mother had inherited not so very long ago. It took us the whole afternoon. He handled the plough which was pulled by two donkeys, I walked in front of the donkeys, leading them by a rope connecting their bridles. Together we egged them on with shouts throughout the warm afternoon. It was more like a summer day. The sun was bright, the sky cloudless and the air quite hot. I discarded my boots and like Henna worked barefoot. We worked the soil, turning it over into lumpy, mushy rows of dark chocolate-brown earth smelling of a mixture of human and fresh cow dung. It sprooshed between my toes as I ploughed, and seen from an angle the tiny flying insects rising from their upturned dwelling places hovered like silver mites against the westering sun.

All afternoon we sweated, and in the evening we stopped work, outspanned the donkeys, picked up our trappings and went home. For a souvenir I had a burst blister on my small finger, caused by pulling on the rope, leading the donkeys. But at least it was an honourable wound and I could say afterwards that I had taken part in the ploughing.   .

TUESDAY, JULY 7

Heavy mist in the mornings now and extremely cold. Frosty landscapes and a vague sun hidden away in the naked branches of the trees and spiderwebs glitteringly hung in hedges. The ground is wet under our feet, the road too, and cloddy clay gums up our boots as we walk at the tail-end of the flock. Winter keeps us company as we walk down the road in the mist. Dickie and I keep our hands stuck deep into our warm pockets but the cold encases our feet. Our toes inside our wet leather boots feel frozen.

'Dis koud, né?' Dickie says.

'Jong, maar dis *koud*,' I say.

This is my first experience of winter shepherding and he sees that I am impressed. I remember last year when we lost some sheep on the mountains and searched all between high rocky crags and against open slopes through driving wind and pelting rain. Later, when we had found the sheep, we sat eating our bread behind a large boulder.

Dickie had said, very ruefully, 'Jy sien. Maar dié's nog niks. Jy moet skape in die winter oppas … en hulle in die berge verloor. En dan *stoksiel alleen*, in die koue reën en wind vir hulle gaan soek. *Dan* sal jy weet wat skape oppas regtig is.'

I had listened to the bitter tone. There was anger in his voice and his boots were completely ripped apart. He was terribly poor and could not afford to buy another pair of boots at all. He was seventeen at the time. If he had been younger he would probably have burst into tears even though I was there. But after a while he had calmed down and spoke gently and I realised that his anger had been directed not against his poverty but against the absolutely persistent stupidity of sheep.

Winter this year has been rather mild, very cold at times but not too wet. But today it rained. There is a mountain range that rises gently at first from between Solitaire and the farm Dunghye Park, and then it goes more dramatically higher as it continues in the direction of the Shaws Mountain Pass, beyond which is a peak, Babilonstoring, that is the highest in the Hermanus-Caledon district, I am told. Sometimes it is vague in the hazy distance. But the people of Teslaarsdal look for signs of rain, not to the great distant peak, but to the dramatic rise of mountain some miles beyond Solitaire.

The shepherds took their overcoats with them. Later the wisps of cloud descended on those peaks and the rain drizzled and soaked the old, worn-out overcoats and all exposed clothing and the unwaterproofed leather boots. Leslie joined Dickie and I and spent the day with us and his flock mingled with ours. I had brought along a bottle of wine in my bag and so after we had our morning coffee and bread, we drank the wine huddling around a twig fire.

Later, when the rain came down still heavier, we sheltered in a warm, partly hollowed-out haystack, leaving the sheep to graze. Occasionally we climbed out of our shelter to see that they did not wander across to the cultivated lands where the wheat was pushing up a flush of tender green shoots. In the haystack we discussed sex and various aspects of love and the everlasting and eternally dismal and disappointingly frustrating lack of young unmarried women in the village. Inevitably these discussions take place when the young men gather. Then, I think, we compare with a pack of dogs. It is rather funny. But we couldn't stay in the haystack all day and the sheep flock – the rain pouring, our feet wet and cold – and moved on over to a koppie. In places the shepherds had stacked large stones to make rough semi-circular shelters from the wind and, to a certain extent, the rain. By then we had decided not to take notice of the rain and cold and of our wet

clothes and soaked boots and cold feet. We were hungry and it was lunchtime, so we picked up dryish twigs and dead roots and made a fire inside the koppie's 'windskerm'. Then we sat back and ate lunch and drank very cold coffee from our wine bottles, and the rain pelted down on us and the fire warmed us and, at the same time, smoked us and burned our eyes; and Dickie's puppy, Bugler, whom he wants to become a sheepdog, cuddled against him for warmth and whined softly in his sleep while the rain fell, sprinkling tiny water drops on him that nestled, jewel-like, on his soft fluffy fur.

Inevitably, I think, the longest, dreariest days for the shepherd always turn out to be like this, wet days, rain and wind and cold together. Long, drawn-out and seemingly never going to end – and when they are alone. Sometimes the rain goes on all day from early morning to night so one never catches a glimpse of the sun. There is no dawn because the day becomes vaguely light and there is no sunset, the day merely darkens into night.

Towards evening the rain stopped and the bean-soup yellow clouds opened slightly above the sunset area, far, far beyond that highest peak, somewhere in the direction of Hermanus, beyond Hermanus. The shepherds came along, sodden, looking homewards now that the day was closing, feeling cold. The sheep all grazed again because there was no rain. So while they grazed we pulled up large bunches of dead twigs, roots and scrub and made a great blazing final fire and stood talking around its searing heat. There were five of us then, Dickie, Leslie, I, Sarel and Oom Piet Julies, and of us Oom Piet was the oldest, being in his seventies, and Dickie at seventeen, was the youngest. Days begin and days end and the time goes from season to season and year to year and the shepherds are shepherds for a long, long time if they herd sheep all their lives. Oom Piet is old and grizzled and has lived the full span of his life. Sarel is a few years older than me, Leslie is my age but Dickie is

much younger and has so far to get yet on his journey through life. One wonders. Because he is my friend I hope his way won't be too hard.

Finally it was time to go and Dickie, Leslie and I trekked homewards and Sarel and Oom Piet followed. The yellow sunset folded close in the western distance with the sun unseen. The day had ended.

In the mornings mist blankets the village, lying thick in the valleys and below the rounded hills and down toward the plains. Underfoot and along pathways the grass is frosted, the dew chiplets of white ice. The cold pinches the fingertips and the toes. Distance is half-seen. Silence is a vagueness beneath the blanket of mist. There is the odd animal sound, the odd child voice. Then you see one or two children, barefooted, on their way somewhere. And it is *cold*. The fowls perch in their runs, not too keen on coming out until the sun has come through. The cows stand about, undecided. Afterwards, when I go across to meet Dickie and we go to the kraal, the sheep are still resting, awake now, on their haunches. We have to shout at them and prod them with our sticks before they rise and snortingly shake off their lethargy.

The mist usually lifts round about 10 o'clock. Then the sun comes out and the sky is blue, not grey, and almost clear except for some wisps of almost transparent cloud very high up. The air is fresh and nippy. We sat at a point just on the outer side of the ridge, near to that big hollowed-out haystack, and from there we could watch the grazing sheep and eat at the same time and look right down the road to the point where the Wolfgat road branches off.

Towards noon it became fairly warm. We worked our way right down to the point where the Solitaire road turns into the main road to Caledon and crosses over to Wolfgat. Sarel was in that area on the other side of the road. With the warm sun out he was

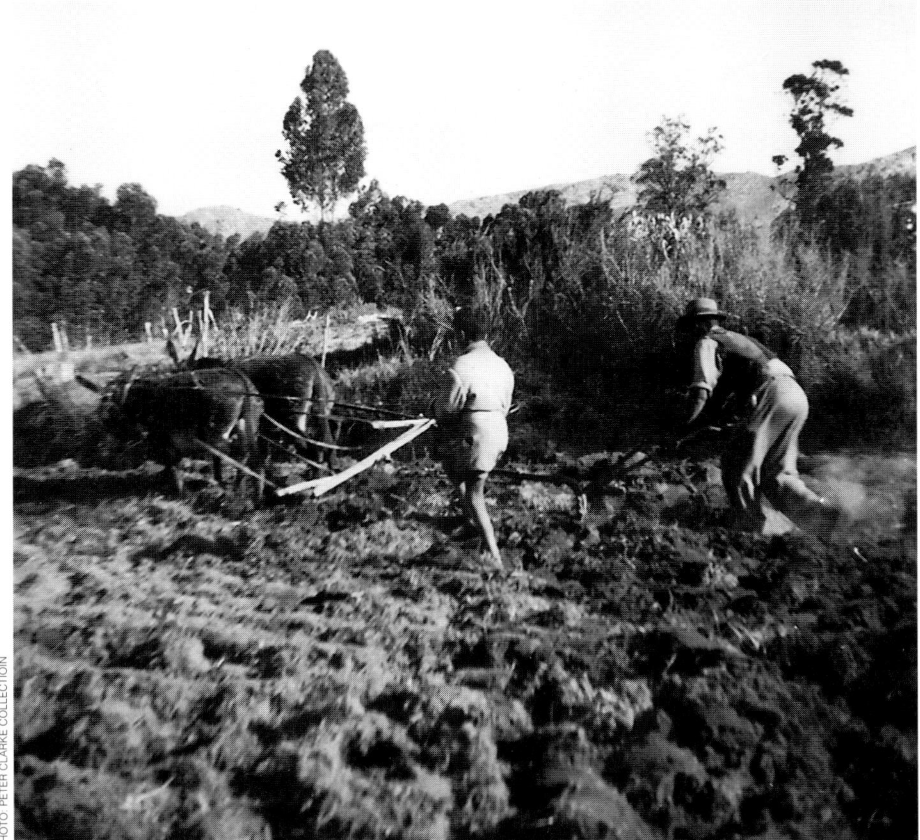

Spring ploughing at Tesselaarsdal, Alfred Matomela assisted by Awie Henn: 'We worked the soil, turning it over into lumpy, mushy rows of dark chocolate-brown earth smelling of a mixture of human and fresh cow dung'. 1959.

feeling sorry for himself. He came over to watch me sketching and said he had a very bad cold. It became so warm I could remove my jacket and walk about in my cotton jersey. It certainly turned out beautiful.

I sketched in my book, a blue book, a blue sky with frilly strato-nimbus clouds and below it a curve of green and brown land and the road going out to Caledon and off to Solitaire and far in the background, across the plain, a distant range of pale grey mountains.

After that I ate lunch of fried fish and home-made bread sandwiches and cold coffee and I smoked. Then, because I felt so damn good, I lay on my back on the ground and rested with the sun warm on me. I wanted to make the most of it. Spring was coming. If I lifted myself I could look sideways and see a whole field of purple-pink petalled oxalis and yellow-headed sorrel and the

flock, spread out now, and some ewes that would lamb in a few weeks' time. And the lands sloped away and rose into gentle hills here and there. Across the road I could see Sarel talking to another shepherd whose flock was feeding in a grassy pocket between ploughed spaces, and on the other side of our flock, Dickie was sitting, smoking his pipe. I guessed he was thinking that tomorrow would be Friday and that I was leaving Saturday morning and I realized that when I do go away I miss him a lot because he is like a brother to me when I am here.

In the early afternoon I let Dickie rest. While he was sleeping I went for a walk and I saw a buck for a few seconds before it disappeared into a valley. The hunting season is open now and one does see buck. Tuesday afternoon, last week, Henna and I watched three of them. Sarel's two dogs chased

one. This was on the Wolfgat road ridge and we were about half a mile away. Going swiftly and elegantly it bounded away, leaving the dogs behind. We couldn't say what kind of buck they were because they were too far away. The sun turned them blackish in the distance. I don't know if anyone here hunts seriously during the open season.

Late last year while with the sheep, Dickie and I found a pheasant's nest one morning. The wheat had been cut by a harvester machine towed by a tractor, the nest with four eggs in it remaining miraculously unscathed. The hen had fled away at my approach and stayed away. There was no sense in talking the eggs home and trying to incubate them. So we left them hoping the hen would return. But she didn't come back that evening. The evening Dickie and his friend Julius stalked the nest and found the hen sitting. Julius, who is a fairly crack shot with his catapult, got her with one stone before she could get away. I had never tasted pheasant so a small portion of roasted breast was saved for me. Unfortunately, the ants raided the kitchen cupboard so it ended up by being given to the cat. Someday yet I shall eat pheasant.

As the afternoon went on we crossed over the road and grazed a while at the dam some distance from the Wolfgat-Teslaarsdal fork roads. The afternoon was still sunny but a cool wind came up so we ducked down in the low scrub and made a fire. Then after an hour we moved again, in the direction of Wolfgat, to Ridley's camp, wire-enclosed and tree shaded. Here we stayed a longish while. There was time to rest but the air was so cold and there was no shelter at all and we had to lie flat down on the ground to avoid the wind cutting into us. At times we wrestled in order to keep warm. In various ways Dickie is maturer. He has grown taller, I think, and the shoulders have a firmer cut to them and the tone of the voice has tended to level into a man's voice without boyish edges. And the face is changing into a man's and he talks with an adult's sensibility – or very nearly. Having been away from his company for months I am most aware of this change in him and I can't help thinking of it and feeling about it as a kind of strange and beautiful miracle. And I am quite glad.

FRIDAY, JULY 10
My heart is in this place and I love it. That is so true and so definite. There is always a place, a kind of extra-special one, that a man sees and is attracted to and loves intensely, in the same way that he sees and admires and loves one particular woman above every other woman, with everything that is in him because that particular place, like that one woman, holds everything that his soul seeks.

When the mist dispersed, we moved up the hill, up that uneven grassy track from the Carelse's place, past Appels' and Richter's cottages. We went through the bushes starting to flower now. Lots of big black furry proteas and the commoner 'suikerkan' proteas, those with the sticky outer red petals. Going further up to the fringes of Kleinberg, beyond the pine tree grove, one encountered the other, brighter pink variety – Elim proteas, I think they are called.

What amazed me too was a smallish flower, or a plant that could easily be related to the protea family. Its narrow petals were a kind of mustard brown and it had leaves about 14 inches long that looked more like blades of tough grass. The plant grew low, unobtrusively beneath other shrubs and bushes, with the flowers looming on the level of the ground. This 'protea' was completely unknown to me but Dickie said it was quite common in the area. I did a watercolour sketch of one in my sketchbook when we reached that outcrop of gigantic rocks on the fringe of Kleinberg.

A gloriously sunny day and we enjoyed it. Quite warm at lunchtime but as the afternoon came on it turned cooler. But having the sun shining made it pleasant. From our position so high up one could see miles away in various directions. But the village itself was hidden behind the curve of the mountain. A few farms were visible.

Sound travels far here, these days particularly. Wandering about on the veld yesterday with the flock we heard a locomotive and I was positive that the sound was coming from Solitaire. But there is no railway at Solitaire, the nearest railway station is at Caledon which is 14 miles away. I was told, yes, it was an engine shunting at Caledon.

Yesterday evening we took notice of the pink sky as we came home, 'shepherd's delight'. If the sun has to rise above a high bank of clouds in the morning sky before being seen, then it means wind. A ring around the sun means wind as also a ring at night around the moon. We unintentionally delayed our homeward journey and so were late. Coming down from the rocky out-crop we discovered that it was just about sunset and we raced through the bushes to the road. But it was nearly 6 p.m. and the sun was

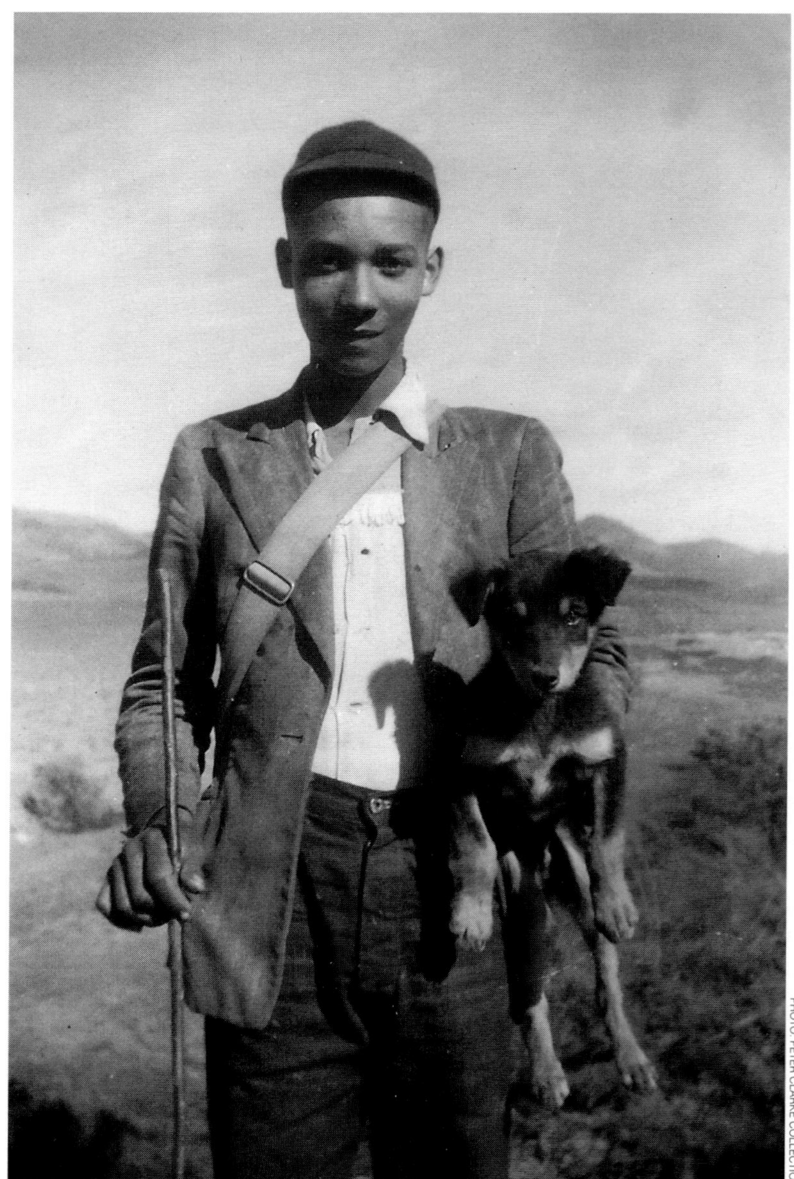

Dickie Wyngaard with his puppy, Bugler, which he wanted to train as a sheep-dog. 1959.

58

Triptych

for Peter Clarke

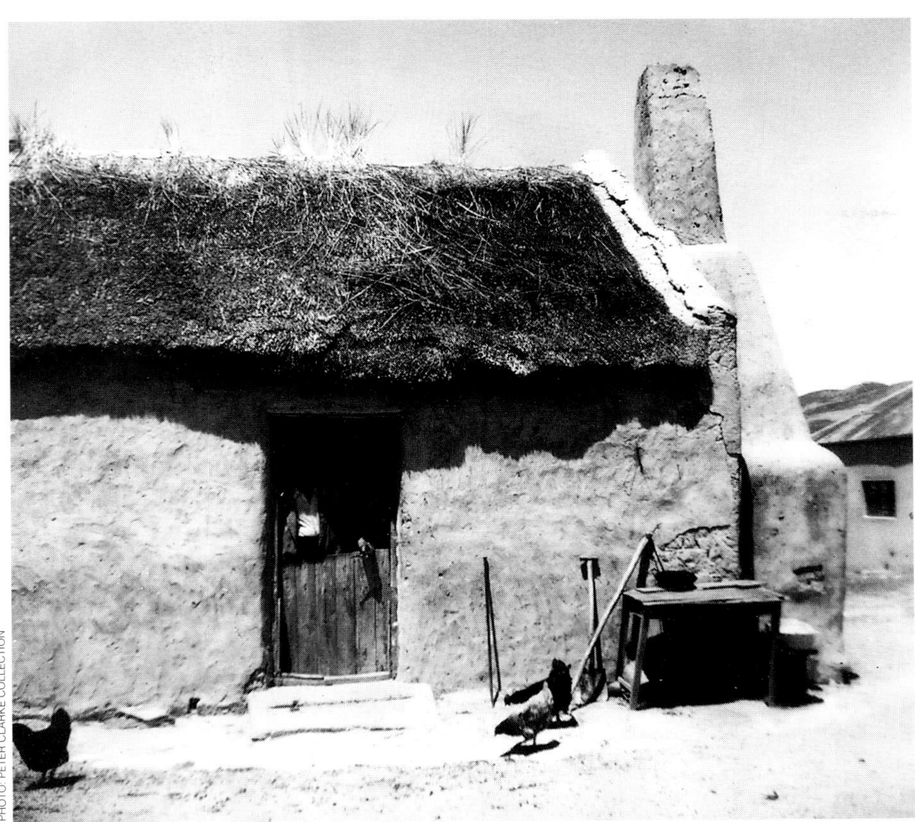

PHOTO: PETER CLARKE COLLECTION

The cottage at Tesselaarsdal where Clarke's friends, Dickie and Karlie Wyngaard, lived. 1959.

gone. It was dusk and the rose-tinted sky was filled with red and pink clouds that were so amazingly beautiful that we didn't mind at all being late. Also, the sheep had grazed well, and we had made the most of it. By the time we chased the sheep into the kraal the evening sky was beginning to fill with the first stars.

I went to the Julius' to have supper. There were guests from Bredasdorp and the supper was lavish. Mrs Julius cooks excellently. There was roast beef, pork, fowl and potatoes, boiled cauliflower, baked pumpkin, white and yellow rice, gravy sauce, grated carrot and orange salad and lettuce, followed by peaches and cream and frothy gelatine plum pudding with custard. There was coffee with which to wash it down.

Some chaps I know were intending to have a drinking party after supper. It worked out very cheaply. Two of the fellows, not working this afternoon, walked over the hills to a nearby farm to buy wine. They bought 'vaaljapie'. They said it wasn't first class wine but it didn't drink badly. They had also two bottles of wine from their private stock, stuff issued to them when they worked on a farm earlier in the week for a few days.

The 'vaaljapie', of which they had bought a gallon glass can, was really not bad at all if one wasn't a connoisseur. The other wine, the 'tot' wine, was muck. It made one drunk and apparently with the farmers, that is the important thing. The 'vaaljapie' had a much cleaner taste and was not at all unpleasant and it made us nice inside and talkative and the conversation as we sat drinking by the fire we had made outside a house, was lively and interesting and uninhibited.

Then it was half an hour after midnight and the wine was finished and we were feeling nice and tight and the fire burned itself out.

Triptych

for Peter Clarke

ELZA MILES

One: Art scene, Cape Town

> fitting neatly here,
> positioned as it is
> Between past and future.[1]

On Wednesday 8 October 1947, a photograph appeared in the *Cape Argus*.[2] It showed an evening art class at St Philip's School in Chapel Street, Woodstock. There at the school, twice per week, John Coplans taught art. He gave tuition in life drawing on Tuesday nights and painting on Saturday afternoons.

The photograph in the *Cape Argus* reflects the energetic bustle of creative people at work. That evening the group of artists had a male model posing in trunks. To relieve him there were two boys waiting their turns. The group consisted mostly of school teachers, but there were also the son of Cissy Gool, Rustum (later Doctor Rustum Gool), the 'bright eyed' schoolboy from Athlone, Albert Adams, and the young dockworker from Simon's Town, Peter Clarke. Louis Maurice, William Diamond and S.V. Petersen appear in the photograph in the foreground. In the mid distance, with his back turned to the viewer, in front of his easel, stands Roland Alexander.

At the time, Maurice, who was teaching art at the Zonnebloem Training College, was already known in Cape Town as a sculptor. He held his first solo exhibition at the Argus Gallery in 1942 and in 1944 shared a show with the painter, Gerard Sekoto, at the Jerome Galleries. Apart from attending these classes to draw from a life model, Maurice enjoyed the camaraderie of other artists such as Sheila Fort, Lippy Lipshitz and Solly Disner. Petersen, an acknowledged poet, had a second volume of poetry on hand and was writing his only novel, *As die son ondergaan*.[3]

The article that accompanies the photograph is entitled 'Eager students at art classes for Coloureds'. Both the article and the photograph encapsulate the creative energy prevalent in Cape Town at the time. On evenings like these, artists, workers, teachers, doctors and students mixed, shared as well as exchanged ideas, and created.

Old photographs and yellowed newspaper clippings inevitably evoke mixed feelings. In the first place one is pleasantly reminded of the 'good old times'. But subsequently the reality of the passage of events dawns on one. Of Diamond we have no further records. Adams, Alexander and Maurice all left to settle in England, where Alexander and Maurice died.

Bohemian life in Cape Town always seemed invigorating. George Hallett – today at the height of his photographic career – recalls his youthful days when he was not only encouraged but inspired by artists and writers such as Uys Krige, Ingrid Jonker, Jan Rabie, Peter Clarke, Amos Langdown, Marjorie Wallace and James Matthews. Matthews encouraged him to photo-document District Six and Clarke once gave him a piece of clay for modelling.

Even after apartheid had been imposed on South Africans, artists carried on with their lives and worked beyond the barriers enforced by segregation. They made art, and young inexperienced artists benefited from those more skilled and experienced in their craft. One is tempted to call it a tradition of altruistic and creative interplay, which became the norm among Cape artists. There seems to have always been an enduring fellowship between young recipients and older professional artists at the Cape.

Gladys Mgudlandlu was self-taught when she

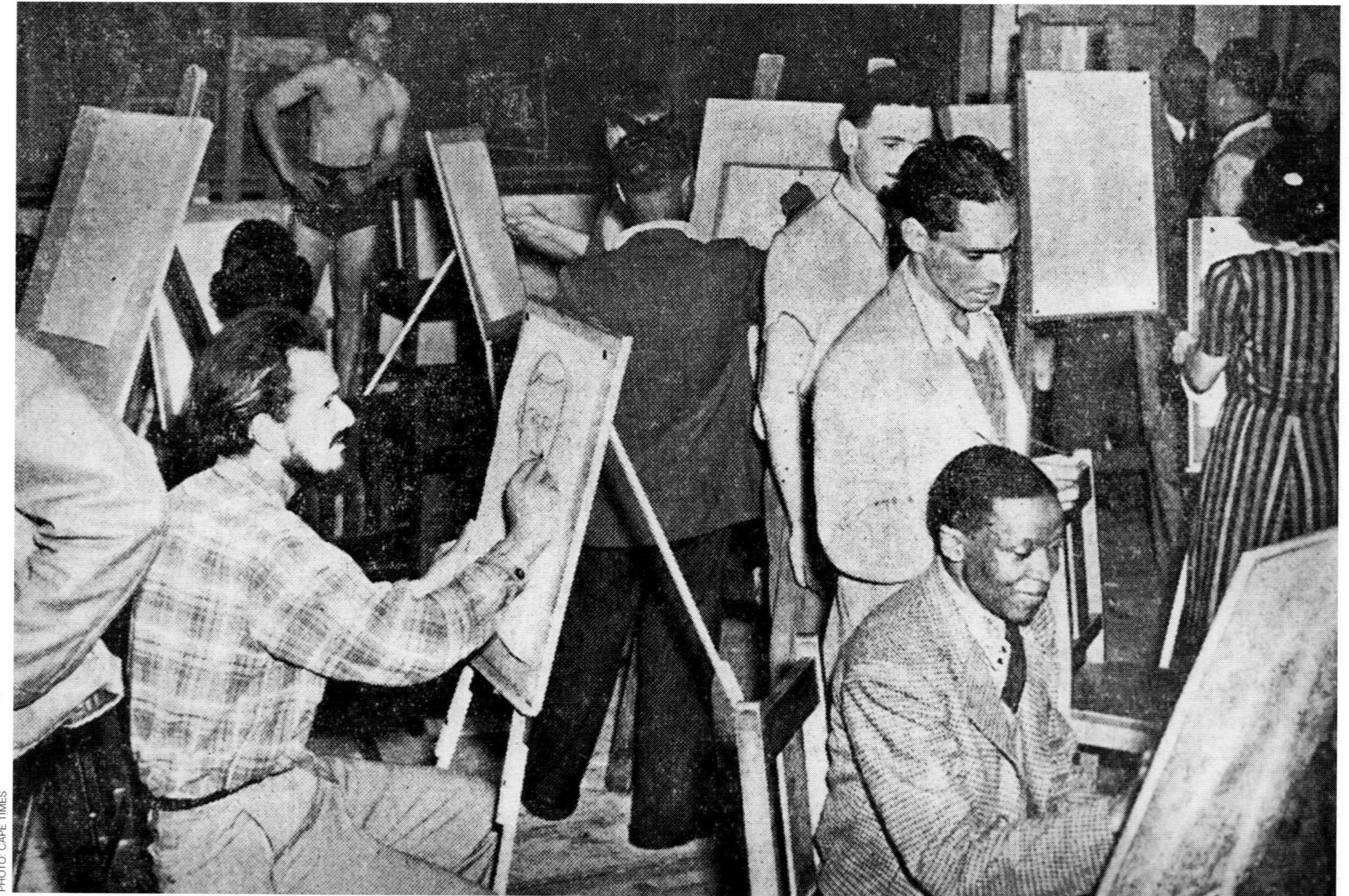

Evening Art Class at St Philip's School in Woodstock: from left to right, Louis Maurice, William Diamond (obscured), S.V. Petersen, Clarke. With his back turned is Roland Alexander. 1947.

exhibited in Cape Town in 1961. The vibrancy of her palette, vigorous brushwork and original imagery immediately caught one's attention. When she subsequently sought technical advice she could turn to Marjorie Wallace, May Hillhouse, Gregoire Boonzaier and Katrine Harries. Likewise Peter Clarke could turn to Lesley Cope and Katrine Harries; and Conrad Theys was welcomed into the studio of Gregoire Boonzaier. After Cecil Skotnes had settled in Cape Town his guidance was sought by Wilfred Delporte and in more recent times by Willie Bester.

This camaraderie had its roots still earlier. When Ernest Mancoba arrived in Cape Town in 1935 he was introduced to Lippy Lipshitz. The latter shared with him his discovery of African sculpture, introducing him to *Primitive Negro Sculpture*, a book by Paul Guillaume and Thomas Munro. A formal language unfolded for Mancoba, quite different to the ecclesiastical one he knew.

Then in 1942 another artist arrived from the north: Gerard Sekoto. He too found accommodation in District Six and befriended Lipshitz. Unlike Mancoba's brief stay, Sekoto lived and painted in District Six for two years, enabling him to forge lasting friendships with Louis Maurice and Solly Disner. Both these friendships remained, long after Sekoto's departure for Paris. Concerned about an outlet for his paintings, Maurice wrote many years later in a letter from London to Disner: 'Gerard has not sent any pictures. He sent me a letter to Cape Town which was re-directed here. He promises that at Xmas when I see him, we can discuss it and I shall for my part see what I can send immediately.'[4]

In a letter to Peter Clarke in 1953, Louis Maurice articulates genuine concern about the creative process, as well as artistic growth.[5] The open-mindedness of the older artist is revealing because at times he also expresses doubts. When Maurice wrote the letter, he had already spent a few months in London, studying independently at the Slade School of Fine Art. He was

62

working extremely hard and three of his sculptures were accepted for the Exhibition of Contemporary British Sculpture. Jacob Epstein was among the artists selected for the exhibition.

Around 1949–50 Peter Clarke and some fellow artists had formed an art group that worked together on Saturdays. By the time Maurice arrived in London, the group had ceased to exist. In the same letter to Clarke, in 1953, Maurice replies sympathetically to the news:

I am sorry to hear that the fellows are not continuing – but then so very few of us having the staying power – I sometimes feel myself like ceasing work and making money – lots of it, but then one goes on and on – I sometimes wonder where to. However I am glad to know you are working, I do hope you will keep at it – even though it is difficult for I believe that if one is worth anything the art must survive – So Peter, the very best of luck. I too need that luck and perseverance to go on somewhere somehow.[6]

In the same year – 1942 – that Sekoto arrived in Cape Town, a child protégé, Valerie Desmore, held her first solo exhibition at the Argus Gallery under the auspices of the New Group. At the time she was 16 years old. The history of her beginning is also testimony to the encouragement and interaction with older artists. Initially Desmore worked under the guidance of Rosa van Gelderen who established the Yellow Window Studio in the Gardens for the benefit of all children interested in art. Moreover, Van Gelderen ran dynamic art classes at the Girls' Central School where she invited professionals like Wolf Kibel to teach. Apart from Van Gelderen's guidance, Desmore was also encouraged by Lippy Lipshitz, Gregoire Boonzaier and Irma Stern.

Desmore left Cape Town in 1946 after she had been accepted by the Slade School of Fine Art in London to further her art studies. Though her talent was acclaimed at the art school she found the approach there too stifling and academic, and eventually studied under Oskar Kokoschka, who at the time had a studio in London.

Almost a decade later, in 1957, another young artist from Cape Town was inspired by Kokoschka. It was Albert Adams, the 'bright-eyed' schoolboy of the St Philip's evening art classes. After he had completed his course in Fine Art at the Slade School of Fine Art, he continued his studies on a Bavarian State Scholarship at the University of Munich. That summer he attended Kokoschka's School of Vision in Salzburg. When Adams held an exhibition in Cape Town two years later, a message recorded by Kokoschka for the occasion was played at the opening. The grand old master laid emphasis on the importance of the artist's commitment and his message was significant for South Africa:

We live with closed eyes, not daring to see the misery we create on earth. The task of the artist is to see. In the years between and after the world wars an artistic movement became the fashion even in countries far away from Paris where it started. It did away with the artistic heritage of humanity. Now this so-called 'non-objective art' is only a signal of the general romantic spirit of modern man, who would rather visit the moon, than reconcile his individual

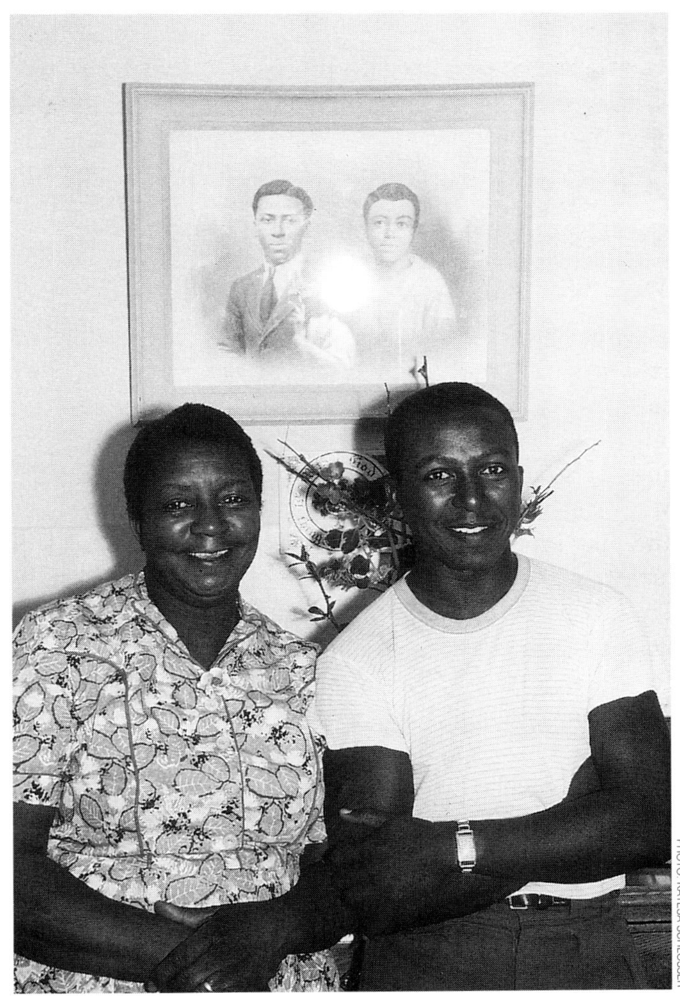

Clarke with his mother, Rose, at their home in Waterfall Road, Simon's Town, 1959. The photograph on the wall shows his parents.

*existence with the changing environment conditioned
by modern technical civilization.*

*My humble opinion always was (and is) that, first
of all, an artist has to provide his fellow men with
visual information. This must be derived from individual experience if it is to be of any importance to
others.*[7]

Apart from the congenial atmosphere that Albert
Adams and Peter Clarke experienced at St Philip's in
1947 and 1948, they had also been exposed to inspir-
ing extra-curricular art classes at Livingstone High
School in Claremont. Here Mr H. J. Esterhuizen, the
art teacher, put at the disposal of students interested
in art, a classroom, art materials and art journals such
as *The Studio*. They could work there, in the afternoons, to their hearts' content. Through *The Studio*
Clarke became familiar with printmaking, especially
with the woodcuts of the German Expressionists,
and the prints of Japanese and Mexican artists.

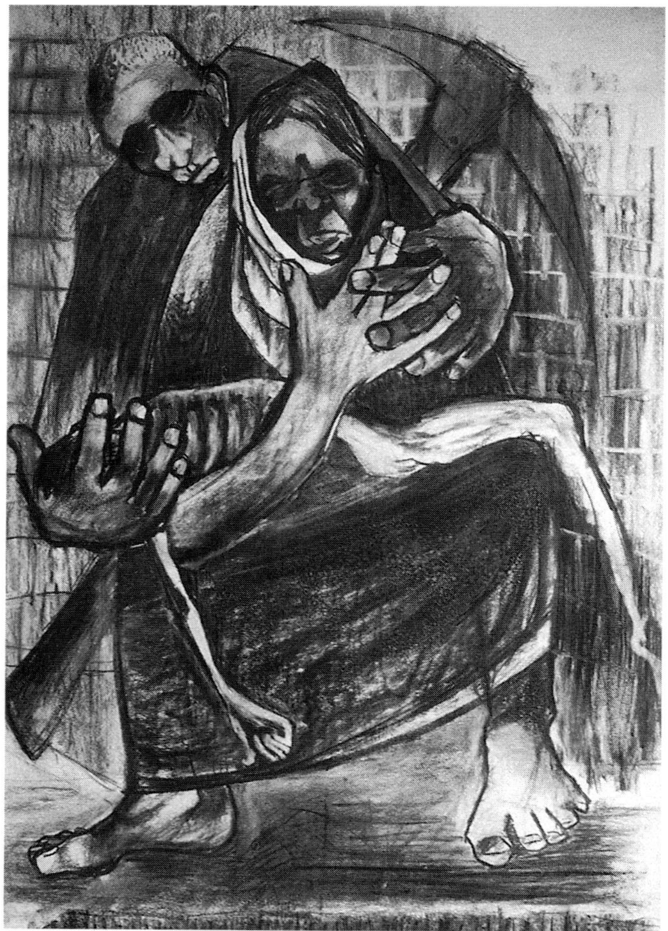

Albert Adams, *The family*, 1948, charcoal on paper, 99 x 68.5.
Bowmint Collection, Pretoria.

Clarke and Adams were still further exposed, after
they had left school, to German Expressionist prints
in private collections held by Capetonians. Many
emigrants from Lithuania and Germany arrived in
Cape Town in the 1930s.

Clarke left school at the end of standard seven in
1944 and took a job as a dockworker in Simon's
Town. Adams, who was head prefect at Livingstone
High School and editor of the school magazine,
matriculated in 1948; then enrolled at Hewat College
and became a teacher. At Hewat, Adams was head
student and editor of the annual magazine in 1951.

Whereas Albert Adams was inspired primarily by
Käthe Kollwitz's images of social criticism that he
saw in the collection of Baron Rudolf von Frieling,
Clarke's role models were Mexican artists: Diego
Rivera, David Alfaro Siqueiros and José Clemente
Orozco. He also observed the art of Ben Shan. In
addition, Clarke's paintings of the people of
Tesselaarsdal and the Cape Flats show a correspondence with those of other Mexican printmakers such
as Alfredo Zalce, Abelardo Avila and Jose Chavez
Morado. Charcoal drawings of 1948 by Adams
exploring the misery of a worker family, show affinity with Kollwitz's images of his mother and a dead
child. Adams sublimates these images by evoking
Pièta configurations. By doing this he underscores
the art critic of *Die Burger*, F.L. Alexander's view:
'Social criticism is often founded on a hidden religious attitude to life. The *Passion of Christ* in
medieval art was a sermon against the sin of man.
This sermon as the artist's theme has been replaced
in our contemporary art by sharp social criticism.'[8]

Clarke continued making art when Coplans's
classes ceased at St Philip's. In 1948 he attended the
classes Johannes Meintjes and Nerine Desmond held
at the Technical College in Roeland Street. From
that time he still retains a portrait in pencil that he
made of a child of District Six. They did not have
regular models to draw and occasionally a model was
called from the street, as happened in the case of the
child's portrait.

Clarke also explored the suffering of Christ on the
cross in a carbon pencil drawing (1957), but he saw
his own concerns reflected rather in the images of
the Mexican revolutionary artists. In Clarke's own
words, 'The history behind those pictures was almost
familiar.'[9] *Women with Lanterns* (1957) clearly shows
his affinity with Rivera.

Mexican art, especially printmaking, was for much

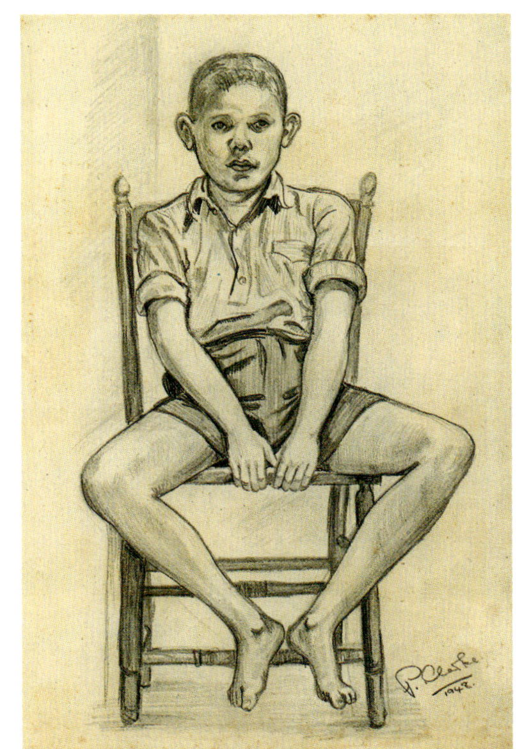

Right: *The boy*, 1948, pencil on paper, 42 x 29.5. Artist's collection, Ocean View. Clarke and his artist friends did not make use of professional models, and people, like this boy, were often called in from the streets during their art classes
Bottom: *Women with Lanterns*, 1957, ink on paper, 16.5 x 24.7. Bowmint Collection, Pretoria.

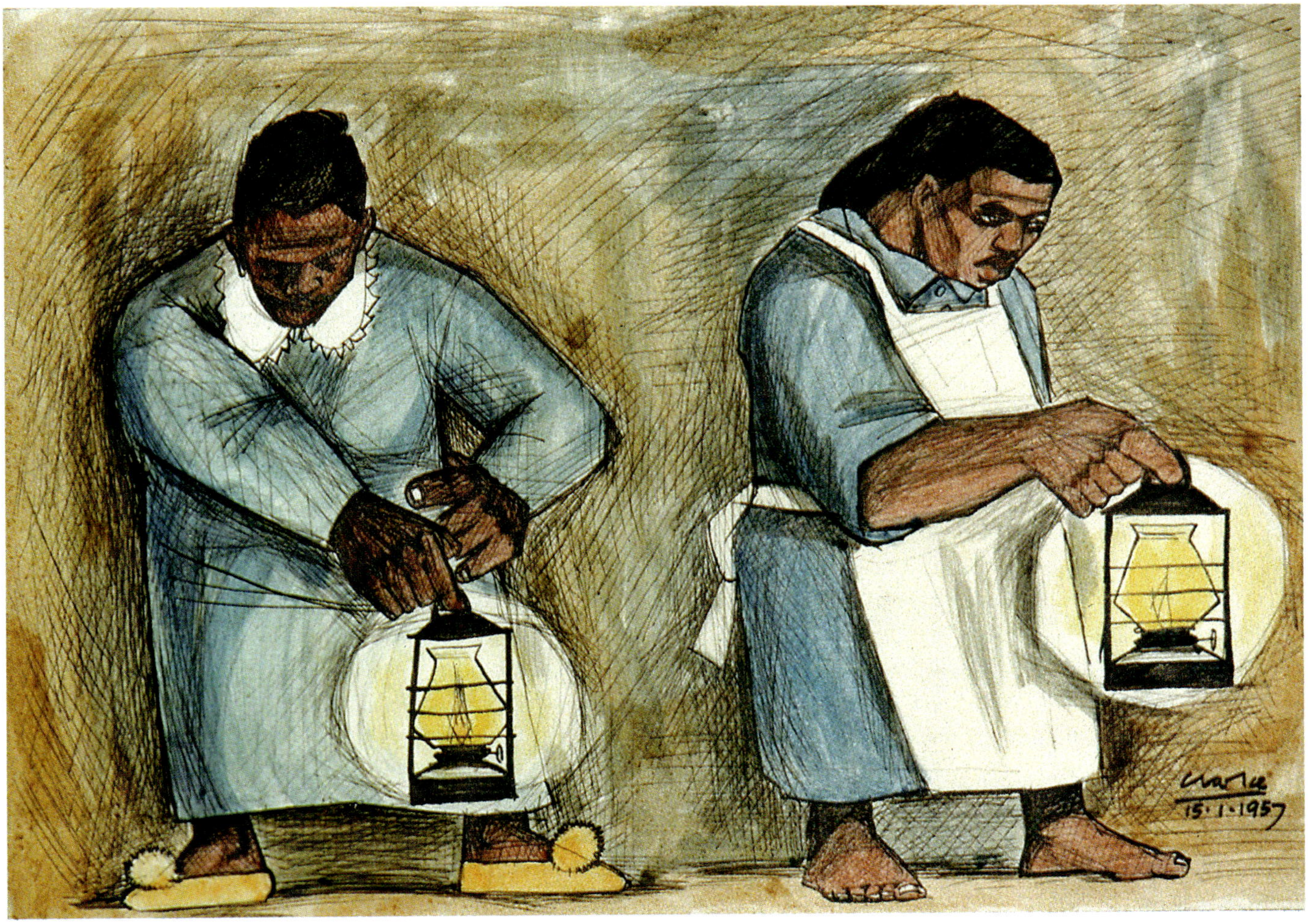

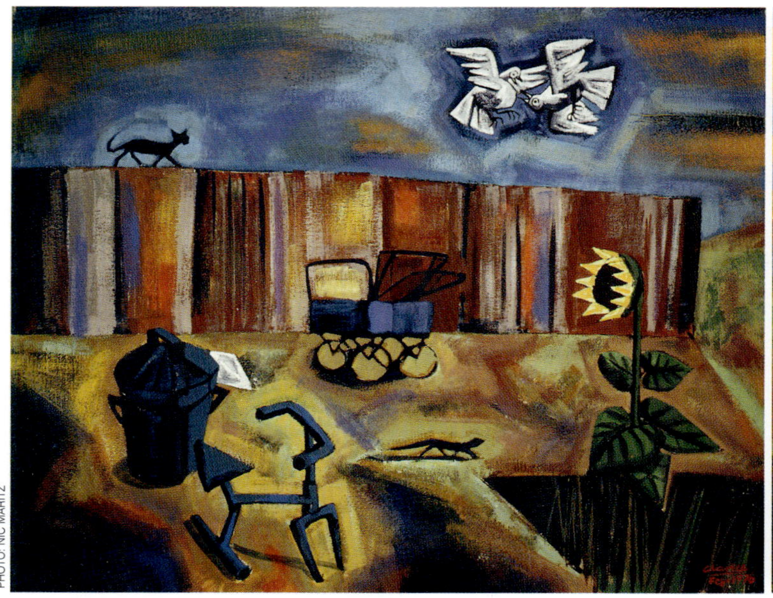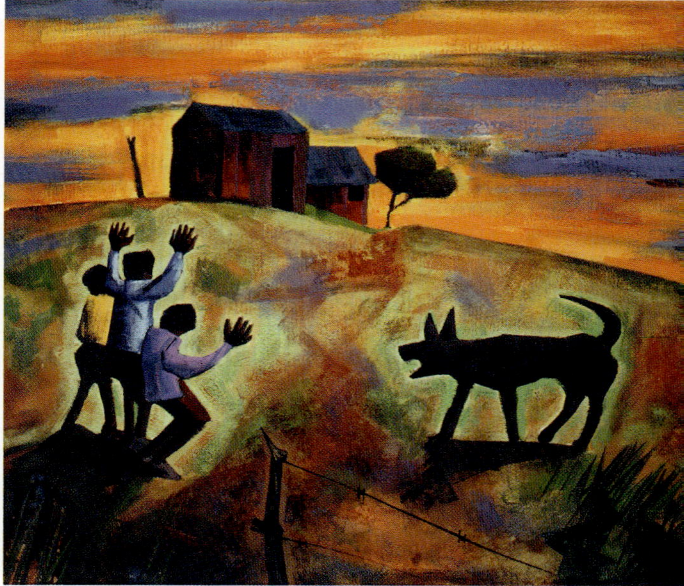

Haunted Landscape, 1976, acrylic on canvas, each panel 55 x 71. Bowmint Collection, Pretoria.

of the 20th century directed against dictatorship. It was an instrument 'for the furtherance of the Mexican Revolution against oppressive, strong-arm governments struggling to keep the lid on explosive agrarian revolts'.[10]

Racial classification became a *fait accompli* after 1948 and perceptions such as 'Coloured culture', 'Coloured art' and 'Coloured artist' emerged. Yet the work produced by so-called coloured artists contradicted the government's system of racial categorisation. Their images, whether they were two or three dimensional, showed that categories such as these were fantasies. It is not surprising, therefore, that E. Kai ended an article for the *Cape Times Magazine* on six Cape artists in the following way: 'These artists – Coloured to those who would regard them primarily as such – debunk not so much by word but by their works the idea of a so-called "Coloured culture."'[11]

Kai interviewed Peter Clarke, who at that time had returned from his studies at the Rijksakademie for Fine Arts in Amsterdam and had held exhibitions in South Africa as well as in New York, Boston and Ljubljana in Yugoslavia. The other artists who took part in the exhibition were the printmaker and painter, Amos Langdown (who was then teaching at the Teachers' Training College at Paarl and who also had studied overseas); the sculptor and welder James Mitchell (who was encouraged by Clarke); the sculptor Frank Brown – Clarke's cousin – who eventually settled in Boston, USA; Ismail Solker and the painter-teacher Gladys Mgudlandlu.

There were other artists whose work debunked the notion of 'Coloured culture' or 'Coloured art'. Conrad Theys explored an arid Cape landscape showing the tenacious growth of quiver trees while Kenneth (Kenny) Baker looked at the intimacy between the streets, buildings and people of District Six and lifted the curtain on abuse and poverty. Christopher Julius not only discovered the logic blueprint of entanglement in his drawings but also the regal gesture in eroding forms. In one painting Henry Jordaan saw a Dufy-like spirit of merrymaking in people strolling in parks on Sundays and holidays; in another he caught the fervour of the lay-preacher on the Parade, calling the people *To repent before it is too late*. Ferdinand Cloete again captured the peace of the village of Genadendal. Sensitively he unfolds it in paintings of metaphysical enchantment. While Hekkie Moos – printmaker and painter – shows how the sensuous curves of a body correspond with its surroundings, Harold Julius emphasised the bulkiness of archetypal earth goddesses in his sculptures.

Whereas exhibitions based on racial distinctions grouped people together, the *oeuvres* of individual artists belonging to the respective groups reflected a wealth of expressions. To showpiece its policy of segregation, the Nationalist government's Department of Coloured Affairs held exhibitions in the seventies to promote 'Coloured art'. When looking in retrospect at those exhibitions, one notices two mainstreams which more or less correspond with the opportunities experienced by the individual artists. On the one

66

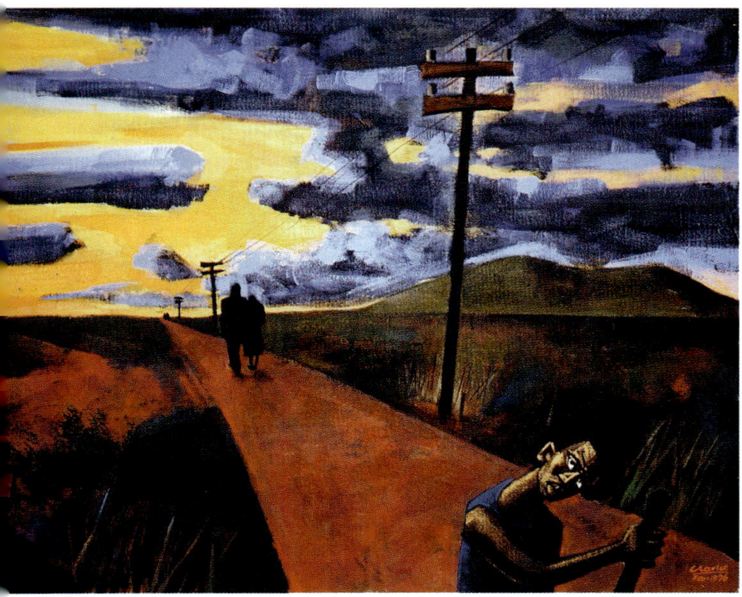

hand there is an approach reflecting local pictorial overtones as in the work of Kenny Baker and Conrad Theys. On the other hand there is work reflecting broader modernist affinities, thus shifting local parameters to encompass broader horizons, as in the diversity of the work of Louis Maurice, Valerie Desmore, Peter Clarke and Albert Adams.

With reference to Clarke the artist, Eleanor Esmonde-White commented on the ridiculousness of racial classification:

We find ourselves in a curious society at the present time – a society where real definitions have become lost and a jargon of colour has taken over. We talk of a European artist or of a coloured artist, forgetting that in the world of the creative person there is no such yardstick. An artist is either good or bad. Peter Clarke has earned his right to be regarded as one of South Africa's best graphic artists.[12]

Two: Simon's Town and Tesselaarsdal

Those family faces
in old photo enlargements show
stages in intimate history.
Khoisan, Boer, Brit bloodstreams interflow.
Framed flyblotched,
they hang expressionless
suspended there in timelessness.[13]

Peter Edward Clarke grew up in Simon's Town where he was born on the 2 June 1929 in an old stone cottage high up on the mountainside. Later the Clarkes moved to Waterfall Road where they lived at Flat 19, Block 5 – until the winter of 1973 when they were moved under the Group Areas Act to 14 Alpha Way in Ocean View, where Peter still lives and works in his bedroom-cum-studio. He had been drawing ever since he could hold a pencil.

Peter was the third of six children to Rose (née Macauley) and Peter James Clarke. Simon's Town was a British Naval Base until 1957 and Peter's father worked as a plumber's mate on the docks.[14]

Peter was fascinated with the bustle of life in Simon's Town. Images gazed at and events wondered at, in his youth were to recur in his art. Children, adults, wagons, birds, sea, rolling hills, fences, masks, houses, roads, plants and dogs all comprise Peter's artistic vocabulary.

There was the wagon and its horses of Mr Runciman's grocery shop, always en route either to the harbour to load cargo or elsewhere to deliver goods, yet constantly on the move. Then there were the derelict wagons of old Albertyn, who ran a downtown cartage concern and lived in a house facing the foreshore. These abandoned wagons were left to the mercy of the elements 'on the edge of the Bus Company's property overlooking the shore'.[15] Here in the wagon graveyard the school children enjoyed their eleven o'clock break. Reminiscences of these glorious breaks are revived in Clarke's short story 'Eleven o'clock the wagons the shore' which was awarded a prize in an *Encounter* BBC short story competition in 1958.[16]

There was also the minesweeper out in Simon's Bay because the world was at war from 1939 to 1945. Though Peter and his peers – observing the sailors at exercise – did not grasp the implications of warfare at the time, in later years Peter wondered 'how many of those sailors have survived'.[17]

Peter's surroundings inspired him. He painted in watercolour the sea shore at St James in 1949 and made pen and ink drawings of some historical buildings of his hometown. These drawings, dated 1953 and 1954, were for Christmas cards, respectively showing *The town clock*, *Roman Rock lighthouse* and *Admiralty House*. When he designed containers for the African Container Co. Ltd in 1960, he used different sea shells for his design because 'of the perfection of their construction and the variety of their form and colours which class them among the most practical and beautiful of Nature's containers'.[18]

Simon's Town, an enclave of the British Empire, celebrated Guy Fawkes Day annually on 5 November. Hence – for Clarke – began a lifelong fascination with masks. On 5 November children either masked their faces with make-up or wore masks (*mombakkiese*) of their own designs as in Clarke's drawing, *Father and Son* (1957). The children also made straw dolls – guys – which were dropped into the bonfire that was lit on the evening of 5 November. His drawings of masked figures at Guy Fawkes celebrations inspired the writer James Matthews to write a short story, 'Penny for the guy', published by *Drum* magazine in November 1956. Two drawings by Clarke illustrated Matthews's story. Both illustra-

tions show little boys wearing masks, giving their heads the significance of adulthood and causing a discrepancy between the puerile body and manly head. The illustration *Jannie sang, plucking the guy up and down in time with music* (1954) shows the masquerade of a grimacing child carrying and dragging a fully clad guy sardonically to its destination. The boy's bravado and the helpless resignation of the guy reveal the silent dialogue between man and his alter ego. Clarke describes the masked one in the following way:

You, on the inside, behind the mask, have taken on the external face of another character ... You can go on questioning yourself about your true existence disguised as someone else – until ... you find yourself wondering why a stranger's mind and thoughts inhabit the face behind the mask.[19]

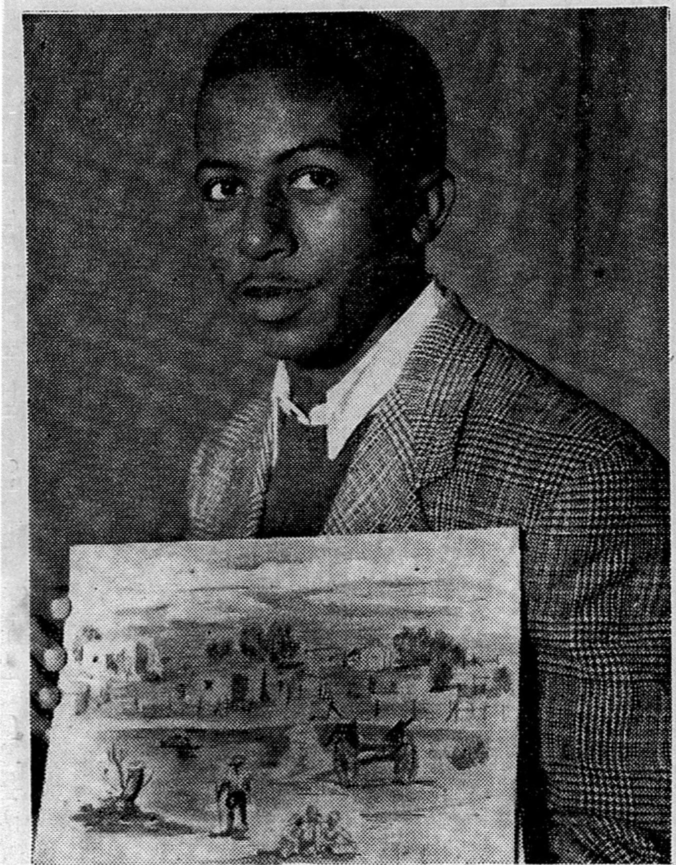

Clarke's early ambitions to paint and to write short stories are expressed in this newspaper clipping from 1952.

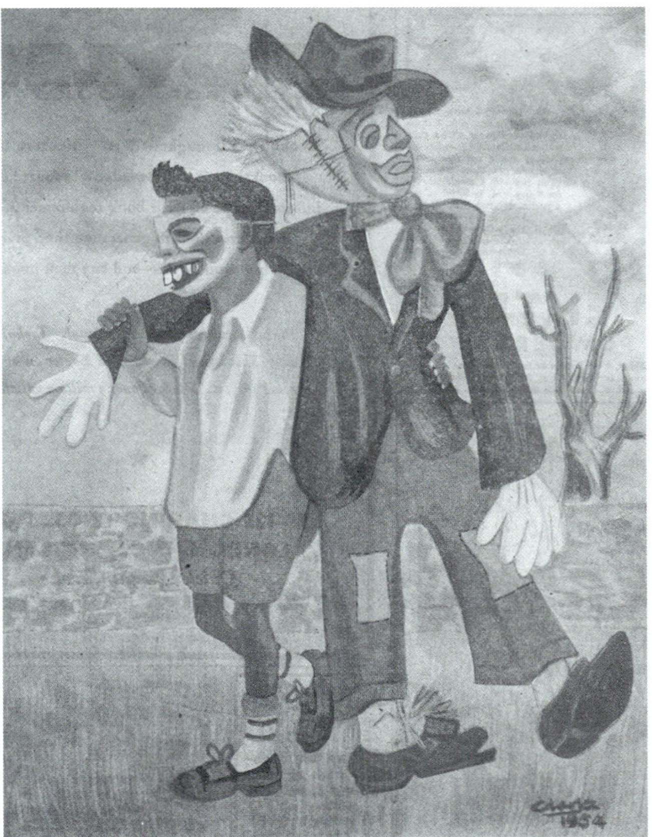

Jannie sang, plucking the guy up and down in time with the music, Clarke's illustration for James Matthews's story, 'Penny for the guy'. 1956.

Still part of the masquerades of Clarke' youth is a Mr Bluff's, an expatriat from Sierra Leone, performance on Wiener's day – a day of commemoration to a local philantropist – marked by sporting events across the Peninsula. For the occasion, this man from Sierra Leone wore a patchwork costume made from hessian and he mimed the 'whites only' long distance walk from Jubilee Square to Simon's Town and back. He, the comedian, ran about with a tin collecting coins as if he 'was gathering remnants of his past'.[20] Years afterward, Clarke read an article on masquerades in *African Arts* and realised that Mr Bluff had been reviving a custom of which the meaning was lost to the spectators. Moreover, Mr Bluff's mimicry was a prelude to Clarke's interest in the art of Central and West Africa.

But Sierra Leone also held other connotations for Peter Clarke: his grandfather hailed from Sierra Leone. He explores this personal history in 'D. J. Ancestor':

Strange to think
a long time ago
he had been a young seaman
ebony skinned out of Sierra Leone
in naval white dress,
British Seaman, in port a Black Romeo
with wild oats to sow,
creator of bliss with his kruman kiss,
dark staff, dark ecstasy.
Passionate progenitor.[21]

For David C. Driskell – head of the Department of Fine Arts at the Fisk University, Nashville, Tennessee – it is Clarke's African heritage that accounts for the versatility of his artistic expression. Apart from the seaman from Sierra Leone who features in the quoted poem, Clarke's other ancestors arrived in Cape Town as slaves from Mozambique. Driskell says:

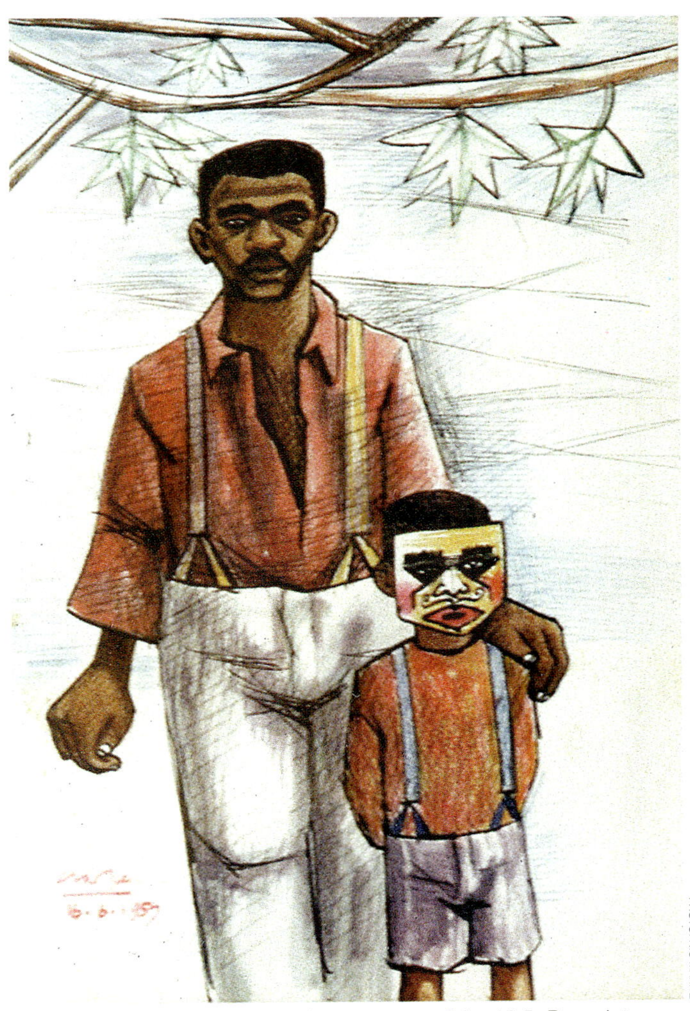

Father and Son, 1957, watercolour on paper, 24 x 16.5. Bowmint Collection, Pretoria.

When Peter left school in 1944 he started to work as a ship painter. Then he ran errands at the harbour for some time and still later became store assistant at the harbour, keeping record of tools and other equipment. He worked from 7 a.m. to 5 p.m. at the dockyard. After work until midnight he pursued his art and on Sundays he went out into the country to paint landscapes.

In 1956 he gave up his job at the harbour and went to sketch and paint for a few months in the idyllic farming village of Tesselaarsdal, situated at the foot of the Kleinriviersberge in the Hartebeest River Valley south of Caledon. Tesselaarsdal is also called Teslaarsdal or Peertjiesdorp. In May 1775 Johannes Jacobus Tesselaar bequeathed the farm to his slaves and underlings, coloured and white respec-tively. Yet property rights were granted, in most cases, only in 1982, after bitter and long disputes among the descendants.[24]

Clarke paid his first visit to Tesselaarsdal in 1949. He spent the December holidays there during 1950 and 1951. From 1956 to 1960 he stayed and worked there annually from spring to just before Christmas.

Tesselaarsdal is Peter Clarke's Pont-Aven or Le Pouldu. Gauguin said of Pont-Aven that it was 'a place with archaic customs and an atmosphere very different from [...] over-civilised surroundings'.[25] It seems that Tesselaarsdal evoked similar connota-tions for Clarke. In some of his Tesselaarsdal land-scapes, he touches on the clarity of Gauguin's 'Synthetism' which implies autonomy of colour, shape and line. If, in these pieces, objects like buildings, trees, people and roads are recognisable, it does not imply that Clarke copied them from life. He followed Gauguin's advice, who taught his friends that it was good to have a model, but if they wanted to paint it, they should draw a curtain over it, 'then the work will be yours – your personal experience'.[26]

Clarke's method of work seems to heed Gauguin's advice. Having observed the model – for instance, the woman carrying two chickens – Clarke will use her as a recurrent motif. Her high cheek bones, *kop-*

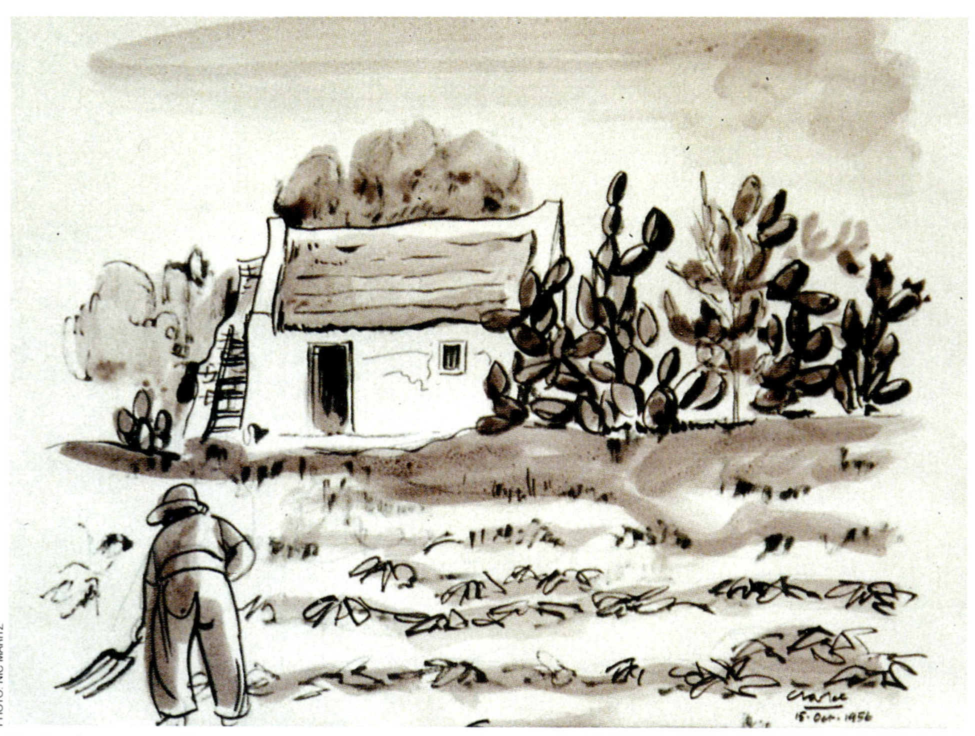

Donkey's cottage, Teslaarsdal, 1956, watercolour on paper, 23 x 29.5. Bowmint Collection, Pretoria.

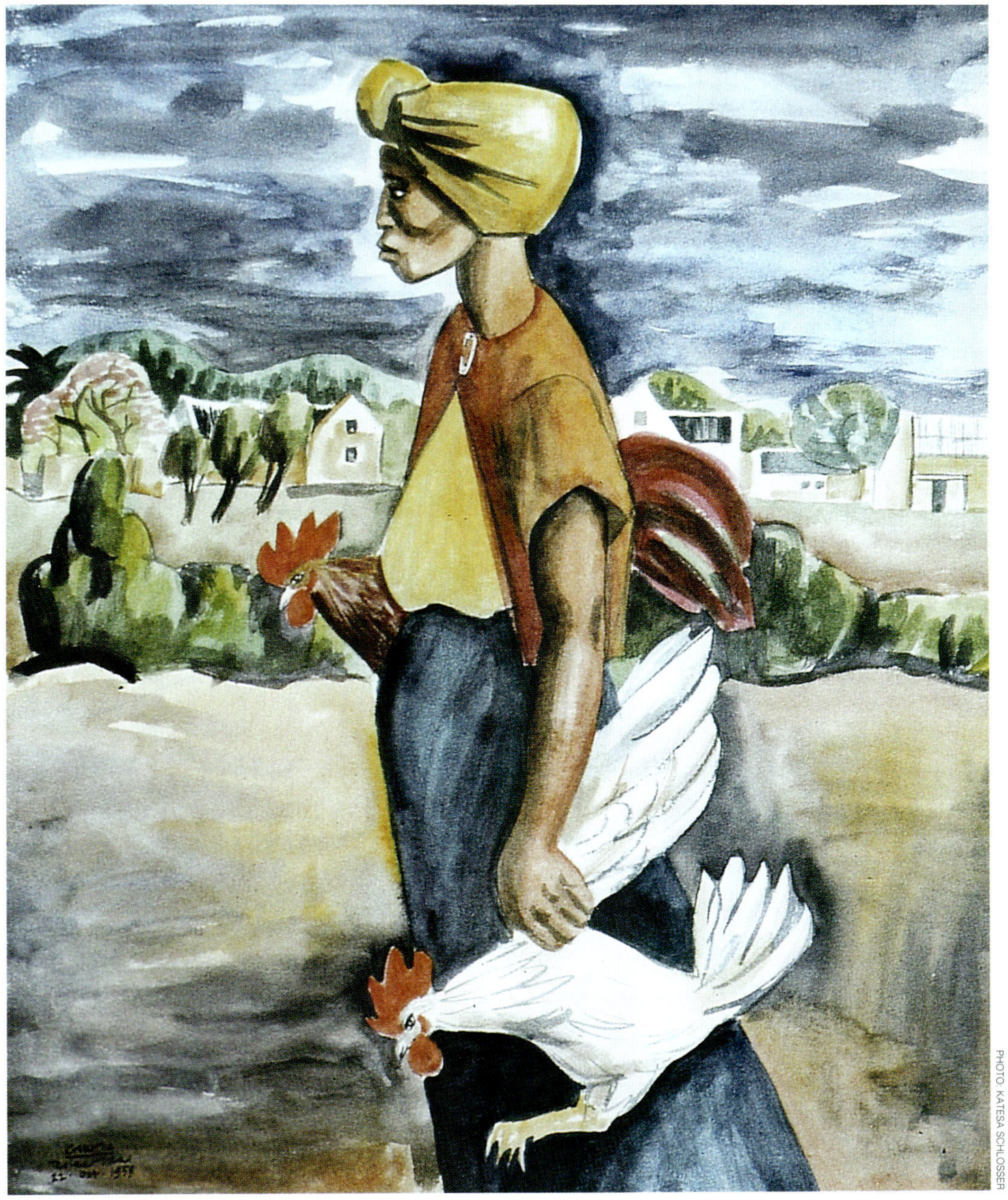

Woman Carrying Cocks, 1958, watercolour on paper, size and location unknown.

doek (turban) and fowls become so familiar that she is more than a mere acquaintance every time we meet her on the road. She appears in at least three of his paintings.

At Tesselaarsdal he got to know the ways of the shepherds intimately as he accompanied them on their daily rounds. The whitewashed and thatched cottages of this farming community, some dating back to 1842, signified hospitality. Here even the donkeys were afforded shelter in a cottage. How different is this concern for animals from the forced removals of people and subsequently their abandoned homes that Clarke would later witness and experience.

At Tesselaarsdal he also tasted the wholesomeness of simple meals. Once the shepherd boy, K., offered him a sweet-squash: '[When] it was cooked he broke it in half and I had one piece and he ate the other piece. And it was the simplest meal I had ever had, this breaking of the vegetable into two pieces, something like a ceremony, a very simple, completely unostentatious ceremony.'[27]

71

Three: Seance

During the fifties several South African artists interpreted the passion of Christ. This is not surprising since South African history had entered a period of conflict and the severe violation of human rights. Anti-white riots erupted at Port Elizabeth and East London; the Registration Act classified all South Africans into separate categories – White, Coloured, African and Indian; Cape Coloured voters were removed from the common roll; Bantu Education and the University Apartheid Acts were implemented. In the light of these events it is not unexpected that artists were drawn to an icon of universal suffering and sacrifice. Louis Maurice showed the pain on the cross both in sculpture and printmaking. Albert Adams evoked the defencelessness of a battered Christ in images of *Ecce Homo* and Robert Hodgins observed *Judas at the home of the high priest*. In 1957 Clarke also made a drawing of Christ on the cross and Matthys Bokhorst, the critic of the *Cape Times* said: '[The] Crucifixion of a Coloured Christ is an unforgettable new approach to the old theme.'[28]

Christ on the cross not only implies a sacrificial death but also reconciliation. The two beams, one vertical and the other horizontal, conjure up the image of paths crossing. When one follows the red

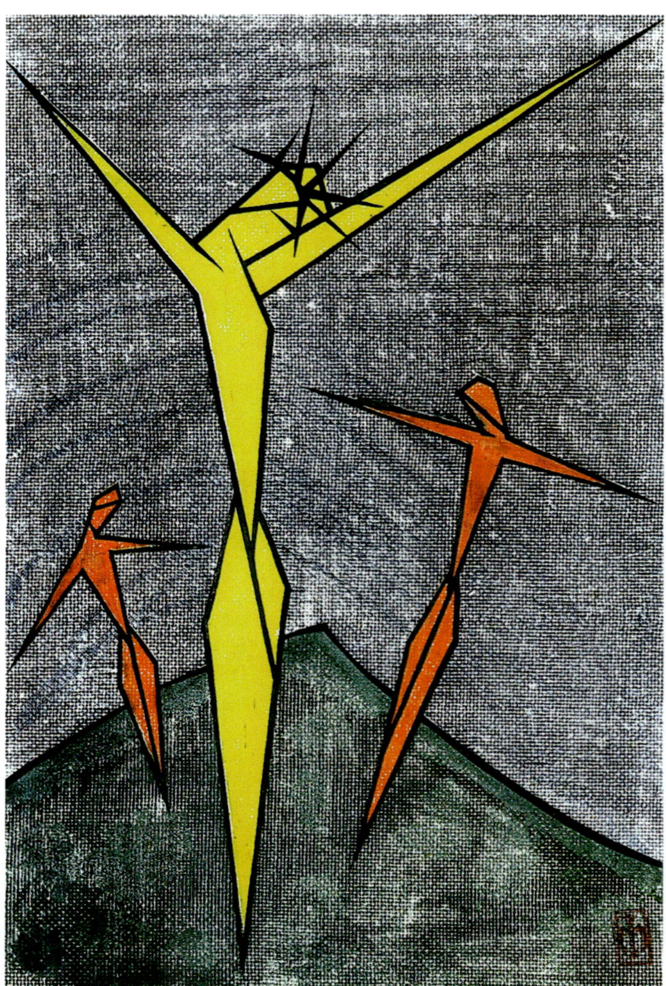

Louis Maurice, *Three Crucified Figures*, 1950, masonite cut and coloured stencils, 47 x 33. Mrs P.M. Henneke, Cape Town.

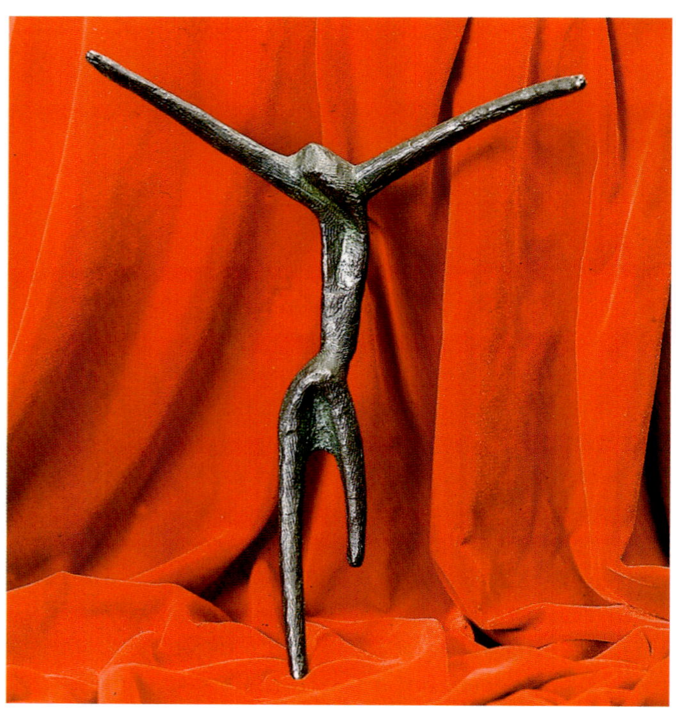

Louis Maurice, *Crucifix*, bronze, 35 20.5. Mrs Isobel Smith.

ochre dust roads moving across idyllic Tesselaarsdal and then the tracts cutting through the forlorn, windblown Cape Flats in Clarke's pictures, one foresees that somewhere these roads are going to intersect and at the intersection:

> You see the four roads disappear
> And know
> The world begins from here[29]

Travellers and their journeys are fascinating, but removals imposed by law unnerve:

When a person is able to travel where ever and when ever he wishes dignity accompanies him as a fellow traveller. But when a person is forced to depart from everything that had been familiar and intimate, when your past, so to speak, is deliberately wiped out of existence as if it was of not the slightest impor-

tance, it takes a long, long time for hatred to release your mind from its grip.[30]

From September 1975 to May 1976 Clarke spent time in the United States of America. He participated in the International Writers' Program in Iowa City where he stayed for three months. At the end of the project he was elected Honorary Fellow in Writing at the University of Iowa. Apart from writing he was also engaged in a joint painting project with two other artists, Dilip Chitre from Bombay and Ahmed Muhamed Imavivic from Yugoslavia. The project was called *The Triple Triptych* and each artist contributed a panel. Clarke painted an Iowa farmscape showing the late afternoon sun.

On completion of the project, Clarke visited friends in Evanston in Illinois. They gave him newspapers with news from southern Africa and in February 1976 he painted in acrylic on canvas another triptych, *Haunted Landscape,* which was exhibited in Cape Town in 1985 at the South African Association of Arts Gallery. Dale Lautenbach, at the time art critic of the *Cape Argus,* singled it out as 'memorable' and said: 'It is a haunting work, threaded

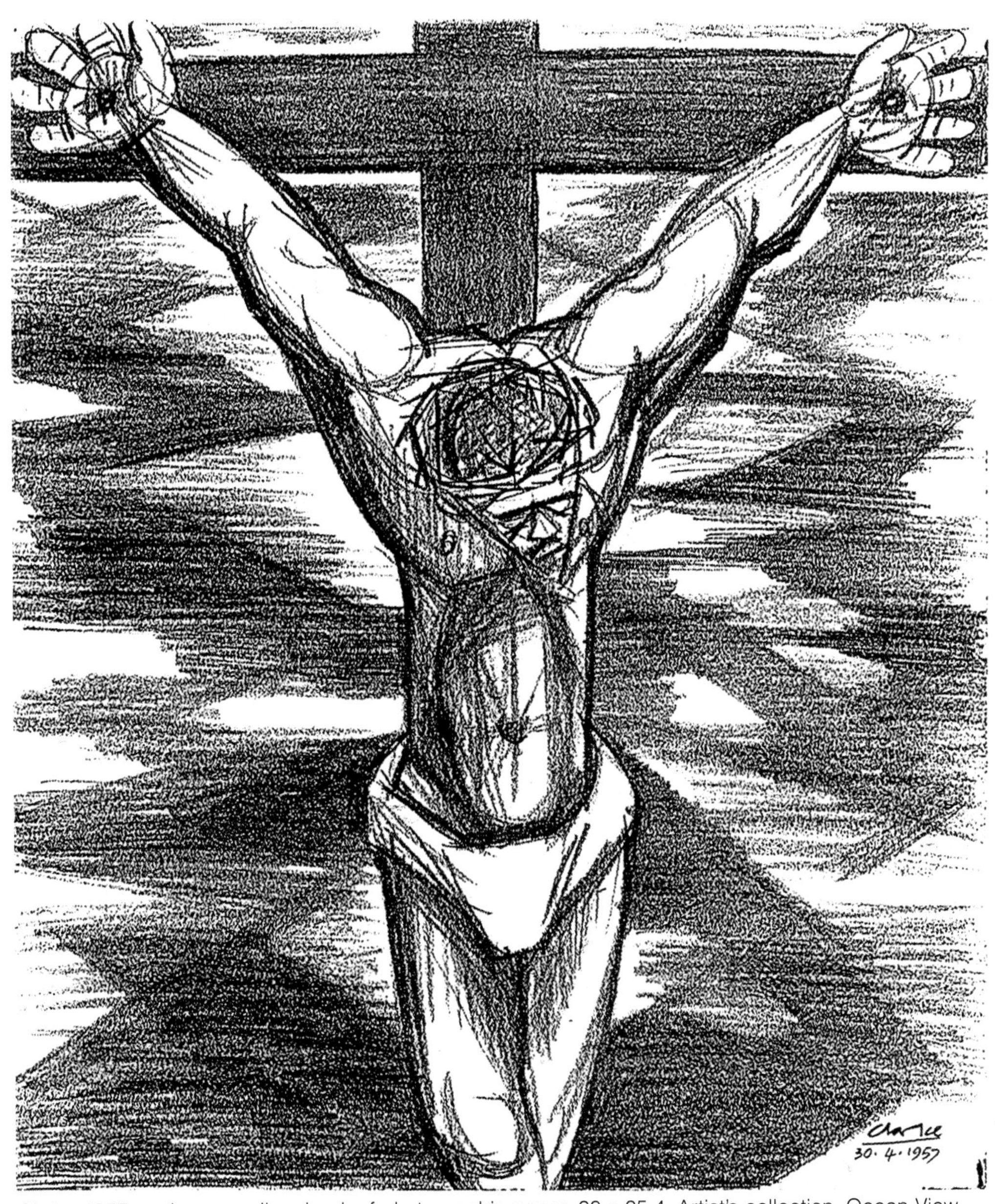

Christ, 1957, carbon pencil on back of photographic paper, 30 x 25.4. Artist's collection, Ocean View.

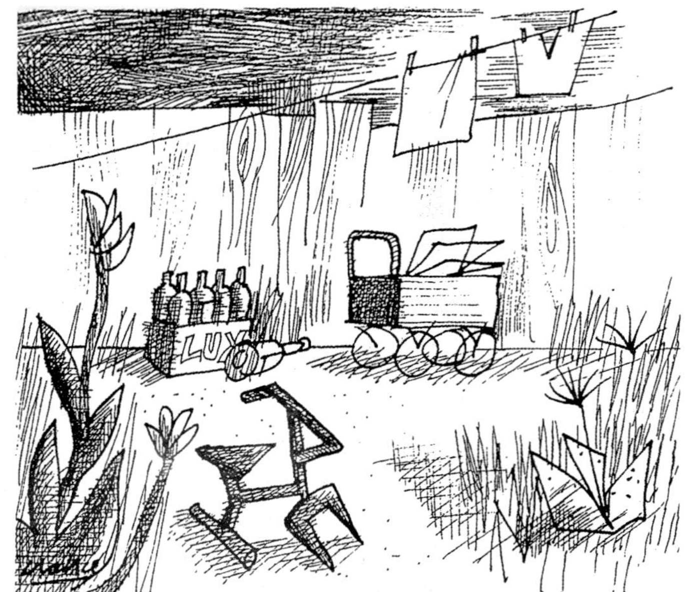

Their backyard, 1984–5.

The main scenes of the triptych correspond with illustrations in 'We shall appear like strolling players', Clarke's unpublished manuscript of 1984–5. The scenes and corresponding illustrations are 'neglected backyard' and *Their backyard*, 'abandoned dwelling against the sky' and *They lived there a long time ago*, 'group of children and dog' and *He won't bite*. Though of later date, these illustrations and Clarke's renderings of a masked girl's performance (*We're not afraid*), people on the move (*Wanderers*) and 'loony'

with subtle contradictions – the beautiful colour from a sky that gives no sun, the broad spaces of a land which confines figures to a narrow road or cramped backyard.'[31]

This triptych and the final lines of Clarke's poem, 'At Effigy Mounds National Monument, Iowa USA 1975', evoke motifs of Clarke's pictorial vocabulary:

> Like us, the Indian ghosts
> wander over these wooded hills,
> their absence following at our backs
> as we tread along the tracks around
> each ghostly-silent mound
> On Effigy Hill.[32]

In discussing *Haunted Landscape*, Clarke told Nic Maritz, curator of the Bowmint Collection in Pretoria, that he wanted to express his thoughts about South Africa: 'So I set to work on this painting [...] partly based on drawings that I'd done beforehand and also partly on elements that came to mind.'[33]

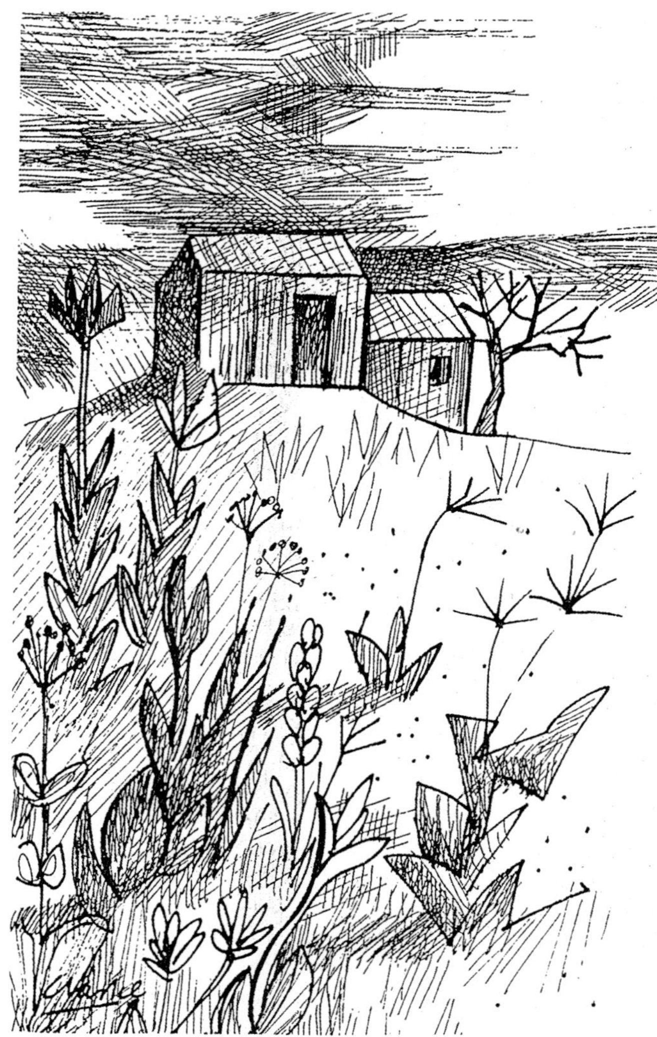

They lived there a long time age, 1984–5.

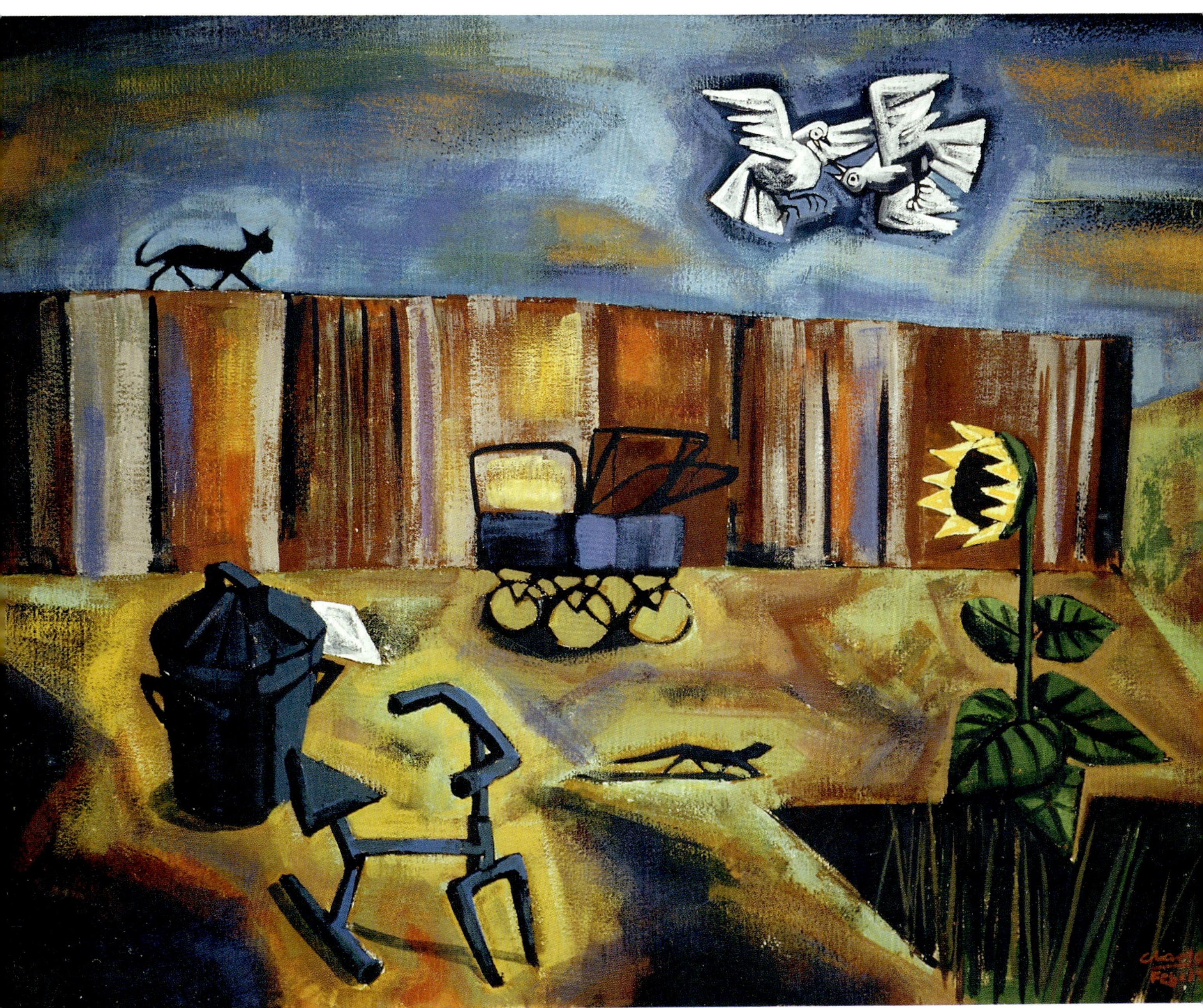

Haunted Landscape I, 1976, acrylic on canvas, 55 x 71. Bowmint Collection, Pretoria.

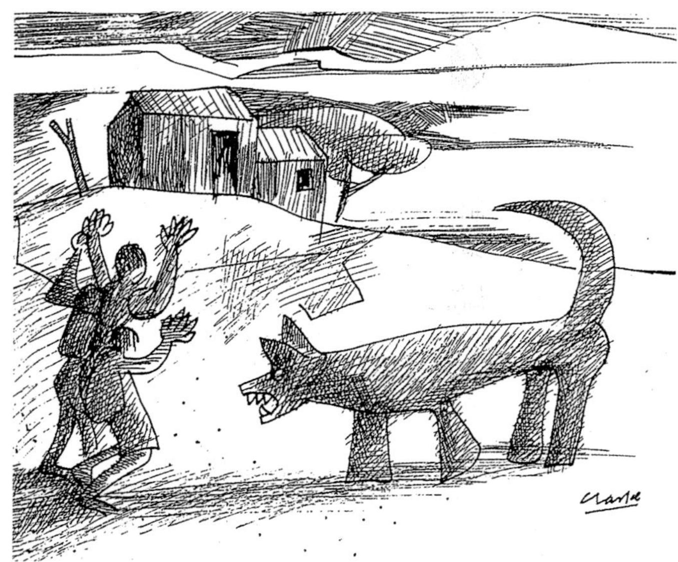

He won't bite, 1984–5.

(Between earth and moon), also from the same text, reflect on the triptych and add significantly to its iconography. Subsequently *Haunted Landscape*, the transcript of the recorded conversation between Clarke and Maritz, and 'We shall appear like strolling players' evoke a seance which unfolds a period in South African history.

Haunted Landscape consists of three separate panels of equal size held together by a continuous landscape at sunset. In the first panel two white doves are fighting in the sky above an abandoned backyard where a corrugated iron fence encloses a garbage bin, derelict pram and tricycle, lizard and sunflower. On the fence, like a sentinel of doom, stalks a black cat. The two doves are oblivious of what is taking place on the ground behind the fence. At the time, the two white birds signified, for Clarke, the 'two political or parliamentary parties'.[34] While they were opposing each other in the isolation of parliamentary debates, they did not notice the deprivation to which the youth was exposed.

In the central piece a group of three children seem to be alarmed by a huge dog. On the horizon next to a windblown tree looms an ominous two-roomed dwelling. The encounter between the dog and children is set between two posts, one next to the house and the other one in the foreground anchoring a neglected barbed wire fence. It seems as if an imaginary curtain has been raised between the posts above the *dramatis personae*. Clarke explains:

To me looking at the dog, it was if they, the children and the dog, were caught up in some kind of drama or even comedy or melodrama … The children are looking, perhaps, not at the dog which to me represents the police activity in South Africa, because at that stage dogs were already being used by the police and I felt it was extremely inhuman to use dogs as weapons against other human beings.[35]

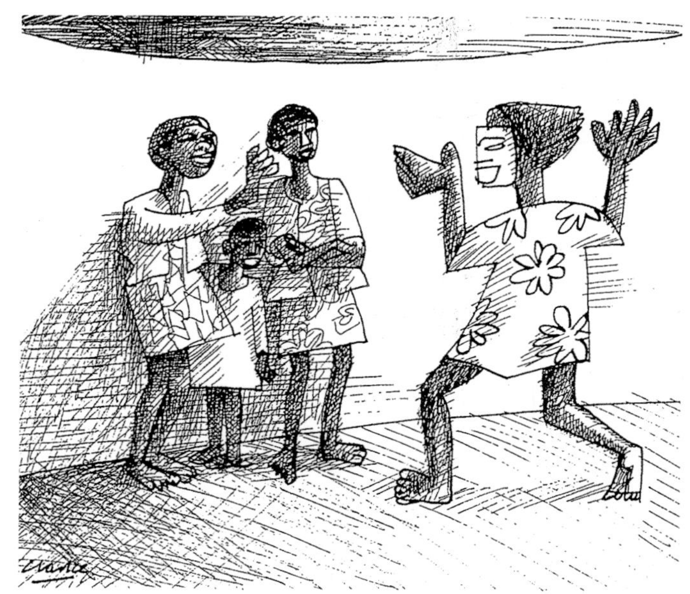

We're not afraid, 1984–5.

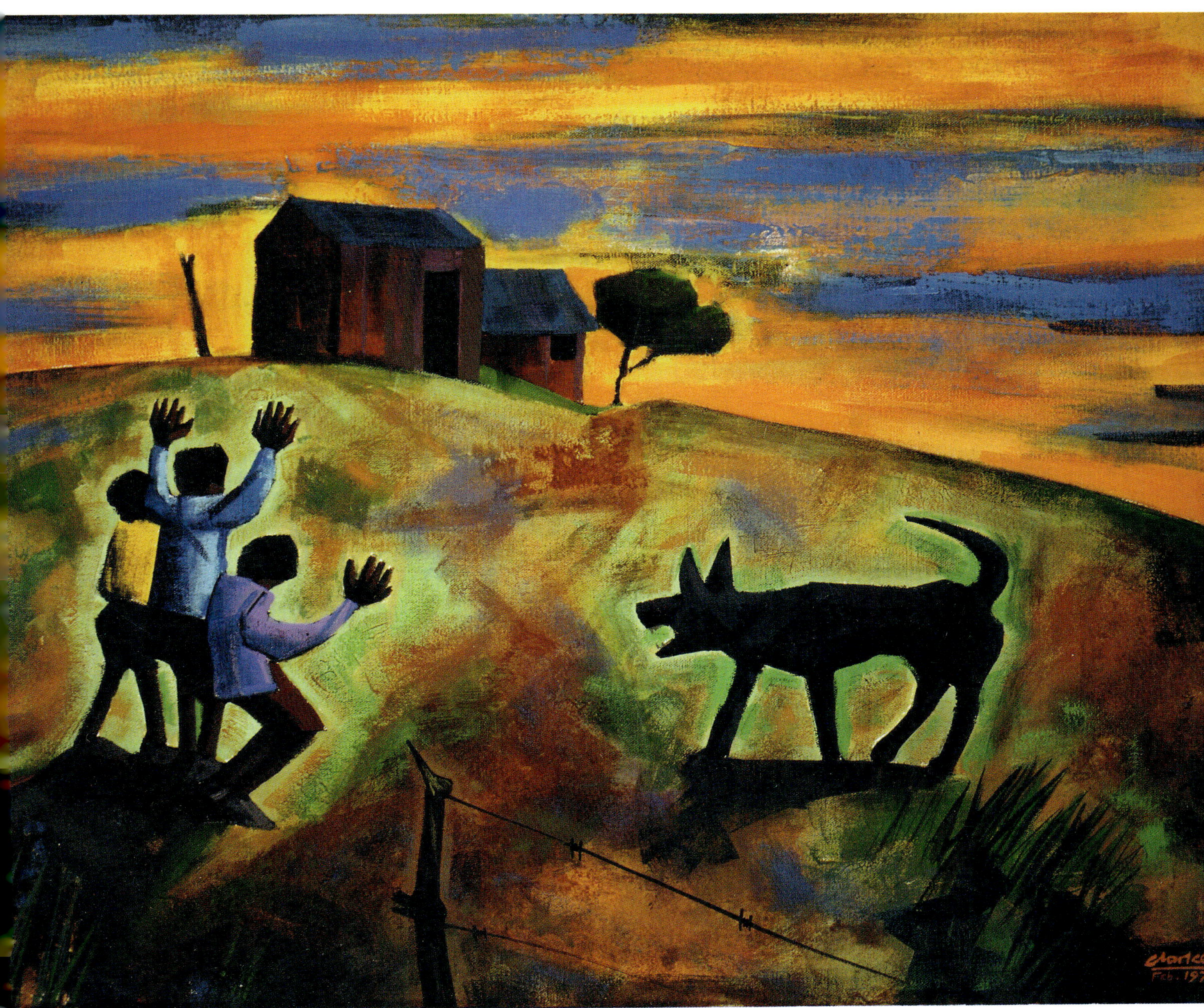

Haunted Landscape II, acrylic on canvas, 55 x 71. Bowmint Collection, Pretoria.

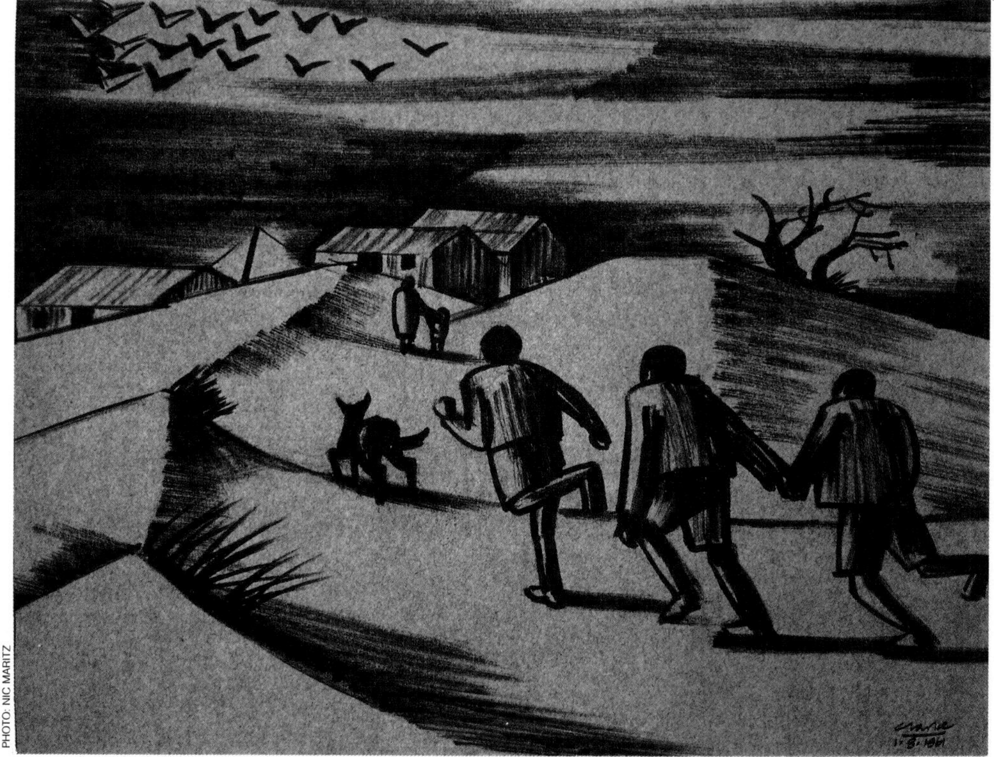

Boys Running, 1961, koki pen on paper, 23.5 x 30.5. Bowmint Collection, Pretoria.

Clarke also says that it is unclear whether the children are alarmed by the dog or whether they and the dog are horrified by the 'haunted' house. In 1961, he had explored a similar ambiguous situation, also involving a dog and three children. But instead of being alarmed by the dog, the boys in the drawing are either chasing it or jogging along with it. They may even all be heading for home.

The mimicry of the masked girl (*We're not afraid*) recalls another illustration, *He won't bite,* from 'We Shall Appear Like Strolling Players'. Behind the mask, the friend becomes a stranger, in the same way that friends become strangers when they are turned on you in the inhumane world of 'urban group areas acts' and in the name of 'law and order'. Then 'she has become a combination of the unreal and the real. Her physical actions, the movements of the fingers and arms, the voice, the peculiar dance-steps emphasise the unreal – and it is as if this that they are looking at is – or could be – the beginnings of some form of lunacy.'[36]

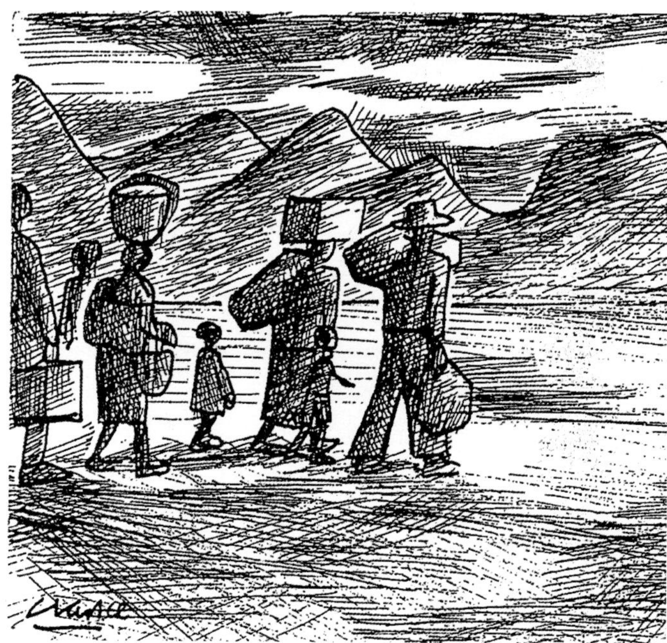

The wanderers, 1984–5.

78

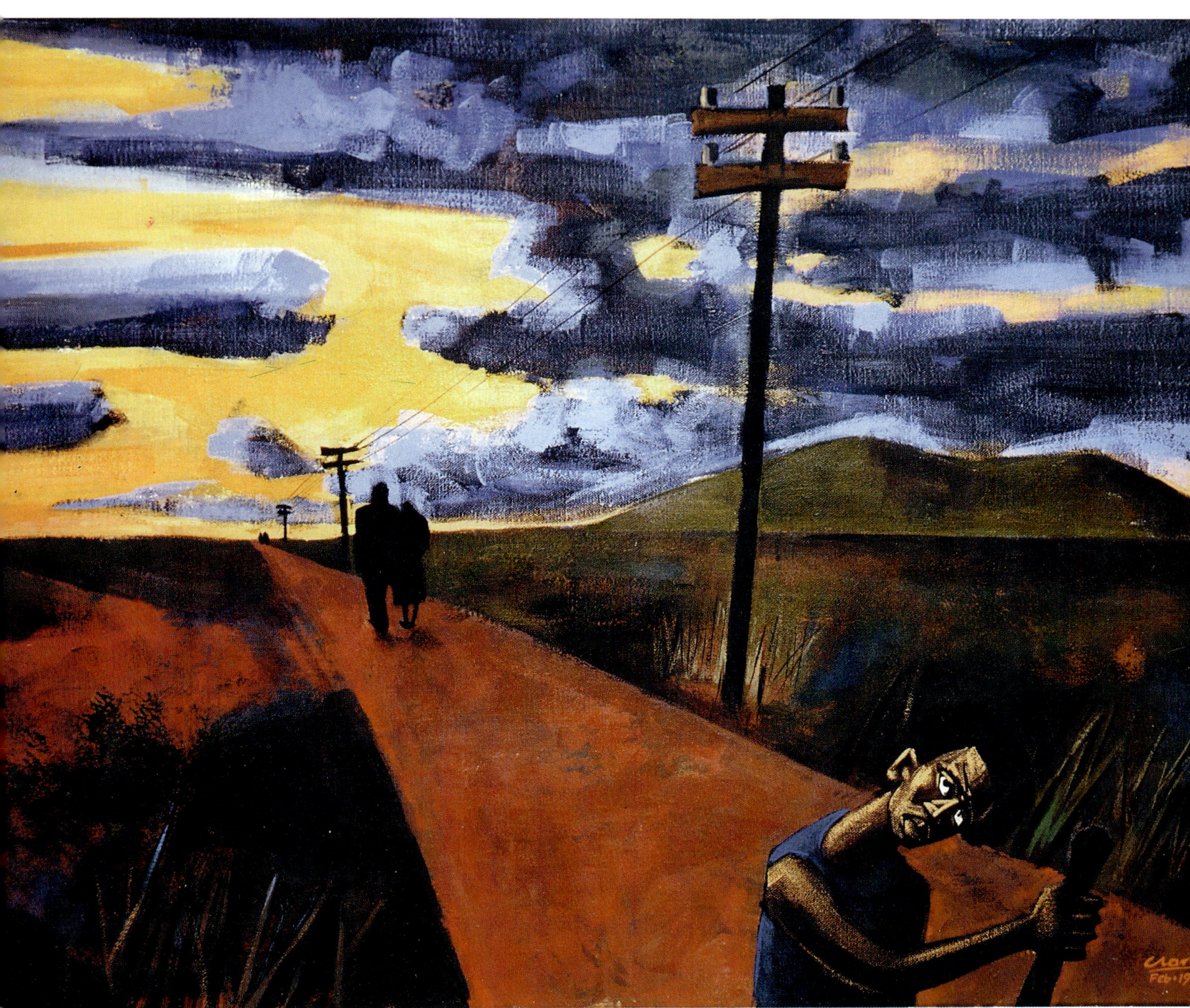

Haunted Landscape III, acrylic on canvas, 55 x 71. Bowmint Collection, Pretoria.

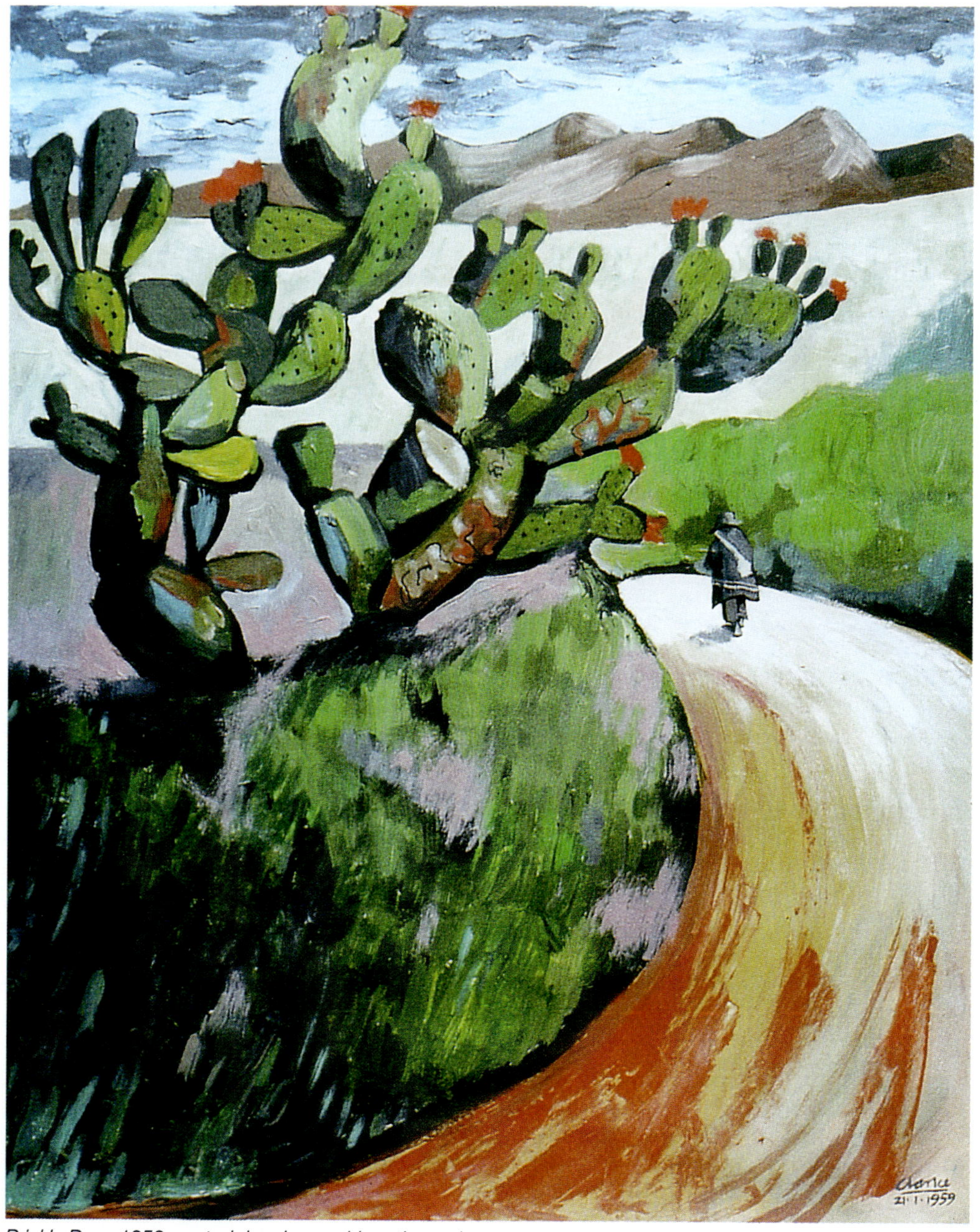

Prickly Pear, 1959, materials, size and location unknown.

In the third panel a burnt sienna road cuts through the gloomy landscape. The road is punctuated in measures of threes by travellers and telephone posts. These cadences seem calculated in comparison with the road curving round a flowering prickly pear at Tesselaarsdal, painted by Clarke in 1959. That road bends and shows colour changes; the wanderer, moving into the distance, is not reduced to an impersonal silhouette as the travellers are in *Haunted Landscape.* He is an individual confidently occupying his space on the road. He is also equipped for the journey as he carries a knapsack. Moreover, this road invites one to follow him because there is nothing that bars you from entering it.

In *Haunted Landscape,* an enigmatic figure (almost Cassandra-like) juts into the foreground and bars one from joining the couples moving and disappearing into the distance. He leans on a staff and his features resemble an African carving. His appearance reminds one of the apparition of Edvard Munch's *Scream,* another bar to entering the picture. Moreover, he resembles the portrayal of the man in

80

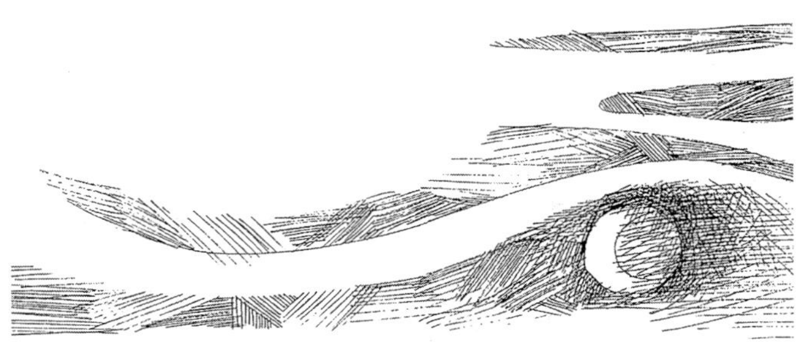

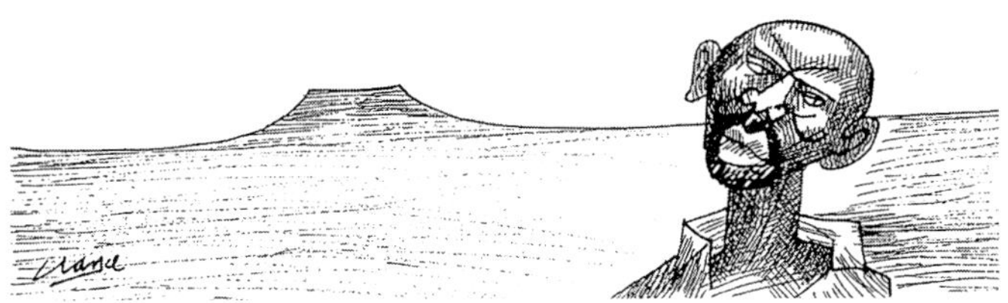

Between earth and moon, 1984–5.

Between earth and moon of 'We shall appear like strolling players'.

The seance becomes real: this man seems entranced and oblivious of what he reveals by tapping his staff. He, the strange one, turns his back on the landscape and faces the viewer. This action forces you to look at a world that displays the remnants of discarded lives. Here children were denied protected childhood and innocent games. Fear, whether of the ferocious animal or the haunted shelter, is their daily companion. When eventually they grow up, their journey leads into desolation.

The crippled one shows the horrors of the past and those still to occur, for he is endowed with supernatural powers:

Perhaps it is not incorrect to say that at certain times he becomes the victim of some invisible tidal pull taking place across thousands of miles of space. One only becomes aware of all these mighty actions that are taking place within his head when this man acts strangely, out of the ordinary, thereby letting you know that he stands, like some godlike figure in some fable, trapped between the earth and the moon.[37]

Not unlike the man described above, Peter Clarke apparently fell 'victim' to 'some invisible tidal pull' when he read the news coverage on South Africa in the Evanston papers. Far from home, he began to reflect on it. Instead of tapping the ground with a walking-stick, Clarke's paintbrush touched the canvas and conjured up subliminal imagery with far-reaching consequences. For a moment the parts of medium and artist merged.

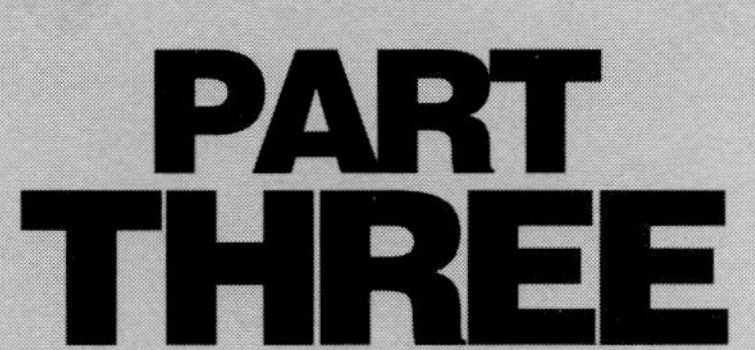

The Contemporaries

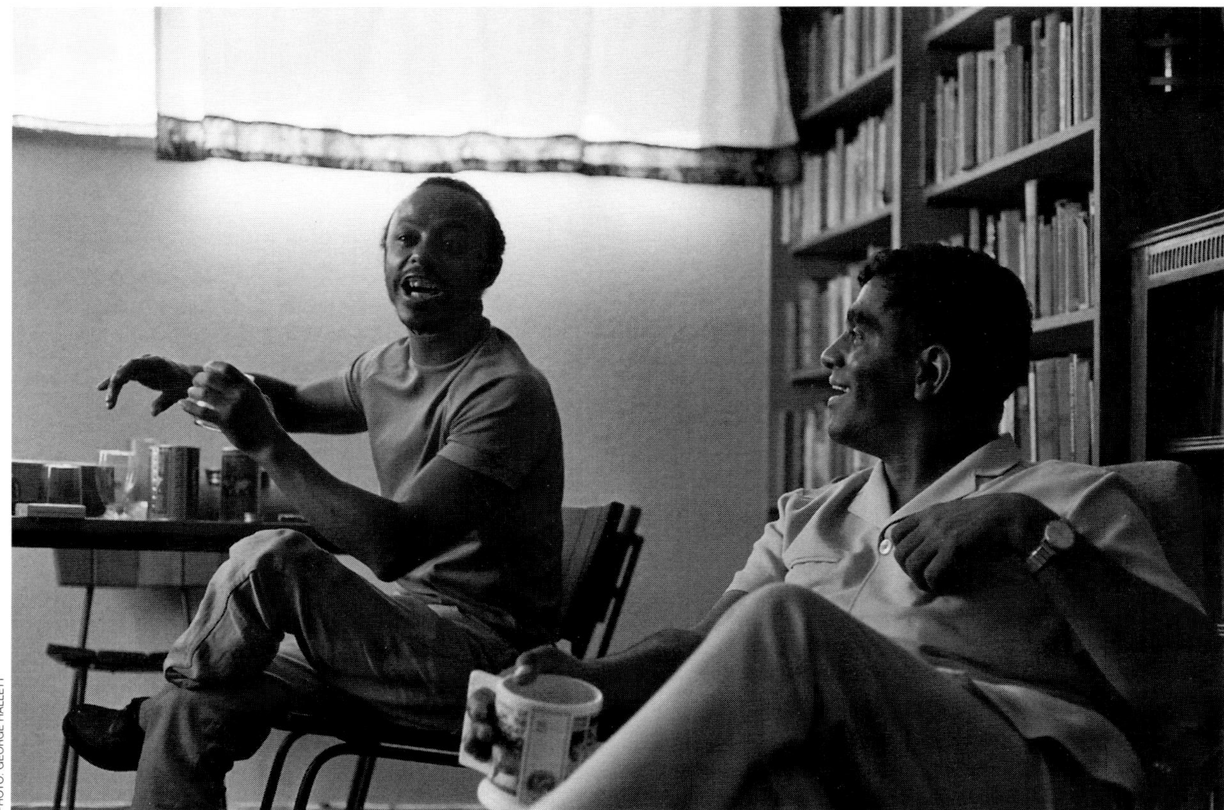

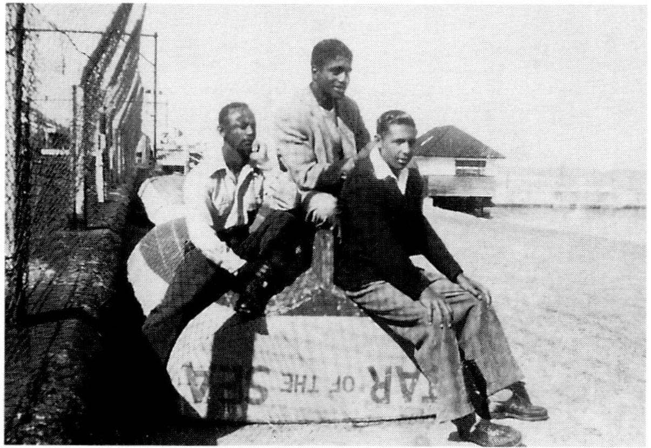

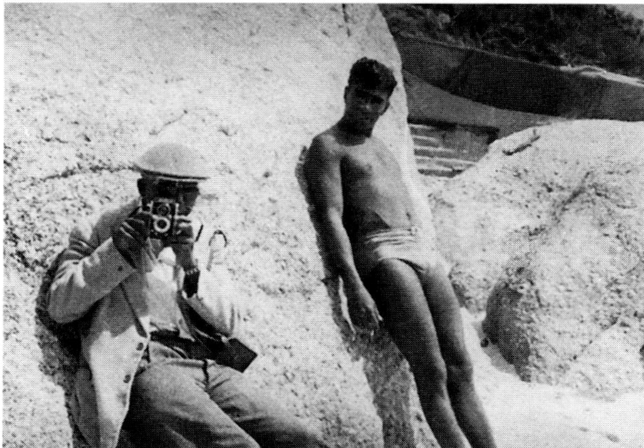

Top: Matthews and Rive share a light-hearted moment at Rive's flat on Rosmead Ave, Kenilworth. Late 1960s.
Bottom left: Matthews, Rive and Fred Miller, on a Sunday afternoon at Kalk Bay harbour. 1955.
Bottom right: Clarke and Rive at the Boulders, Simon's Town. 1957.

Riva

RICHARD M. RIVE

A cold, misty July afternoon about twenty years ago. I first met Riva Lipschitz under the most unusual circumstances. At that time I was a first-year student majoring in English at the university, one of the few 'coloured' students then enrolled at Cape Town. When I first saw her, Riva's age seemed indefinable. Late thirties? Forty perhaps? Certainly more than twenty years older than I was. The place we met in was as unusual as her appearance. The rangers' hut at the top of Table Mountain near the Hely Hutchinson reservoir, three thousand feet above Cape Town.

George, Leonard and I had been climbing all day. George was talkative, an extrovert, given to clowning. Leonard was his exact opposite, shy and introspective. We had gone through high school together but after matriculating they had gone to work while I had won a scholarship which enabled me to proceed to university. We had been climbing without rest all afternoon, scrambling over rugged rocks damp with bracken and heavy with mist. Twice we were lost on the path from India Ravine through Echo Valley. Now soaking wet and tired we were finally in the vicinity of the rangers' hut where we knew we would find shelter and warmth. Some ranger or other would be off duty and keep the fire warm and going. Someone with a sense of humour had called the hut 'At Last'. It couldn't be the rangers for they never spoke English. On the way, we passed the hut belonging to the white Mountain Club; and slightly below that was another hut reserved for members of the 'coloured' Club. I made some remark about the white club house and the fact that prejudice had permeated even to the top of Table Mountain.

'For that matter we would not even be allowed into the so-called Coloured Mountain Club hut,' George remarked, serious for once.

'And why not?'

'Because, dear brother, to get in you mustn't only be so-called coloured, you must also be not too so-called coloured. You must have the right complexion, the right sort of hair, the right address and speak the right sort of Walmer Estate or Wynberg English.'

'You mean I might not make it?' I said in mock horror.

'I mean exactly that.'

I made some rapid calculations. I was dark, had short, curly hair, came from Caledon Street in District Six but spoke English reasonably well. After all I was majoring in it at a white university. What more could anyone require?

'I'm sure that at a pinch I could make it,' I teased George. 'I speak English beautifully and am educated well beyond my intelligence.'

'My dear boy, it won't help. You look far too coloured, University of Cape Town and all. You are far, far too brown. And in addition you have a lousy address.'

I collapsed. 'You can't hold all that against me.'

Leonard grinned. He was not one for saying much.

We trudged on, instinctively skirting both club huts as widely as possible, until we reached 'At Last', which was ten minutes slogging away, just over the next ridge.

A large main room with a very welcome fire going in the cast-iron stove. How the hell did they get that stove up there when our haversacks felt like lead? Running off the main rooms were two tiny bedrooms belonging to each of the rangers. We removed haversacks and sleeping-bags then took off damp boots and stockings. Both rangers were off duty and made room for us at the fire. They were small, wiry Plattelanders; a hard breed of men with wide-eyed, yellow faces, short hair and high cheekbones. They spoke a pleasant, soft, guttural Afrikaans with a distinct Malmesbury brogue, and broke into easy laughter especially when they tried to speak English. The smell of warming bodies filled the room, and steam rose from our wet shirts and shorts. It became uncomfortably hot and I felt sleepy, so decided to retire to one of the bedrooms, crawl into my bag and read myself to sleep. I lit a lantern and quietly left the group. George was teasing the rangers and insisting that they speak English. I was reading a novel about the massacre in the ravines of Babi Yar, gripping and revolting: a bit out of place in the unnatural calm at the top of a cold, wet mountain. I was beginning to doze off comfortably when the main door of the hut burst open and a blast of cold air swept through the entire place, almost extinguishing the lantern. Before I could shout anything there were loud protests from the main room. The door slammed shut again and then followed what sounded like a muffled apology. A long pause, then I made out George saying something. There was a short snort, followed by peals of loud, uncontrolled laughter. I felt it was uncanny. The snort, then the rumbling laughter growing in intensity, then stopping abruptly.

By now I was wide awake and curious to know to whom the laugh belonged, though far too self-conscious to join the group immediately. I strained to hear scraps of conversation. Now and then I could make out George's voice and the low, soft Afrikaans of the rangers. There was also another voice which sounded feminine, but nevertheless harsh and screechy. My curiosity was getting the better of me. I climbed out of the sleeping-bag and as unobtrusively as possible joined the group around the fire. The newcomer was a gaunt, angular white woman, extremely unattractive, looking incongruous in heavy, ill-fitting mountaineering clothes. She was the centre of the discussion and enjoying it. She was in the middle of making a point when she spotted me. Her finger remained poised in mid air.

'And who may I ask is that?' She stared at me. I looked back into her hard, expressionless grey eyes.

'Will someone answer me?'

'Who?' George asked, grinning at my obvious discomfort.

'Him. That's who.'

'Oh, him?' George laughed. 'He's Paul. He's the greatest literary genius the coloured people have produced this decade. He's written a poem.'

'How exciting,' she dismissed me. The other laughed. They were obviously under her spell.

'Let me introduce you. This is Professor Paul. First-year Bachelor of Arts. University of Cape Town.'

'Cut it out,' I said very annoyed at him.

George ignored my remark. 'And you are? I have already forgotten.'

She made a mock, ludicrous bow. 'Riva Lipschitz. Madame Riva Lipschitz. The greatest Jewish watchrepairer and mountaineer in Cape Town. Display shop, 352 Long Street.'

'All right, you've made your point. Professor Paul … Madame Lipschitz.' I mumbled a greeting, keeping well in the background. I was determined not to participate in any conversation. I found George's flattering of her loathsome. The bantering continued, to the amusement of the two rangers. Leonard smiled sympathetically at me. I remained poker-faced, waiting for an opportunity when I could slip away. George made some amusing remark (I was not listening) and Riva snorted and began to laugh. So that was where it came from. She saw the look of surprise on my face and stopped abruptly.

'What's wrong, Professor? Don't you like the way I laugh?'

'I'm sorry, I wasn't even thinking of it.'

'It makes no difference whether you were or not. Nevertheless I hate being ignored. If the others can treat me with the respect due to me, why can't you? I'm like a queen, am I not, George?' I wasn't sure whether she was serious or not.

'You certainly are like a queen,' he laughed.

'Everyone loves me except the Professor. Maybe he thinks too much.'

'Maybe he thinks too much of himself,' George added.

She snored and started to laugh at his witticism. George glowed with pride. I took in her ridiculous figure and dress. She was wearing a little knitted skullcap, far too small for her, from which wisps of mousy hair were sticking. A thin face, hard around the mouth, grey eyes, and a large nose I had seen in caricatures of Jews. She seemed flat-chested under her thick jersey which hung down to stick-

thin legs stuck into heavy woollen stockings and heavily studded climbing-boots.

'Come on, Paul, be nice to Riva,' George encouraged.

'Madame Riva Lipschitz, thank you. Don't you think I look like a queen, Professor?' I maintained my rigid silence.

'Your Professor obviously does not seem over-friendly. Don't you like whites, Professor? I like everyone. I came over specially to be friendly with you people.'

'Who are you referring to as you people?' I was getting angry. She seemed temporarily thrown off her guard at my reaction, but immediately controlled herself and broke into a snort.

'The Professor is extremely sensitive. You should have warned me. He doesn't like me but we shall remain friends all the same; won't we, Professor?'

She shot out her hand for me to kiss. I ignored it. She turned back to George and for the rest of her stay pretended I was not present. When everyone was busy talking I slipped out quietly and returned to the bedroom.

Half asleep I could pick up scraps of conversation. George seemed to be explaining away my reaction, playing clown to her queen. Then they forgot all about me. I must have dozed off for I awoke suddenly to find someone shaking my shoulder. It was Leonard.

'Would you like to come with us?'

'Where to?'

'Riva's Mountain Club hut. She's invited us over for coffee, and to meet Simon, whoever he is.'

'No, I don't think I'll go.'

'You mustn't take her too seriously.'

'I don't intend to. Only I don't like her type and the way George is playing up to her. Who the hell does she think she is, after all? What does she want with us?'

'I really don't know. You heard she said she was a watch-repairer somewhere in Long Street. Be reasonable, Paul. She's just trying to be friendly.'

'While playing the bloody queen?

Who does she think she is because she's white?'

'Don't be like that. Come along with us. She's just another person.' George appeared, grinning widely. He attempted an imitation of Riva's snort.

'You coming or not?' he asked, laughing. For that moment I disliked him intensely.

'I'm certainly not.' I rolled over in my bag to sleep.

'All right, if that's how you feel.'

I heard Riva calling for him, then after a time she shouted. 'Goodbye, Professor, see you again some time.' Then she snorted and they went laughing out at the door. The rangers were speaking softly and I joined them around the fire, then fell asleep there. I dreamt of Riva striding with heavy, impatient boots and stick-thin legs over mountains of dead bodies in the ravines of Babi Yar. She was snorting and laughing while pushing bodies aside, climbing upwards over dead arms and legs.

It must have been much later when I awoke to the door opening and a stream of cold air rushing into the room. The fire had died down and the rangers were sleeping. George and Leonard were stomping and beating the cold out of their bodies.

'You awake, Paul?' George shouted. Leonard shook me gently.

'What scared you?' George asked, 'Why didn't you come and have coffee with the queen of Table Mountain?'

'I can't stand her type. I wonder how you can.'

'Come off it, Paul. She's great fun.' George attempted a snort and then collapsed with laughter.

'Shut up, you fool. You'll wake the rangers. What the hell did she want here anyway?'

George sat up, tears running down his cheeks. He spluttered and it produced more laughter. 'She was just being friendly, dear brother Paul, just being friendly. Fraternal greetings from her Mountain Club.'

'Her white Mountain Club?'

'Well, yes, if you put it that way, her white Mountain Club. She could hardly join the so-called coloured one, now, could she? Wrong hair, wrong address, wrong laugh.'

'I don't care where she goes as long as you keep her away from me. I have no need to play up to whites and Jews.'

'Now really, Paul,' George seemed hurt. 'Are you anti-Semitic as well as being anti-white?' My remark must have hit home.

'No, I'm only anti-Riva Lipschitz.'

'Well, anyhow, I like the way she laughs.' He attempted another imitation, but when he started to snort he choked and collapsed to the floor coughing and spluttering. I rolled over in my bag to sleep.

Three months later I was in the vicinity of Upper Long Street. George worked as a clerk at a furniture store in Bree Street. I had been busy with an assignment in the Hiddingh Hall library and had finished earlier than expected. I had not seen him since we had last gone mountaineering, so strolled across to the place where he worked. I wanted to ask about himself, what he had been doing since last we met, about Riva. A senior clerk told me that he had not come in that day. I wandered around aimlessly, at a loss what to do next. I peered into second-hand shops without any real interest. It was late afternoon on a dull, overcast day and it was rapidly getting darker with the promise of rain in the air. Upper Long Street and its surrounding lanes seemed more depressing, more beaten up than the rest of the city. Even more so than District Six. Victorian double-storied buildings containing mean shops on the ground floors spilled over into mean side-streets and lanes. To catch a bus home meant walking all the way down to the bottom of Adderley Street. I might as well walk all the way back. Caledon Street, the noise, the dirt, the squalor. My mood was as depressing as my immediate surroundings. I did not wish to stay where I was and at the same time did not wish to go home imme-

diately. What was the number she had said? 352 or 325? I peered through the windows of second-hand bookshops without any wish to go inside and browse. 352, yes that was it. Or 325? In any case I had no money to buy books even if I had the inclination. Had George been at work he might have been able to shake me out of this mood, raise my spirits.

I was now past the swimming-baths. A dirty fly-spotted delicatessen store. There was no number on the door, but the name was boldly displayed. Madeira Fruiterers. Must be run by some homesick Portuguese. Next to it what seemed like a dark and dingy watchmakers. Lipschitz – Master Jewellers. This must be it. I decided to enter. A shabby, squat, balding man adjusted an eyepiece he was wearing and looked up from a workbench cluttered with assorted broken watches.

'Excuse me, are you Mr Lipschitz?' I wondered whether I should add 'Master Jeweller'.

'What exactly do you want?' He had not answered my question. He repeated, 'What can I do for you?' His accent was guttural and foreign. I thought of Babi Yar. I was about to apologise and say that I had made some mistake when from the far side of the shop came an unmistakable snort.

'My goodness, if it isn't the Professor!' and then the familiar laugh. Riva came from behind a counter. My eyes had become accustomed to the gloomy interior. The squat man was working from the light filtering in through a dirty window. Rickety showcases and counters cluttered with watches and cheap trinkets. A cat-bin, still wet and smelling pungently, stood against a far counter.

'What brings the Professor here? Coming to visit me?' She nodded to the squat man indicating that all was in order. He had already shoved back his eyepiece and was immersed in his work.

'Come to visit the queen?'

This was absurd, I could not imagine anything less regal, more incongruous. Riva, queen? As gaunt as she had looked in the rangers' hut. Now wearing an unattractive blouse and old-fashioned skirt. Her face as narrow, strained and unattractive as ever. I had to say something, explain my presence.

'I was just passing.'

'That's what they all say. George said so last time.'

What the hell did that mean? I started to feel uncomfortable. She looked at me coyly. Then she turned to the squat man.

'Simon, I think I'll pack up now. I have a visitor.' He showed no sign that he had heard her. She took a shabby coat from a hook.

'Will you be late tonight?' she asked him. Simon grumbled some unintelligible reply. Was this Simon whom George and Leonard had met? Simon the mountaineer? He looked most unlike a mountaineer. Who the hell was he then? Her boss? Husband? Lover? Lipschitz – the Master Jeweller? Or was she Lipschitz, the Master Jeweller? That seemed most unlikely. Riva nodded to me to follow. I did so as there was no alternative. Outside it was dark already.

'I live two blocks down. Come along and have some tea.' She did not wait for a reply but began walking briskly, taking long strides. I followed as best I could half a pace behind.

'Walk next to me,' she almost commanded. I did so. Why was I going with her? The last thing I wanted was tea.

'Nasty weather,' she said, 'bad for climbing.' Table Mountain was wrapped in a dark mist. It was obviously ridiculous for anyone to climb at five o'clock on a weekday afternoon in heavy weather like this. Nobody would be crazy enough. Except George perhaps.

'George,' she said as if reading my thoughts. 'George. What was the other one's name?'

'Leonard.'

'Oh, yes, Leonard. I haven't seen him since the mountain. How is he getting on?'

I was panting to keep up with her.

'I don't see much of them except when we go climbing together. Leonard works in Epping and George in Bree Street.'

'I know about George.' How the hell could she?

'I've just come from his work. I wanted to see him but he hasn't come in today.'

'Yes, I knew he wouldn't be in. So you came to me instead? I somehow knew that one day you would put in an appearance.'

How the hell did she know? Was she in contact with George? Daily contact? I remained quiet, out of breath with the effort of keeping up with her. What on earth made me go into the shop of Lipschitz – Master Jeweller? Who the hell was Lipschitz – Master Jeweller?

The conversation had stopped. She continued the brisk pace, taking her fast, incongruous strides. Like stepping from rock to rock up Blinkwater or Babi Yar.

'Here we are.' She stopped abruptly in front of an old triple-storied Victorian building with brown paint peeling off its walls. On the upper floors were wide balconies ringed with wrought-iron railings. The main entrance was clutttered with spilling refuse bins.

'I'm on the first floor.'

We mounted a rickety staircase, then came to a landing and a long, dark passage lit at intervals by solitary electric bulbs. All the doors, where these could be made out, looked alike. Riva stopped before one and rummaged in her bag for a key. Next to the door was a cat-litter smelling sharply. The same cat?

'Here we are.' She unlocked the door, entered and switched on a light. I was hesitant about following her inside.

'It's quite safe, I won't rape you,' she said and snorted. This was a coarse remark. I waited for her to laugh but she did not. I entered, blinking my eyes. A large, high-ceilinged, cavernous bedsitter with a kitchen and toilet running off it. The room was gloomy and dusty. A double bed, round table,

two comfortable-looking chairs and a dressing-table covered with bric-à-brac. There was a heavy smell of mildew permeating everything. The whole building smelt of mildew. Why a double bed? For her alone or Simon and herself?

'You live here?' It was a silly question and I knew it. I wanted to ask, 'You live here alone or does Simon live here also?' Why should I bother about Simon?

'Yes, I live here. Have a seat. The bed's more comfortable to sit on.' I chose one of the chairs. It creaked as I settled into it. All the furniture must have been bought from second-hand junk shops. Or maybe it came with the room. Nothing was modern. Jewish-Victorian, or what I imagined Jewish-Victorian to be. Dickensian in a sort of decaying nineteenth-century way. Riva took her coat off. She was all hurry and bustle.

'Let's have some tea. I'll put on the water.' Before I could refuse she disappeared into the kitchen. I must leave now. The surroundings were far too depressing. Riva was far too depressing. I remained as if glued to my seat. She reappeared. Now to make my apologies. I spoke as delicately as I could, but it came out all wrongly.

'I'm very sorry, but I won't be able to stay for tea. You see, I really can't stay. I must be home. I have lots of work to do. An exam tomorrow. Social Anthrop.'

'The trouble with you, Professor, is that you are far too clever, but not clever enough.' She sounded annoyed. 'Maybe you work too hard, far too hard. Have some tea before you go.' There was a twinkle in her eye again. 'Or are you afraid of me?' I held my breath, expecting her to laugh but she did not. A long pause.

'No,' I said at last. 'No, I'm not afraid of you. I really do have an exam tomorrow. You must believe me. I was on my way home. I was hoping to see George.'

'Yes, I know, and he wasn't at work. You've said so before.'

'I really must leave now.'

'Without first having tea? That would be anti-social. An intellectual like you should know that.'

'But I don't want any tea, thanks.' The conversation was going around in meaningless circles. Why the hell could I not go if I wished to?

'You really are afraid of me. I can see that.'

'I must go.'

'And not have tea with the queen? Is it because I'm white or Jewish? Or because I live in a room like this?'

I wanted to say, 'It's because you're you. Why can't you leave me alone?' I got up determined to leave.

'Why did you come with me in the first place?'

This was an unfair question. I had not asked to come along. There was a hiss from the kitchen where the water was boiling over on the plate.

'I don't know why I came. Maybe it was because you asked me.'

'You could have refused.'

'I tried to.'

'But not hard enough.'

'Look, I'm going now. I have over-stayed my time.'

'Just a second.' She disappeared into the kitchen. I could hear her switching off the stove, then the clicking of cups. I stood at the door waiting for her to appear before leaving. She entered with a tray containing the tea things and a plate with some assorted biscuits.

'No, thanks,' I said, determined that nothing would keep me. 'Said I was leaving and I am.'

She put the tray on the table. 'All right then, Professor. If you must, then you must. Don't let me keep you any longer.' She looked almost pathetic that moment, staring dejectedly at the tray. This was not the Riva I had learnt to know. She was straining to control herself. I felt dirty, sordid, sorry for her.

'Goodbye,' I said hastily and hurried out into the passage. As I swiftly ran down the stairs I heard her snorting. A short pause and then peals of uncontrolled laughter. I stumbled into Long Street.

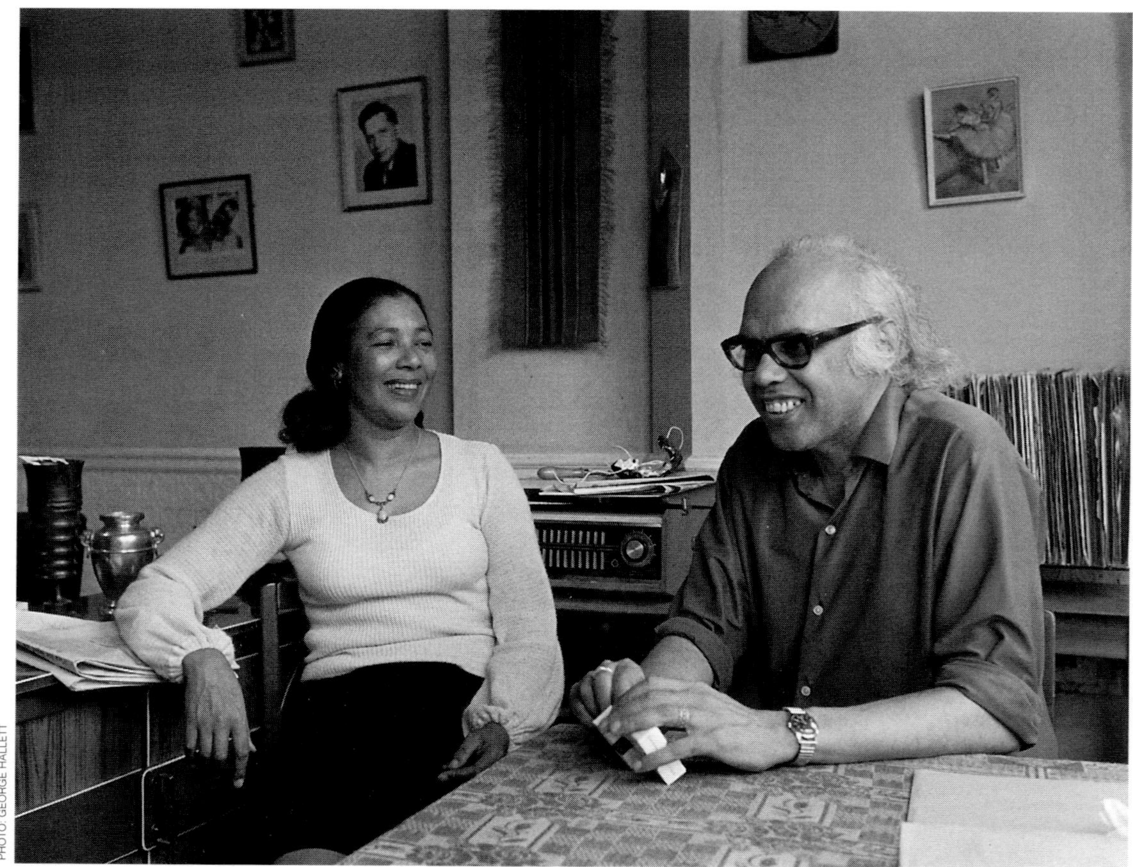

Alex La Guma and his wife, Blanche, at home in Muswell Hill, London. 1975.

Nocturne

ALEX LA GUMA

There were three of them sitting at the table near the window. At that time of the afternoon the Duke's Head was quiet. The plump barman wiped the smooth, stained teak in front of him. At the end of the bar a haggard man sat like a lone penitent in a cathedral and slowly sipped his flat beer. Somewhere across the street somebody was playing a piano. The three at the table were drinking beer and port and talking quietly.

'It's easy,' Moos was saying. 'Frog will be outside holding a candle. You and I, Harry, will get in and floor the watchman. Hell, Harry, you aren't listening.'

Harry was listening to the piano across the street. The music came through the open window, now tinkling like water dripping into a fine china bowl, now throbbing and booming with the sound of many beautiful tuned gongs, rippling away and rising again in great waves.

'God, what playing,' Harry said, as the piece ebbed to a gentle finish. 'Did you rookers hear that?'

'___,' Moos said. 'Classical stuff. Just a helluva noise. Give me a wakker jol any time.' He dismissed the subject by taking a swallow of beer. 'Now listen. We'll go over it again …'

'I know, I know,' Harry said. 'Frog is outside keeping watch. We'll be inside fixing the watchman. Now, what time do we meet?'

'Nine,' Mos answered. 'I'll pick Frog up and we'll get you outside the Modern.'

'How much you think we'll pick up?' Frog asked, drinking some of his port. The piano started again, the music drifting cautiously into the barroom.

'About a hundred and forty or fifty,' Moos said. He was aware of the sound again, but ignored it. Only Harry continued to listen. He sipped his port and let his mind lap at the music. The gentle, perfect notes touched something inside him, and he got a strange feeling, but did not try to fathom it. He kept listening. He tried the air under his breath, struggling with it like a terrier with an expensive slipper, and gave it up to listen again. The piano music quivered and undulated. Once a car passed and drowned it momentarily, but it emerged again, gentle as the drop of tears. It was the *Nocturne No. 2*, in E flat major, by Chopin, but Harry did not know that.

Moos and Frog began talking about other things as the piano drifted into the *Fantasie-Impromptu*. Harry was completely absorbed in the music now. It held him in its spell, tying him to itself with wires of throbbing sound, drugging his mind into a coma of swelling and fading rhythm. The music went on, seemingly inexhaustible: Liszt's *Hungarian Rhapsody* pounded and crashed, the theme from Tchaikowsky's *Pathètique* wept quietly, waltzes and minuets pranced and cavorted, pieces of Beethoven marched somberly, and Spanish gypsy dances whirled and stamped. Schubert's *Serenade* called longingly to some unknown lover in a darkened room. The *Nocturne* came again, drifting with the step of fairies on moonlit grass.

The Duke's Head began to fill up steadily with the six o'clock crowd, until the music was lost in the steady hum of voices. Harry got up and wandered to the bar. The spell was broken. He whistled softly through his teeth, trying to capture a tune, but his mind had not drunk deeply enough of the music. He joined the three-deep line at the bar and shouldered his way through until he could order half-a-pint of white wine. He leaned against the wet teakwood and drank quietly, still trying to remember. Around him men discussed every topic imaginable: work, races, politics, women, wine, bioscope, religion. A dirty and dishevelled man came in, selling pickles and curry pies. At one end of the bar an argument developed, and for a few moments there was uproar, until the plump barman broke it up.

Somebody tapped Harry on the shoulder and he turned his head. It was Moos.

'Nine o'clock. Don't forget.'

'Okay. Okay. See you later.'

Harry did not watch Moos and Frog go out. He finished the white wine and then extricated himself from the jam at the bar and pushed past the swinging doors into the street. He paused on the pavement. It was growing dark, and the street lamps were on. From diagonally across the way the piano music was still going on, a little louder now that he was outside. It came from an old two-story building, one of a row that formed one side of the grimy street.

He stood for a while and listened, and then strolled down the pavement, looking across at the house, drawn by the music like an alley cat drawn by the scent of fresh and tender meat.

Drab and haunted-looking people sat in doorways looking like scarred saints among the ruins of abandoned churches, half listening, gossiping idly, while the pinched children shot at each other with wooden guns from behind overflowing dustbins in the dusk. Harry crossed the street and paused, hesitating, outside the house.

The music gripped him again. It came from a half-open window on the first floor, bubbling out like a spring of cool water in a wasteland. Then he made up his mind suddenly and climbed the chipped front steps and edged into the house. The hallway was dim and smelled of stale cooking and carbolic water. The sound came from the upper landing, slipping down the worn staircase, echoing from the gloomy corners and the high, stained ceiling. He climbed the stairs slowly, advancing into the crescendo of Ravel's *Bolero*.

Outside the door he stopped, nervous now, a little afraid, but soaked in the music. He stood there while the *Bolero* ended in its crashing chords. Sound came again, tirelessly, gently, moonbeam quivering on quiet waters, on trees and grass along a lonely river bank, sighing for love, and he placed his hand on the doorknob and turned it.

The music faded away like a cataract in a little mountain nook quietly running dry, and the girl at the piano looked at him with sudden surprise.

'I'm sorry if I scared you,' he said, holding the door open. 'I've been listening to you playing from across the way. Real good music.'

'Thank you. Do you like it?'

'Don't know anything about it. But it sounds pretty.'

'Come in and sit down if you want to,' she said. 'People around here often come in to listen.'

'Thanks, miss.'

He entered, awkward as a tramp being admitted to a parish tea, and was suddenly conscious of the port-wine smell on his breath. He sat down on a straight chair as if he expected it to collapse under his weight. The room was neat, dustless, polished, the little tables cluttered with bric-à-brac, framed music-school certificates hanging with Queen Victoria, wedding groups, and *God Is Love* along the papered walls. Another door led to an adjoining room. The whole place seemed to struggle for survival with the surrounding dilapidation, like a Siamese cat caught in a sewer.

'You learn to play by yourself?' he asked, scarcely daring to speak aloud.

'Oh, no. I studied in a convent.'

'What's it bring you? It's pretty, but what's it bring you? Money?'

'Money's not everything. People come up here to listen.' She smiled at him and ran her fingers along the keys. Her face was dark and fine and delicate as a costly violin. 'What do you want me to play?'

Harry cleared his throat and said: 'That piece you were playing when I came in. It sounded good.'

'The *Moonlight Sonata*.' And the music welled up again, falling on him like a gentle rain. He sat straight up, listening, and his muscles relaxed and his mind forgot the nervousness and he sank back in the chair.

'I never had a chance to listen to this kind of stuff,' he said, when it had ended. 'High bugs go to the City Hall to hear it.' He wiped his mouth on the back of his hand and went on: 'There's another piece I heard you play. Goes like this.' He pursed his lips and struggled with the tune and managed a few notes while she listened. He tried again and managed a few jumbled bars this time. Then he gave it up, shaking his head and grinning shyly.

But she had caught it and her hands moved again, gentle as the fall of a hair, and the music poured from her fingertips. 'You mean Chopin's *Nocturne*.'

'Is that what it's called? Yes, that's it.'

He leaned back and shut his eyes and whistled soundlessly with the music, taking it in completely. She played it twice and his head nodded in time.

After that the old-fashioned clock on the sideboard caught his eye and he remembered with a little start that Moos and Frog would be waiting for him. He got up quickly and said: 'I won't keep you any longer. I've got to be going, anyhow.'

'Did you enjoy it?'

'Really. I'd like to come again, some other time.'

'Of course. Come any evening.'

'Thanks, miss. Well, good luck.'

'Good-bye. Thanks for coming in to listen.'

He was out in the dark street again and hurried up it. The doorstep sitters had withdrawn now and the windows of the tenements were yellow with lamplight. Babies wailed here and there, hangers-on lounged against walls, couples made furtive love in doorways. Somewhere beyond, neon signs made a glare against the sky, like a city after a bombardment.

Moos and Frog were waiting impatiently in the light of a shopfront, smoking and cursing fretfully.

'Where the ___ you been?' Moos asked angrily. 'We been waiting.'

'Awright, awright. I'm here now,' Harry said. 'Let's go.'

They walked down the street together. Harry was still thinking about the girl who played the piano, and that he didn't even know her name. He whistled quietly. Knock something, she had said it was. Funny name. He thought, sentimentally, that it would be real smart to have a goose that played the piano like that.

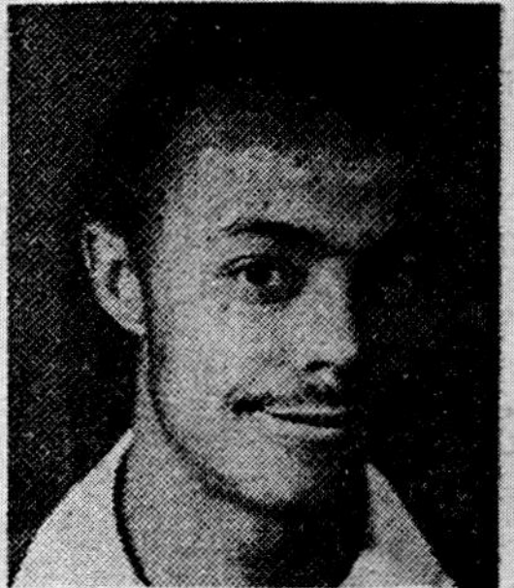

JAMES MATTHEWS

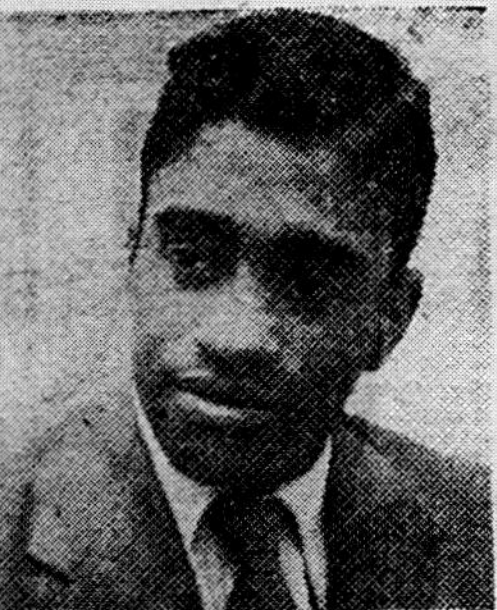

RICHARD M. RIVE

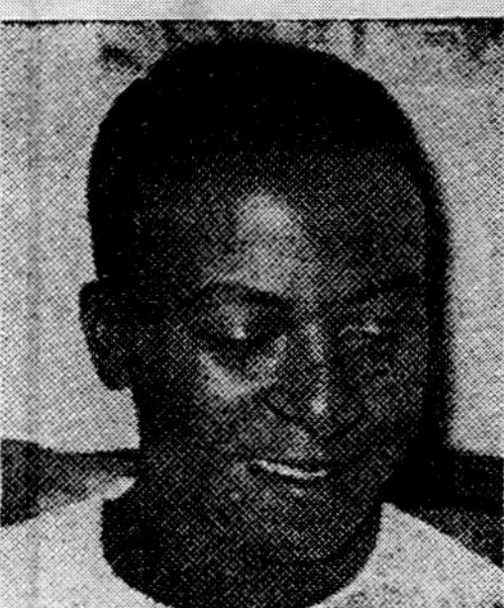

PETER E. CLARKE

Three famous Cape writers do a three-in-one story on a boy they all knew, called:

Willy-Boy!

THE DOWNFALL

By James Matthews

"WILLIE-BOY" . . . "Willie-boy" . . . "Willie-boy!" His mother's voice rose above the roar of the street noises: the children engaged in games in which the main requirement seemed the emptying of their lungs with the maximum of sound; the cries of two hawkers perched on top of a cart stacked with vegetables, the horse straining in the harness and the leather irritating the open sores on its flanks; the lorry whose driver impatiently sounded his horn as he tried to pass the cart in the narrow street.

Willie-boy walked around the corner out of sight of his mother, but her voice followed him and hung in the air like notes from a battered bugle, the bugler blowing with apathy for a listless audience.

The weather had taken its toll of the houses leaning against each other for support. Their original colours had long disappeared and they were left with a uniformity of drabness. In front of each door played a brood of half-naked children. At the corners the older ones lounged against the walls and poles. From a doorway tumbled a drunk. The children watched his progress as he weaved from side to side. He stopped and turned to stare at them, and for no apparent reason burst into tears.

A woman, her stockings hanging on her legs like a sagging concertina, walked past, paused, and peered in his face, then walked on shaking her head.

Like a liner battling to dock he manoeuvred himself to the mouth of an alley, where he collapsed, one foot resting in a pool of water.

Willie-boy watched the others as they played klaverjas. Clubs were trumps. He nodded his head in approval as the youth seated in front of him led with the jack of clubs then followed up with the ace.

He made no move for concealment when his mother turned the corner. He concentrated on the game and hoped she wouldn't call him in front of the other youths.

She stood a few steps from them and called him. He made as if he didn't hear.

(Turn over)

THEY THAT MOURN

By Richard Rive

WHEN the world feels hot it's hot as hell in District Six. The sky is sweet red Muscadel and the moon melts. The world then becomes bounded by Hanover Street and Clifton Hill, and some say the world becomes a bit soiled and dirty, but the world laughs back richly and tells you to go to hell. After all the world revolves around District Six and District Six pulls up its nose at the whole damn universe.

A newspaperboy with scurvey, sprawling toes grinned broadly as he tried to persuade a drunk to buy his last tattered copy of the "Cape Argus." Willie-boy watched disinterestedly from the narrow entrance of one of the limitless lanes. The drunk argued thickly, hurling spicy invectives at the newsvendor. Then with an undignified lurch he careered on his way. Willie-boy was bored. This was not what he had expected. He wanted action, or still better wanted to create action.

The chain around his wrist jangled invitingly, enticingly. He watched a well-dressed Malay delicately removing a filter tip cigarette from an - expensive silver case and then affectedly blowing a thin stream of smoke into the hot Cape Town night. Willie-boy wanted action, wanted to sense the feeling of bone crushing under hard iron, of warm blood washing away all his muddled fears, or to compensate for his crushed feelings, his humiliation. To hurt. Not only for the sake of hurting but as compensation.

Willie-boy saw and did not see, felt and did not feel. He felt iron, hard iron against his wrist, felt the heat coming in waves up the street, felt the oppressive confines of the alley. Suddenly his face froze into a mask as two White Policemen strutted down the street. Willie-boy felt an itching sensation all over his body. Sweat running uncomfortably between skin and clothes as fingers ate into the soft sandstone of the brick wall till it rubbed hard and thick under the nails. He shivered involuntarily as the streetlight caught the metal of their badges and buttons. Willie-boy felt like running, felt as if he had committed a crime.

(Turn over)

THE DELINQUENT

By Peter Clarke

NOW that he was so near the end, Willy-boy lay there thinking back to the days of his childhood. Of course then it was nothing more than boyish mischief that led him to doing all those fancy tricks that he had got up to. He remembered the many apples pinched in shops while the owners had their backs turned, the climbing over fences into gardens to pick fruit off the trees, knocking on people's doors and running away, teasing dogs, upsetting dust-bins in the street. All that went to make up the pleasure of his childhood. "Yes," Willy-boy thought, "those were the days." Even though the pain was throbbing in ever-increasing waves through his body, he couldn't help smiling as he thought of all the fun he had had (which, strangely now, made him sad remembering it).

Naturally people thought it was all very well and sometimes gave in to Willy-boy's odd sense of humour and impetuousness. But it became irritating as time went by and he became older because instead of ceasing he just went from bad to worse until it was just too obvious that Willy-boy was turning into an utter rogue.

Yes, he remembered those days, a little drowsily now . . . far off as in a dream . . . and voices saying, "Willy-boy, you'd better stop playing the fool the way you do" . . . "Why don't you listen to me" . . . "God alone knows what is going to happen to you when you are a man" . . . "Willy-boy, you've been smoking dagga again" . . . "She says you're the one who did it to her" . . . "Willy-boy, you're hurting my arm" . . . "Here's your cut" . . . "Listen to me, Willy-boy, I am your mother" . . . "Willy-boy, Willy-boy" . . . The voices lingered like the memory of a warped record then hazily trailed away and died. Yes, Willy-boy thought, regrettably, that was the way things had gone with him, from good to bad, from the fresh sunniness of childhood to this bitter end in the darkness of a filthy city street pavement.

(Turn over)

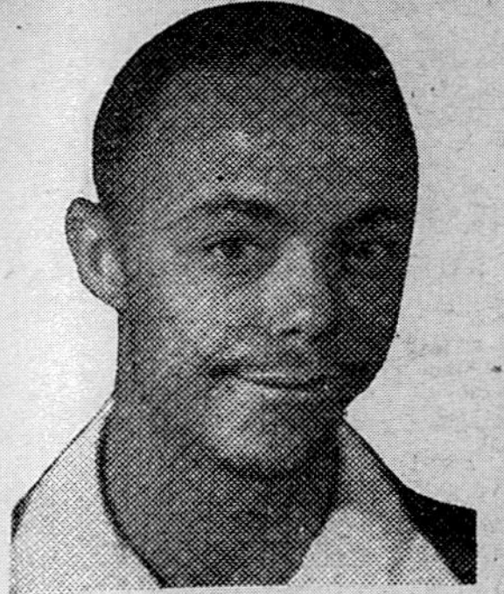

"DOWNFALL"

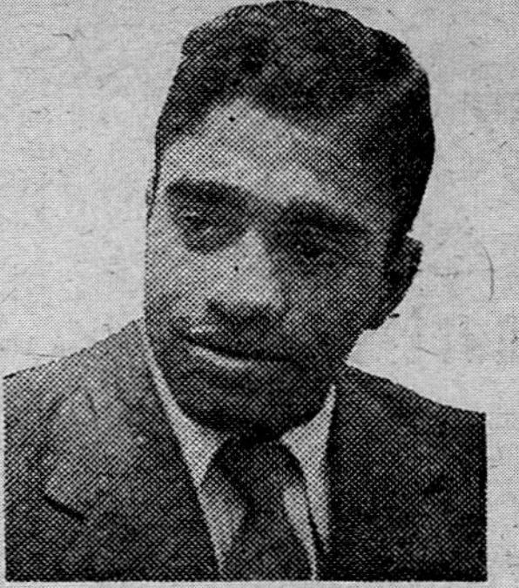

"MOURN"

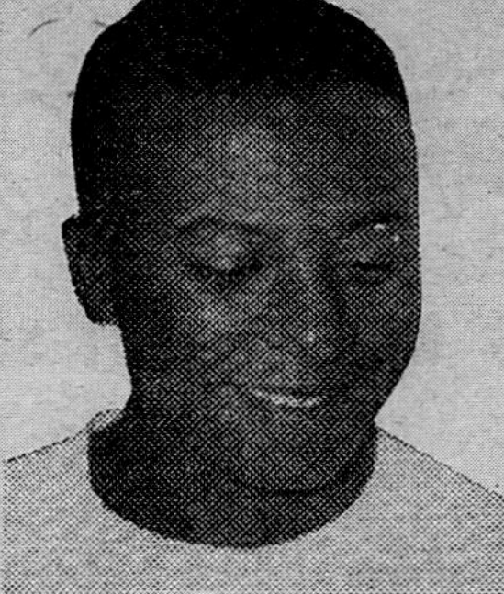

"DELINQUENT"

"Willie-boy!" He cursed softly and walked past her. She walked close at his heels and droned a litany of complaints as they crossed the street. His ears were closed to her laments, and he increased his pace.

"Willie-boy!" He ignored the voice and stood with his back to her. "Willie-boy, when are you going to listen? I have told you so many times to stay away from that corner. Nothing good can come from it. Last week, Kalli and Maila were in trouble through stealing a tyre from Mr. Cohen's lorry, and if it wasn't for the pleas of their mothers and the fact that the tyre was returned, they would have been taken to the police station."

Tears formed in her eyes as she gazed at him. She crossed the room and sat next to him, resting her hand on his head with her fingers entwined in his hair.

He felt uncomfortable under her touch and squirmed his body. He fought the feeling of tenderness which filled him. To counter it he let his mind dwell on the youths at the corner. The theft of the tyre was but one of the incidents his mother knew about. There were several. Some in which he played a part, others where he was too frightened to join.

He could almost see the failure of their plans and their capture. Their appearance in court with his mother weeping in the background and he standing with his head bowed, his hands pressed against his ears to cut off the sound of her weeping.

He got up with an abrupt movement and walked over to the window. He turned and saw the shock mirrored in her eyes, the mouth aquiver. He called out in a loud voice to hide his shame. "I'm a big boy and not a baby!" Then he ran over to her and cradled her in his arms, rocking her to and fro. The tempo of her breathing gradually slackened.

He gazed at her. Her eyes were closed, on her face a contented smile. He bent down and impulsively kissed her on the cheek. She opened her eyes and smiled at him.

"Its almost time for supper and here I'm still sitting daydreaming. I better get busy and start or else I'll be late and you will be hungry." She made no move to get up and continued smiling at him. "Do you want pancake tonight?"

He smiled his thanks.

His unexpected display of affection made her forget her usual caution and she walked over to the dresser where be-

(Turn over).

Felt like running into the street and shouting that he had a chain tied to his wrist and was going to knock hell out of the world to prove to Jamesy that he didn't care a damm.

He had been humiliated in front of the gang. Dragged out of his bioscope seat and beaten up by Jamesy. There was no retaliation. No one ever retaliated against Jamesy. One suffered and murmured under the breath and knocked hell out of the next one. Jamesy was never challenged. Willie-boy again felt the shame as he slunk out of the bioscope with his tail between his legs. Ignoring the derisive laugh of the usher in his dirty khaki uniform. To be beaten up in front of all. Willie-boy felt that he had to let blood flow to compensate for his humiliation, let the world bleed but of course leave Jamesy alone. Leave Jamesy and White Policemen alone. He couldn't remain in the alleyway all night even if the policemen were idling under the streetlight. Willie-boy slunk out of the lane and mustered up all the nonchalance at his disposal. He felt guilt written all over him. Jamesy would not feel the force of his bicycle chain but the rest of the damm world would, and the rest of the damm world was enquiring its way down the next street, was parading in the form of a neatly dressed white man who dared to walk alone in District Six, who dared to stop and ask Willie-boy for a match. Willie-boy felt white heat and fumbled in his windbreaker pocket. To drop the matches and while the white man bent to hit hard and low and revenge his humiliation.

Willie-boy panted like a dog in the lane. He had to redeem himself on some-one . . anyone, that is, of course, except light-brown heads, or heads wearing police helmets. After all the whole bloody world was scared of white faces. They made one pant in alleyways and grip convulsively on iron chains. They made one remember a different world, of mothers, and funerals and all the hell rest.

That was the night he wept hot tears. The neighbours clicking their tongues and fussing around his mother lying cold and impassive. He

(Turn over).

It was there that he met Ernie and Jumbo and Al and soon they were friends because of their mutual interests and came from the same district in Cape Town which in itself demanded a certain amount of loyalty. Except for Jumbo, who felt he wanted to go home sooner but was brought back and sentenced to a longer period of "reforming," they left the Reformatory all about the same time. Back home again they got up to their old tricks, much to the despair of everyone with whom they came into contact. Life was made unpleasant by these bullies.

People clucked their tongues and Willy-boy's mother shook her head and said, "That Willy-boy, he's so wild, I can't do anything with him. He won't listen to me." She would say to nobody in particular, "He's my own child but I should never've brought him into the world."

Willy-boy wouldn't listen to anyone. Why should he? He was a tough guy and who ever heard of tough guys listening to small talk from other people, even though those people included his own mother.

His father gave him no advice because in his own youthful days he had gone on in the same way and Willy-boy was therefore nothing else but a repetition of what he had been. At 16 Willy-boy was already a big-limbed, lusty man who when drunk thought nothing of challenging his father to fights merely to show off his strength.

They would start fighting, Willy-boy drunk from smoking too much dagga and his father drunk from drinking too much of the cheap wine commonly known as "Joep." The neighbours would shudder and say, "It's Willy-boy at it again." Upstairs, in the second floor apartment of the tenement building where they lived, the two men would be brawling, knocking over furniture and breaking things while they shouted at and cursed each other. Willy-boy's mother and sisters could be heard wailing and uttering high-pitched screeches while imploring, "Willy-boy leave your dadda alone" and, "Ach,

(Turn over).

MATTHEWS: "HE MURDERED HIS MOTHER. WHY?"

neath a stack of newspapers she kept her purse. She took some money from it and replaced it. He watched her movements with affected indifference.

"You light the primus while I go to the shop and get some flour and bread."

He nodded his head and took the matches she offered.

The squeaks from the stairs told of her progress and he waited until it was quiet then he dropped the matches on the table and ran to the dresser. Taking care not to disturb the pattern of the pile of newspaper he lifted it and withdrew the purse.

He stood with the purse in his hand, afraid to open it. He could feel the coins through the thin material.

A sound from the stairs gave warning of his mother's return. He hurriedly released the clasp of the purse with a little pressure. Inside were three florins and a ten shilling note, the coins wrapped in the note. He removed two of the florins and closed the purse, slipping it back into its hiding place.

The coins jangled in his pocket as he ran from the room. His mother was at the head of the stairs when he reached the landing.

"Willie-boy, where are you running to? Supper won't be long now. I've got everything."

He shook her hands off and shoved her aside. She tottered backwards and her feet slipped on the first step. He stood as if hypnotised as she fell against the bannister, the weight of her body toppling her over. For a moment she was suspended in mid-air like a glass tied to a piece of string - - - then the string was cut.

She uttered no cry while falling and the impact of her body as she hit the floor was like a box smashed against the wall.

He peered over the bannister. One leg was folded under her, her hands covering the lower part of her face and the eyes were open. All his strength seemed to have left him and he dropped to his haunches with tears streaming across his face. From below came the clamour of excited voices as people filled the passage.

THE END

£50! £50! £50!

Watch out for the Winner of Drum's £50 Short Story Contest — next month!

RIVE: "WILLY-BOY WAS JUST A SICK BOY!"

awoke the following morning a changed person who had blotted out all remembrance, because, to believe that she had never died it was essential to believe that she had never lived. Overnight he had become a being who could not react or remember. A machine at fourteen. He read an American comic while the people sang hymns in the dining-room. He hated the smell of flowers, the solemn faces, the stiff black ties. He hated every memory of his mother. The way she stooped to the left as she walked, her gnarled hands, and then, her last words. "Here wees my genadig . . ." God have mercy upon me. God never had mercy upon him. God never entered the sunless hovels in which he lived. God could not have bothered about his world of cheap wine and violence. God must have forgotten Willie-boy, because Willie-boy had decided to forget all about God. And that happened when the last heavy sods fell on the lid of the coffin.

Willie-boy staggered out of the lane, and the craving to be back inside the bioscope and at peace with Jamesy was wild inside him. To be back in bioscope, drunk with pleasure. To laugh and swear and hurl invectives at the opposite row. Or to be a youngster again . . . in a world of prayer-meetings and church socials and mothers with gnarled hands. And pleasant old men. And fussy old women, like the one coming down the road. A fussy old woman who stooped slightly to the left as she walked. Whose face spoke poverty.

Willie-boy muttered as he approached her, swearing at the world, swearing at her. She was frightened and Willie-boy felt a curious satisfaction at seeing the fear in her eyes, felt like playing with her, torturing her, paying Jamesy back. Shouting even louder and louder while fear shot through her eyes. Grabbing her coat and pushing her against the wall and letting her feel the way he felt when he slunk out of the bioscope. Fear or humiliation, or both. To bully an old Coloured woman who offered less resistance than a White Policeman. To knock hell out of her. To feel her mumble in sheer terror, "Here wees my genadig" . . . . . And then to turn white hot and drop his hands.

And then Willie-boy covered his face in his hands and wept the way he had never wept at his mother's funeral. And a passing newspaper boy grinned and whistled to his screaming companions to come and see a grown skolly weeping alone in the grimy midst of a District Six street.

THE END

CLARKE: "YES, WILLY-BOY WAS A SAD CASE!"

man, Willy-boy, stop fighting with your dadda."

Next morning the mother, who was soft-hearted, would be apologising to all the neighbours for the disturbance of the night before. "I don't know what is the matter with Willy-boy. We want to be respectable people and he acts like a skolly. Oh, this world is full-up with trouble."

One day Ernie looked from a "BUGS BUNNY" comic, which happened to be his favourite reading matter, to remark, "I say, Jumbo's home." Jumbo's term in the reformatory was over.

"Mm. Then we'll have to celebrate," said Willy-boy, who was sitting admiring the sunlight glinting on the pitch-black rims of his finger-nails.

That evening they took Jumbo on a round of all the old haunts. As they walked along a street, a drunk approached, rolling his way home, wherever that was. That drunk was so fuddled he didn't even notice Willy-boy trip him. He fell against them, muttering apologetically, "Shorry gent-sh, shorry gent-sh." They were in too much of a good mood to beat him up as they would normally have done, so they merely laughed and helped him to his feet and said there was no harm done and so on. The drunk was sent on his way home but not before Willy-boy had quickly fingered him and removed a bottle of brandy from his back pocket and slipped it into his own.

"T'anks, pal," the drunk was calling back to them and they laughingly shouted, "An' t'anks to you, too, pal."

Willy-boy vaguely remembered the gun he had in his pocket which he had got that day from an acquaintance living across town. "Look, fellows, look at what I've got." His hand shook awkwardly as he showed it to them, holding it with the muzzle pointed towards them. A wave of drunken protest. "Hey, be careful." "Put it away." "Something'll happen."

"But look," Willy-boy insisted, "look," while he continued to point and his arm straightened, "because I'm going to press the trigger," he laughed wildly.

The other three lunged awkwardly at him and tried to grab hold of the gun, but Willy-boy held tight and they swayed this way and that way as they struggled. Suddenly there was a loud report followed immediately by another out of which emerged a hideous scream. The strugglers fell apart and, suddenly sober, gaped. It was Willy-boy. He had been shot in the chest. Even in the semi-darkness they could discern the blood pouring out of his body as he knelt and then fell over on to his face.

THE END

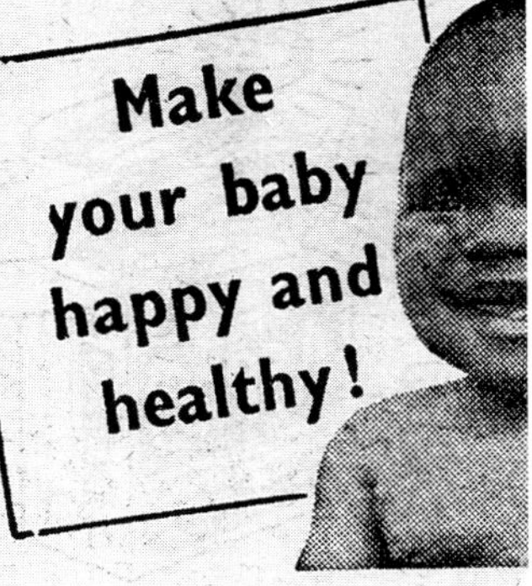

Don't let your baby suffer! Whe growing baby often feels pain and c he becomes thin and cries often. baby has pains in his stomach When this happens baby needs safe, good medicine to take the pain away. Wise mothers all over the world give babies Ashton & Parsons Infants' Powders because they are the best.

Ashton & Pa
WORLD FAMOU
Infants' Pow
1/6 for 20 Powder:

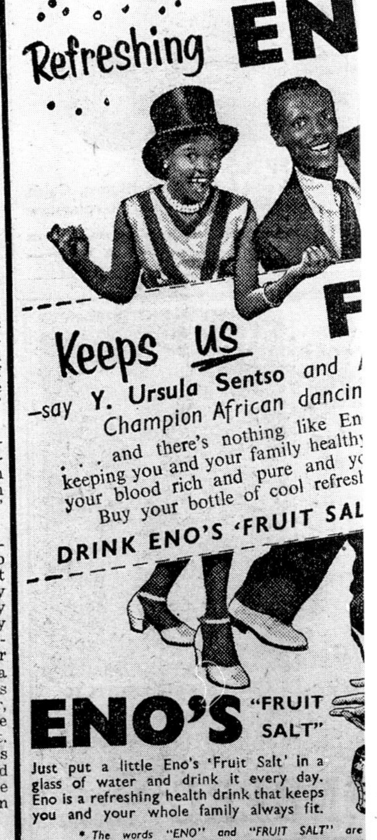

Just put a little Eno's 'Fruit Salt' in a glass of water and drink it every day. Eno is a refreshing health drink that keeps you and your whole family always fit.

* The words "ENO" and "FRUIT SALT" are

PART FOUR

James Matthews

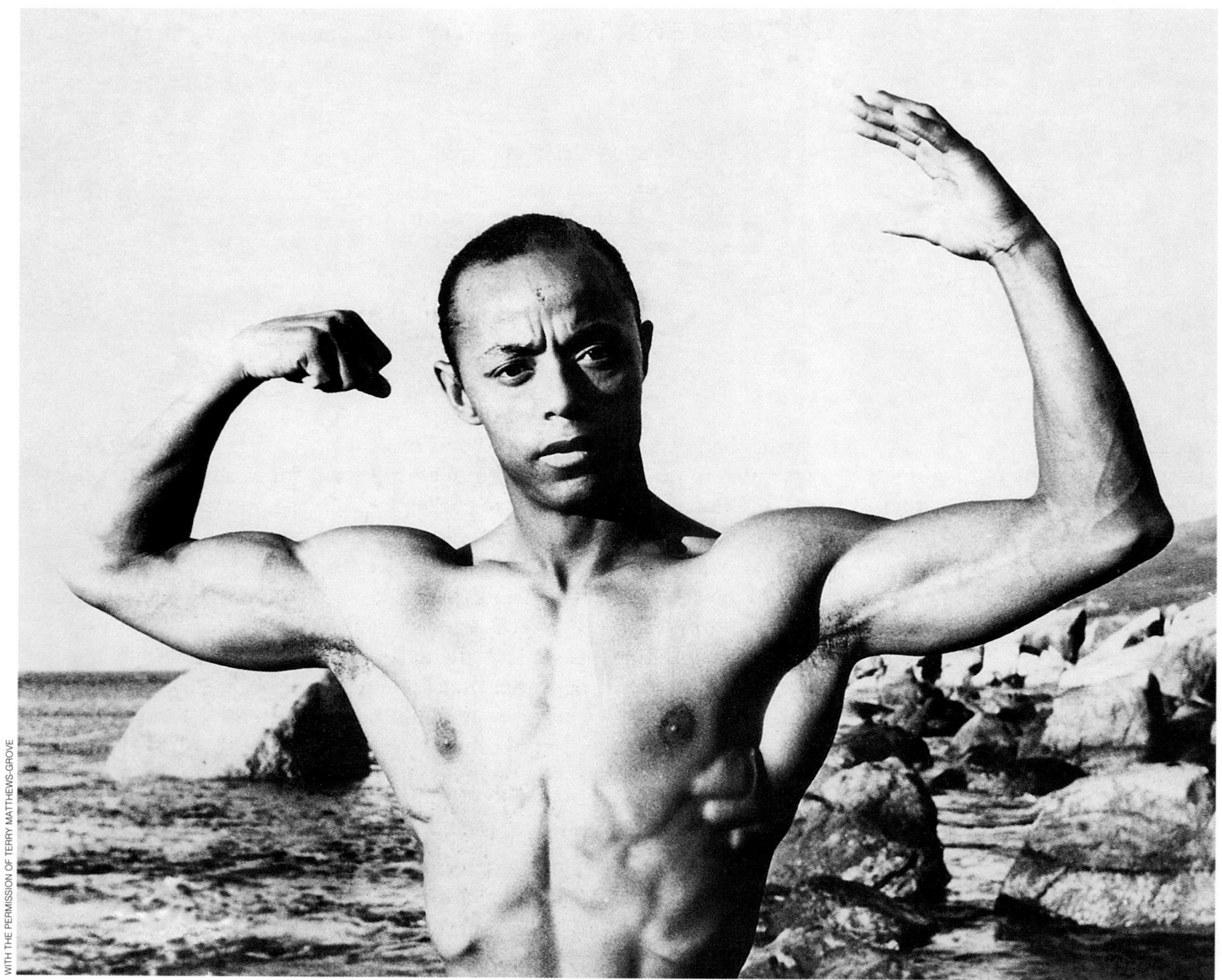

As a young adult Matthews took up body-building at the YMCA on Chiappini Street, in Bo-Kaap. The photograph was taken along the False Bay coast, possibly in the late 1940s, early 1950s.

The pictures swirling in my mind

JAMES MATTHEWS

The genesis of my creative writing came at the age of about ten, with the realisation that I was able to formulate the pictures swirling in my mind into descriptive passages on paper. The stringing of words into meaningful passages always fascinated me. Its growth developed when I wrote a composition at high school. I was thirteen and in standard seven. Miss Meredith, my English teacher, scored the composition above the class average. She stated that I had written a short story and not a composition, praising me for the originality of my approach. I wrote about a group of hoboes. I had often seen them lounging in front of the Salvation Army Hostel near Prestwich Street Primary School which I attended before moving on to Trafalgar High. For me, it was just a composition but it indicated that I had taken the first step to becoming a writer. I will never forget Miss Meredith.

At school, I procured books from the Hyman Liberman Institute in District Six, and row upon row of books in the library heightened my enchantment.

A fall from a high stoep in my youth left lasting effects. Georgie, my uncle, three years older than myself, carried me on his back to the clinic in Hof Street. The clinic did not have an X-ray machine and we were given bus fare to Groote Schuur Hospital. In spite of the severe concussion I suffered, we were sent home, again by bus. I was told not to attend school for two months. The healing process did not occur as I suffered concentration and memory lapses on my return to school. Maths classes became problematic. I stopped schooling. I am still suffering from the same affliction.

Getting a job as messenger on the *Cape Times* helped in a small measure to ease the strain on the family finances. I was introduced to the South African Library in Government Avenue – then a lending library – when I returned books for a female member of the editorial staff. I was overwhelmed by the sight of stacks of books placed in regimented rows, dwarfing the display offered by the District Six library.

I was not aware that blacks were members of the library and was filled with trepidation as I used her card to take out a book by Balzac, Zola or Maupassant. While at high school, Miss Meredith had suggested that I should read the works of these writers, as it would help me to understand how they presented their stories. I intended to start taking out books alphabetically. But I was soon struck with the absurdity of my decision as books written by authors whose surnames started with an A filled more than half of the first towering stand. It would take time beyond measure before I would reach Steinbeck, my favourite author at that period. His *Grapes of Wrath* overwhelmed me. Even at my tender age I empathised with the characters and their poverty.

At seventeen, I emerged in print in the pages of *The Sun*, a weekly newspaper serving the needs of mainly middle-class coloureds. The editor of *The Sun* was George Golding, principal of Upper Ashley Primary School, who later headed the Coloured Representative Council, the National Party's second-class parliament for coloureds.

I had embellished a visit to a dentist with the waiting-room filled with woe-faced patients, adding fictional touches. The pleasure of seeing my name in print eased my disappointment, lingered on even after I discovered that I was not to be given a monetary reward for the publication of my 'masterpiece'. I made a silent vow that in future I would not allow anything I had written to appear in print without a fee attached. From that moment, I regarded myself as a professional writer.

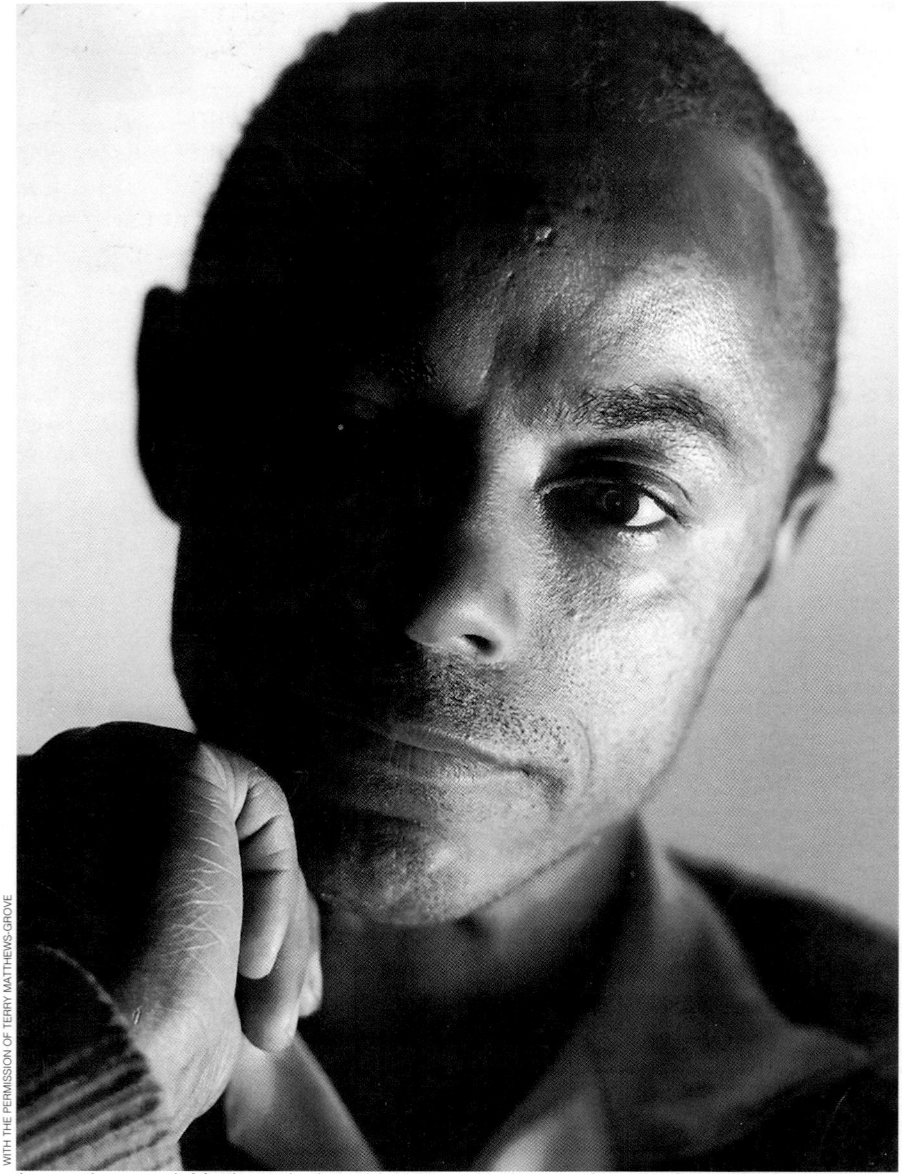

In pensive mood, Matthews in the mid-1950s, with the scar from the fall in his youth which 'left him with lasting effects', clearly visible. Photograph undated.

My parents shared the delight of seeing my name at the head of the piece. My mother was a domestic servant. I often accompanied her on her rounds to her 'madam' when I was younger and helped her polish floors. My father was an illiterate dock labourer and only learned how to spell his name during his short spell in the Cape Corps which he joined not out of patriotism but because of the depression in the ranks of the poor. He was not even given a bicycle, as promised by General Smuts to all those who volunteered, when he was boarded from the army. To my regret, my father was not very forthcoming to us about his army experiences, and I had often wondered how

he could have been promoted to the rank of corporal being illiterate. The only conclusion I could come to is that his promotion came about because of his forceful personality. I must include glimpses of my father's army bit when I do get around to finally doing a series of stories centred on my growing-up period in the Bo-Kaap.

I was an anomaly on our street corner – the only one in our group who read books beyond Westerns, James Hadley Chase or Mickey Spillane, the only one who dabbled in words. A 'slimmetjie'.

My muse was in accord with my desire to prove that I was a writer. The report in print was the incen-

100

tive to couple my imagination and creativity as I became more disciplined to produce more short stories.

My efforts were rewarded with the appearance of a story in the *Cape Times* weekend magazine, to be followed later with one in the *Cape Argus*. The attitude of members of the staff changed towards me with the publication of the stories. I adopted an air of indifference at their congratulations although secretly pleased. Here was someone who ran their errands and placed a cup of tea on their desk having stories published in the paper they worked on as journalists. My position on the editorial floor had shifted. Reporters addressed me with familiarity – not the familiarity of a boy-boss relationship but one of almost acceptance, while the younger ones approached me with diffidence as my creative writing was superior to their mundane reports. This changed relationship reflected the two worlds I inhabited. At home, in the evenings, I would join my friends on the corner playing rummy, smoking marijuana and participating in gang fights. I was a Cluster-Buster gang member. On the editorial floor they were looking at me as a burgeoning short story writer.

It was a repeat of the scenario of my days at Trafalgar High. There, most of my schoolmates were from a fairly affluent background while I was ghetto born. When I left school in the afternoons it was to go and sell newspapers on street corners to help ease the financial difficulties at home.

One of the people who helped direct me in the way I was going, was the late George Manuel, a person to whom I will always be indebted. He was the manager of The Star bioscope in District Six, editor of the *Cape Standard*, a weekly newspaper vastly different from the mainstream papers in serving the needs of its coloured readership. He introduced me one evening to Peter Abrahams who was staying with him at his home in District Six. Overawed, I could just mumble the inanities of social intercourse as I

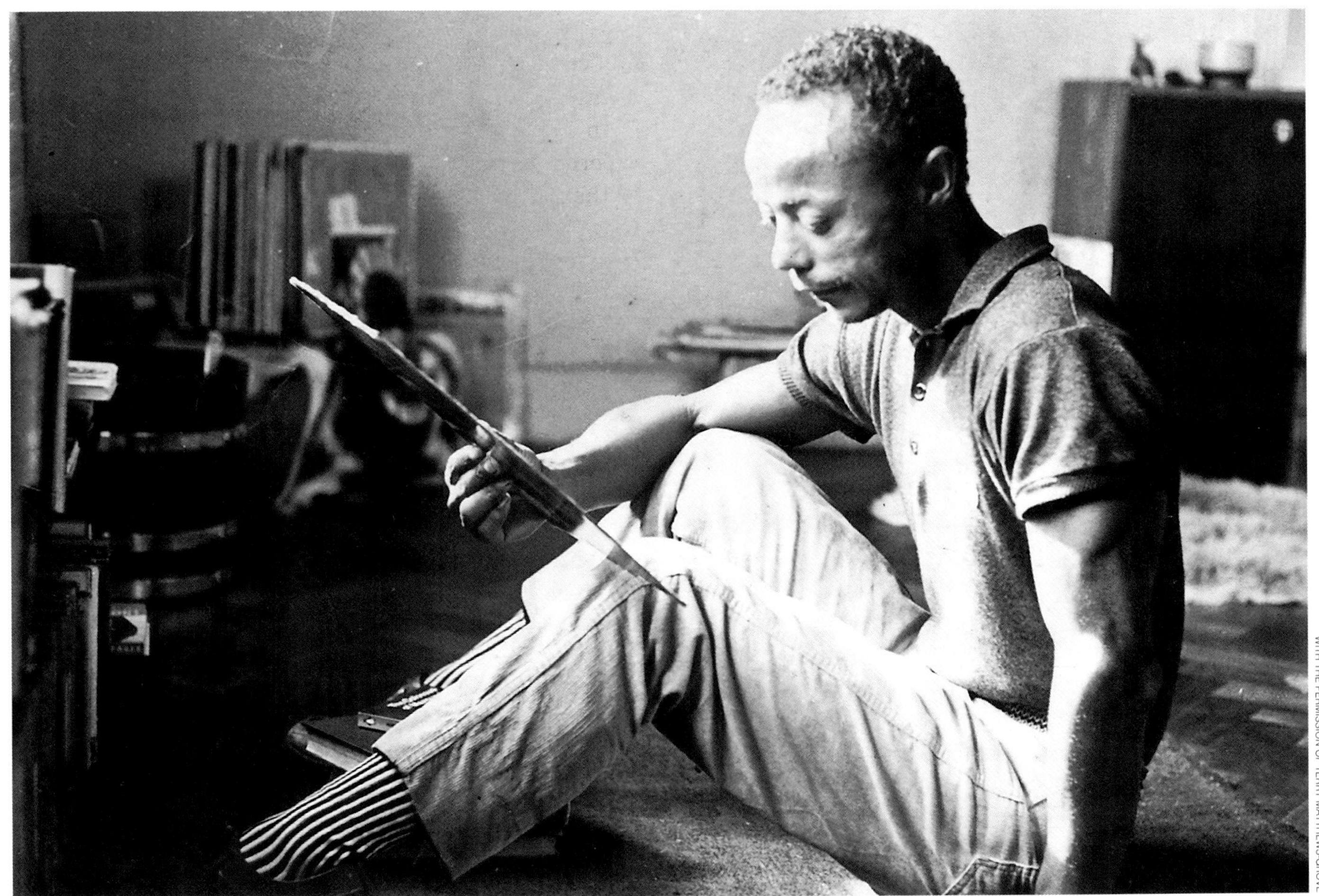

Matthews has a catholic taste in music, and attributes his love of European classical music to the influence of Richard Rive. Photograph undated.

thrust out my hand towards a short, slender man with bulging eyes. George must have told Peter Abrahams that I was writing. I was hesitant in my brief reply to his questions. I was turned inarticulate by the presence of Peter Abrahams, whose *Path of Thunder* I had read several times. It tells of a love shared by a coloured man and a white woman, and the tragedy it caused, a pattern of love across the colour bar that not even the National Party at a later stage could break completely with its Immorality Act. Peter Abrahams was the only writer of colour that I knew, and my awe of him prevented me from expressing my admiration of his work.

I was beginning to think of myself as a writer as the number of my stories published increased in the weekend magazines of the *Cape Times* and the *Cape Argus*.

My stories always depicted my background. Though not overtly political, the characters reflected the disadvantaged surroundings in which they were placed and how they related to them. Chris Kavanagh, editor of the *Argus* weekend magazine, was so impressed by the authenticity of my stories that he asked me to his office. I was hesitant. My insecurity caged me in a dilemma of my own making. He knew me only as a contributing writer and not as a coloured who writes. I sought George Manuel's counsel; he soothed my anxiety, assuring me that the worth of my writing should transcend the fear I had that pigmentation would be an obstacle to my acceptance. Chris Kavanagh's cordial congratulations dispelled my disquiet and brought about the awareness that colour would no longer enchain me to a place positioned by a hierarchy bolstered by racism.

It was at that time that Peter Clarke came into my orbit. My stories had come to his attention. I suspect that he also, at times, must have felt a sense of alienation in his surroundings. An artist and a writer burgeoning in a black working-class area were not quite the norm. Peter's council flats in Simon's Town were more stable than Shortmarket Street in the Bo-Kaap, but we were both anomalies: two spirits striving to display their creativity through art – Peter spreading paint on canvas and myself lining paper with words.

A knock on the door announced his arrival on a Saturday afternoon. Peter Clarke topped my short stature by a few inches, a short-cropped head above a stocky figure, his address one of reserve. His reserve soon melted, to be replaced by the warmth of his spirit after I had introduced him to my friends – not my Cluster-Buster friends on the corner – but those who were members of the YMCA body-building club in Chiappini Street, round the corner from where I stayed. I looked forward to the Saturday visit from Peter as he introduced me to the world of fine art. A strong bond developed with the increase of visits from Peter. At a much later stage, when I had moved to Silvertown, a township on the Cape Flats, Peter became the godfather of my daughter, Terry.

Through Peter, I met Richard Rive. At first, I was wary of Richard – a high-school teacher, self-assured and articulate. Although born in an area similar to mine, he had long fled the decaying slum of District Six. He was at ease in a world of which I had no knowledge. He could speak of Uys Krige, Jack Cope, Jan Rabie, Marjorie Wallace and Ingrid Jonker. I was aware of Krige and Cope because their books were on the library shelves.

Apart from Peter and Richard, Alex La Guma was the only other coloured writer I was aware of locally. Alex, at that time, was working as a clerk at Caltex. His writings appeared mainly in *Fighting Talk* and *New Age*.

In 1956, I had advanced from editorial clerk to reporter, 'journalist' if I wanted to flatter myself. Prior to that, I had contributed news reports to *Golden City Post* on a freelance basis. I now no longer had to care for the needs of the news staff. I had joined their ranks. I was now on the payroll of Drum Publications – a reporter on the *Golden City Post*.

The Crescent Café, next to the Avalon Cinema in District Six, was our meeting place on Saturday afternoons. Peter, Richard and myself as writers, Lionel Oostendorp as photographer, and Kays, a new addition to the *Post* staff, would sit and discuss the world's troubles and our role to explore it through photographs and words. The Crescent Café became our cultural oasis.

Being the sole representative in Cape Town of *Golden City Post*, I saw to it that its readers were kept informed of the criminal and anti-social activities of their milieu. Lionel Oostendorp and myself became part of each family we interviewed who had a member outraged or brutally killed over the weekend. I raised it with Jim Bailey, owner of Drum Publications, that we should, at least, carry news of a more edifying nature as the other papers did. His reply was that the *Argus* and *Times* were better

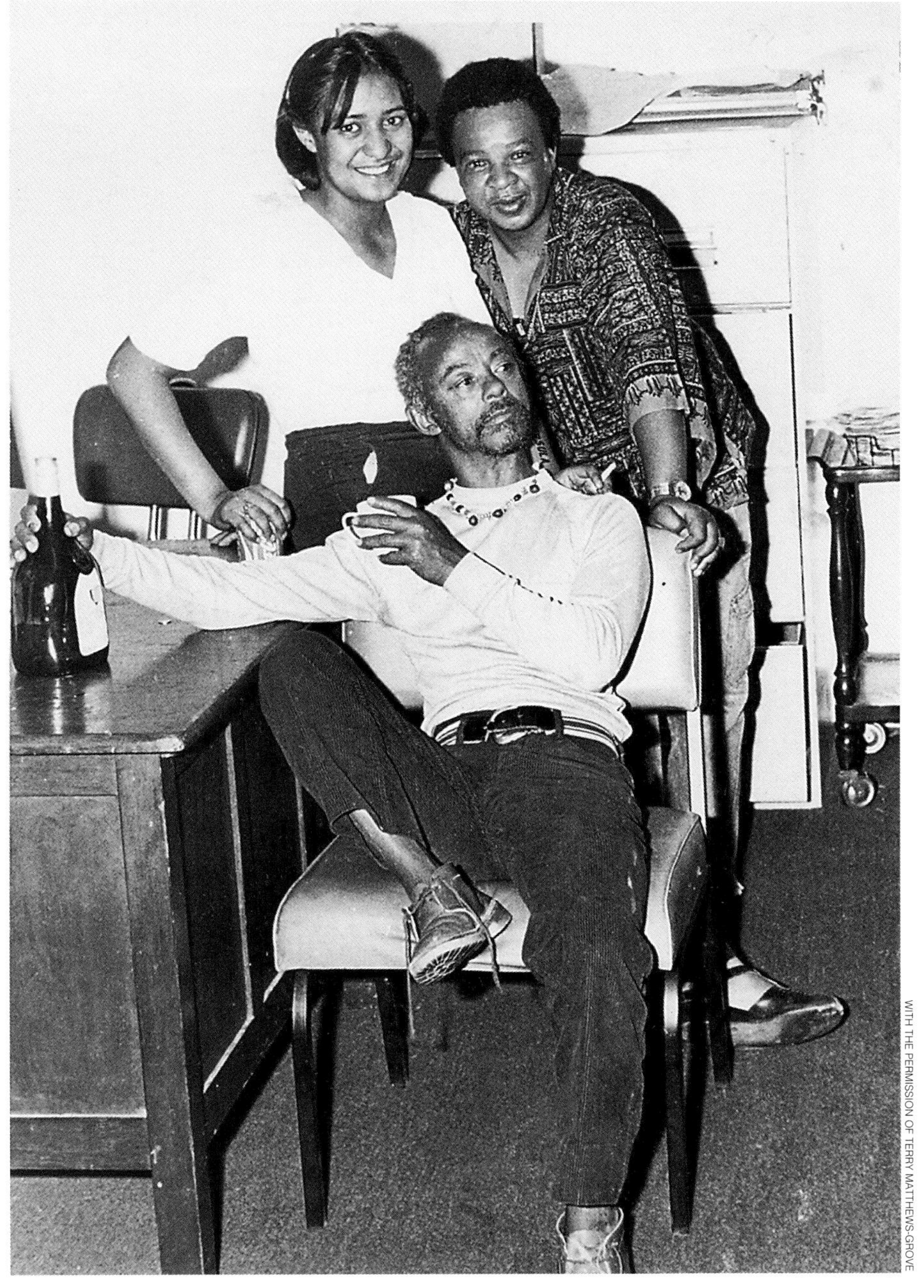

Matthews in characteristic mood with Ursula Marshall and Thabo Serote, younger brother of the poet, Mongane Wally Serote, in the offices of the short-lived Johannesburg newspaper, *The Voice*. 1978.

papers than the *Post* but *Post* could certainly 'out-rape' them.

A joint story contributed by Peter, Richard and myself was published – a story I felt that was above the level of most stories published. The three of us selected a character we named Willy-Boy and each of us constructed a piece to show how we saw Willy-Boy. It was the one and only time a story of that nature was published in *Drum*. Although having had some short stories published in *Drum*, I was not a member of the *Drum* school of writers.

My time on *Golden City Post* was an enriching period but I left after eighteen months. It was balm to the spirit and bolstered my dignity to be engaged in work that was formerly only available for whites. But it was not sweet enough to flavour the financial exploitation that went with the position. I earned less as a journalist than I did as a clerk at the *Cape Times*.

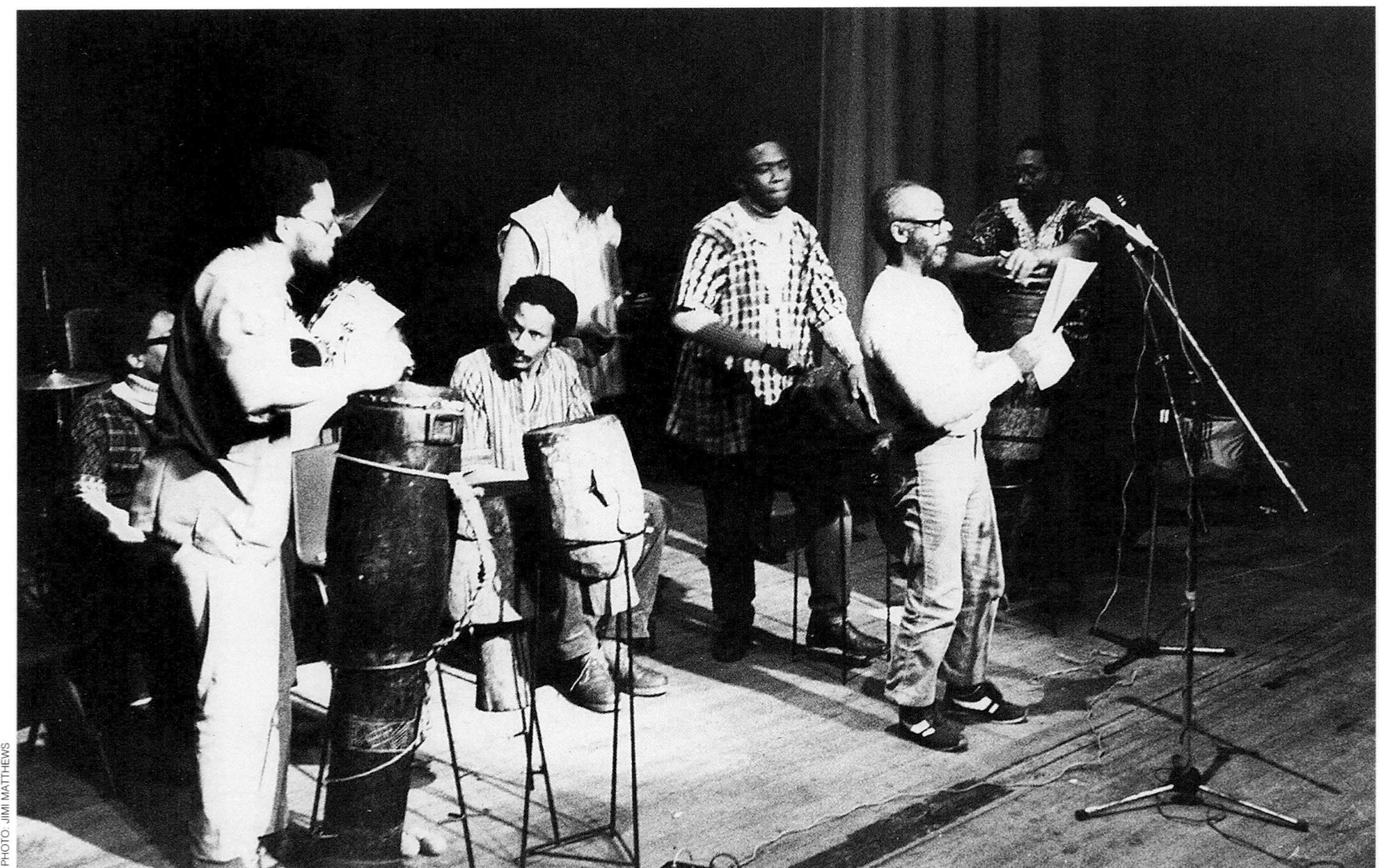

Matthews reading at a performance of Pula Arts Commune, a group of exiled South Africans, at the Commonwealth Centre, London. 1980.

My political awareness was crystallised through the lessons I imbibed with Wolfie Kodesh's talks to us on the corner as he sold *New Age*, the communist paper, in the neighbourhood. If it were not for my determination to maintain my identity and not allow others to make decisions for me, I would have joined the Communist Party as he certainly enlightened me to the circumstances of our position. My stories started illustrating the plight of the disfranchised.

'The park', a story depicting the vileness of a regime that robbed a little child of the joy of experiencing the pleasure of a swing in a public park, depicts the horrendous nature of apartheid. It was published in Uganda in 1958 because of the censorious nature of the apartheid regime. Of the short stories that I have had published, apart from 'Azikwelwa', 'The park' is probably the apex as it has been given prominence by its appearance in several anthologies and it has been translated into different languages.

'The park' was also the first story that aroused the ire of the state. I was invited to attend the first African Writers' Conference at Makarere University, Kampala, Uganda. The state showed its displeasure by issuing my passport three weeks after the conference had ended.

Harassment by the state lacked all subtlety. It seemed that the state was engaged in playing a cat-and-mouse game. Sometimes my mail was intercepted, then I would receive a letter and the writer would enquire why I had not replied to previous letters. Had I had a telephone, it would certainly have been tapped. I had been asked to come to the offices of the Special Branch a few times but I had ignored their call. All this made me become very despondent.

My despondency drove me to the United States Consulate to find out whether I could emigrate to what I thought would be a place of sanctuary. Emotionally, it was a downer. The United States would have given me sanctuary if I had been a shepherd. Shepherds were needed by farmers in the Utah mountains. An approach to Botswana was equally negative. Plumbers and carpenters were needed, but not impoverished writers.

104

Another call came from the Special Branch stressing the urgency of my attendance.

What if I should suddenly disappear after an after-midnight visit from them? Being a single parent, I was inwardly filled with worry about the well-being of my children. I thought it best to respond to the Special Branch's invitation.

The office in which I was waiting was not any different from any other office. There were two chairs on either side of the desk. In one corner a huge filing cabinet. My two interrogators entering the office quickly dispelled any feeling of ease the ordinariness of the office might have evoked. Confronted by the Van Wyk brothers filled me with fear. I was fully aware of the nefarious actions of the brothers Van Wyk. They were the state's instruments of torture.

When I challenged a question asked, I knew that I was in trouble when the elder Van Wyk brother snapped the pencil he had been using. To ease the rising aggression, the other brother said that they were aware that I was trying to leave the country.

I explained that my efforts had not been successful.

With an almost benign smile the younger Van Wyk said that they had the solution to my problem.

It could be arranged that I would be able to leave for Botswana. My gratitude would be displayed by informing on my fellow-blacks in residence and receiving payment for a job well done.

I politely declined. Mentally, I decided that South African winters were not that bad.

Outside, I took deep breaths to calm myself. I did not expect that I would be allowed to leave after I had refused their offer.

Writing political short stories for publication in South Africa during the apartheid period was a

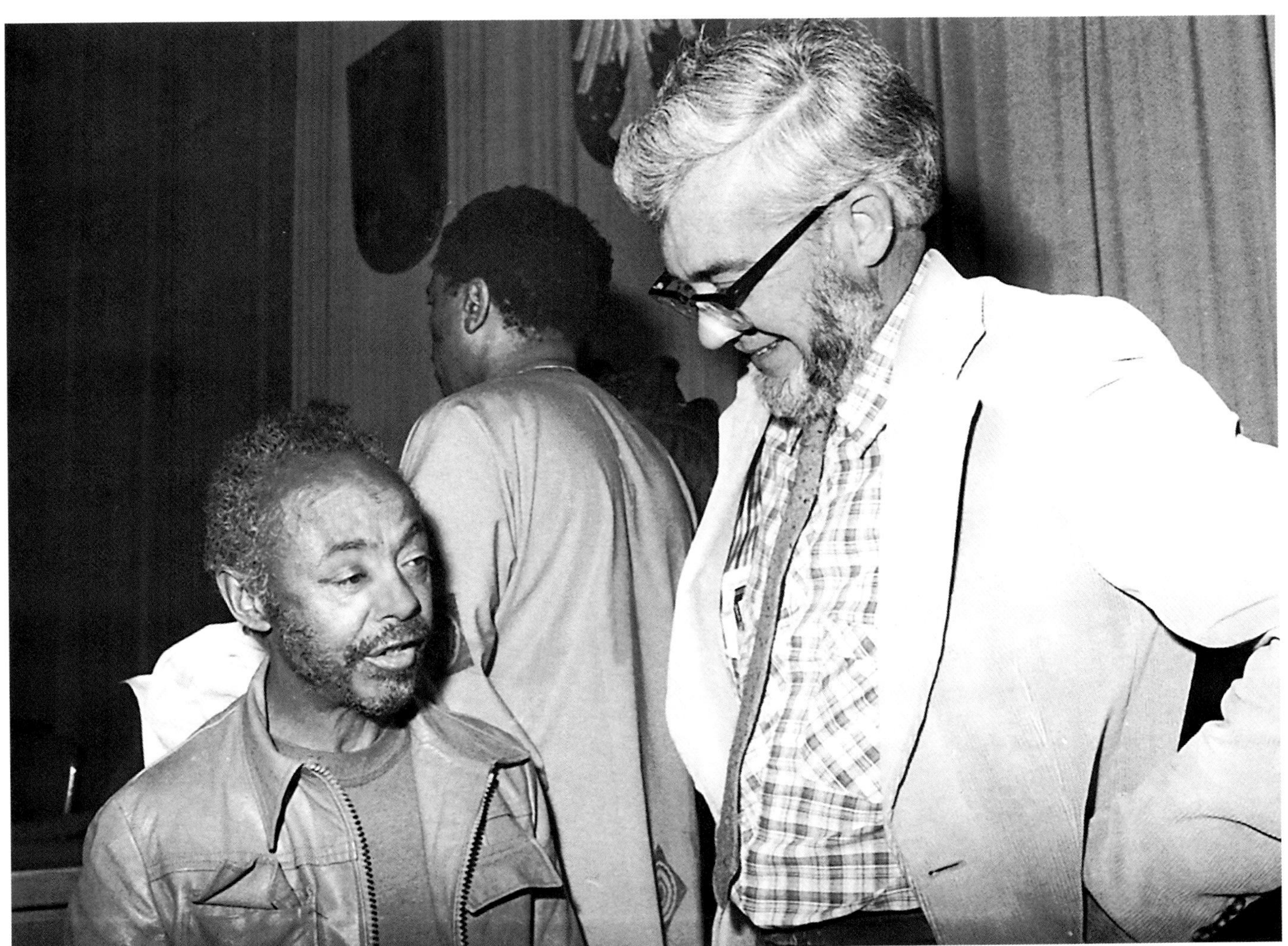

Matthews with the publisher of *Cry Rage!*, Peter Randall; in the background is Sipho Sepamla, Frankfurt Book Fair. Frankfurt am Main, 1980.

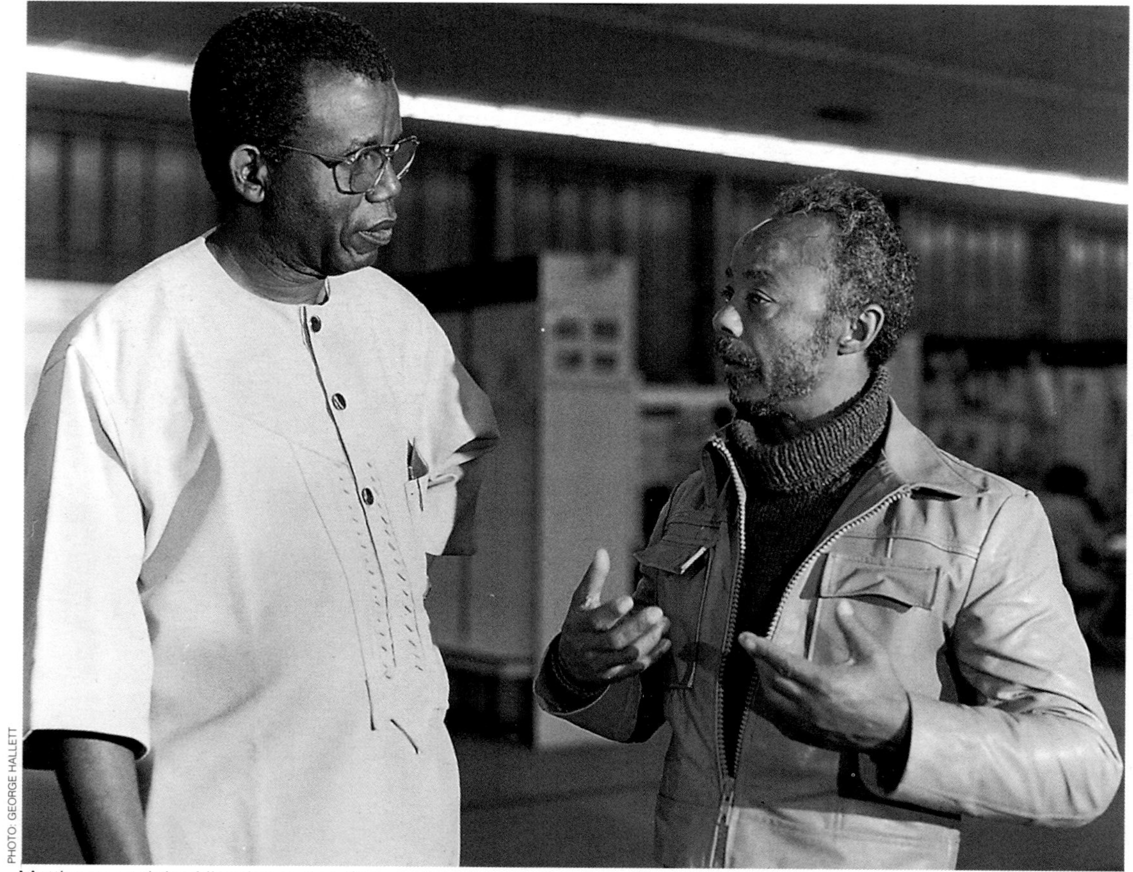

Matthews and the Nigerian writer, Chinua Achebe. Frankfurt am Main, 1980.

daunting challenge. Firstly, almost all the publishing houses were reluctant to bring out a book challenging the state, particularly if the writer was black. Secondly, I was fearful about how my incarceration or banning would affect my young children. I ceased to write political short stories and turned to writing poetry with political content, which I read and distributed at small gatherings.

I could not contain my anger at the injustice of racial laws and my political poetry climaxed with Spro-cas (later Ravan Press) publishing *Cry Rage!* in 1972 – the first book of poetry discussed in parliament by the Herrenvolk law-makers. They could not decide whether it was poetry or a petrol bomb. They banned the book.

The banning of *Cry Rage!* did not deter me from producing further works. I enlisted the aid of fellow-poets – Wally Serote, Mafika Gwala and Ilva Mackay, among others – who shared my disgust of a regime that needed iniquitous laws and arms to maintain its stand.

Not out of fear but for financial reasons, Spro-cas suggested that I should attempt to publish the anthology myself. I could understand their rationale. They could continue to be active with other needed pursuits less damaging to their financial well-being.

With no money but the support of S & S Printers, I started a publishing house – BLAC – and brought out *Black Voices Shout!*

The book shared the same fate as *Cry Rage!*

106

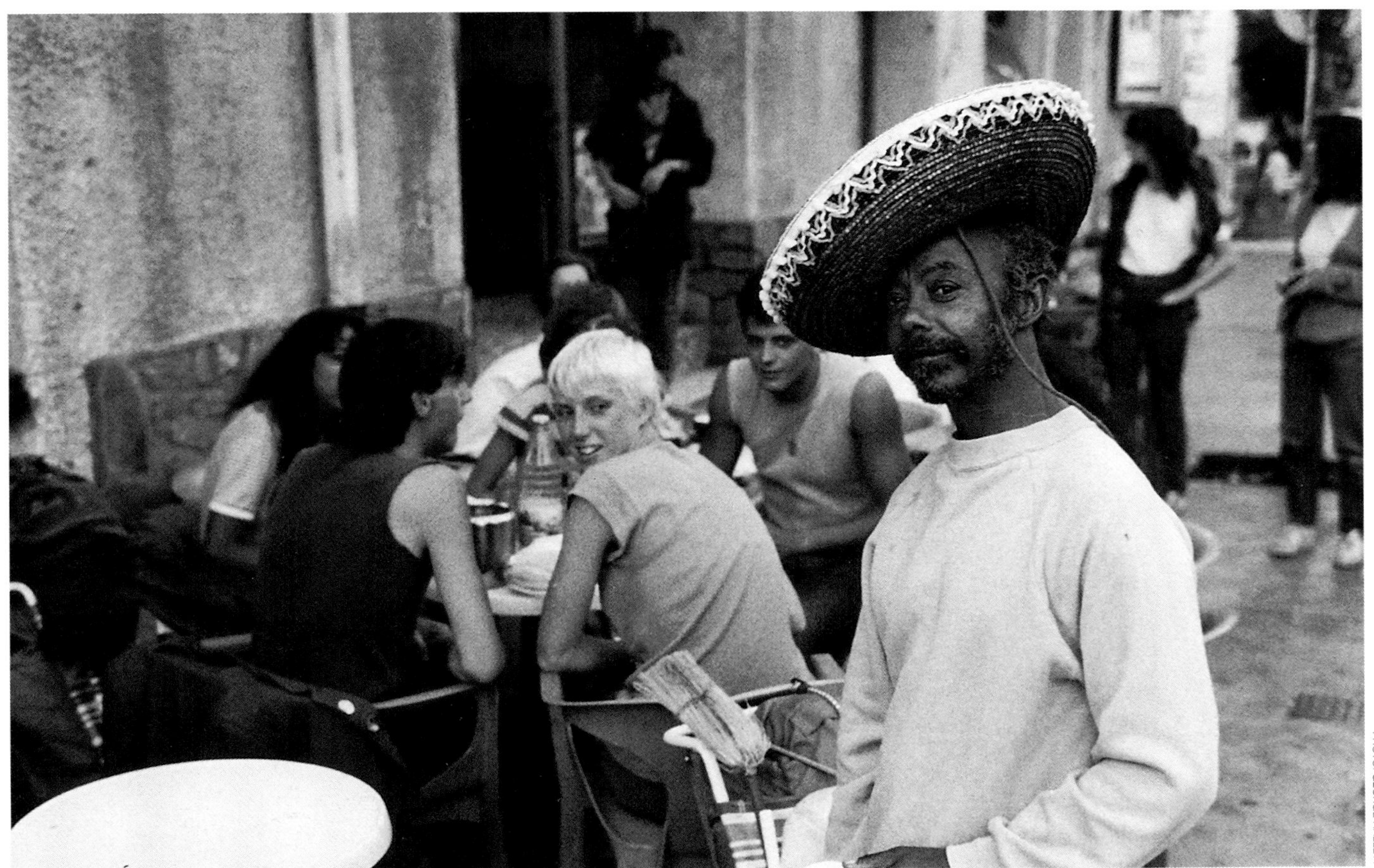

The day the poet, disguised as a Mexican, wandered through the city centre of Perpignan, in the south of France. 1980.

It was banned after three weeks, leaving me with a printer's bill.

The harassment by the state only made me more determined to face its onslaught.

With many others, 1976 saw me taking a vacation in Victor Verster Maximum Prison. I was kept in detention for almost six months because of my writing.

All in all, BLAC produced nine books and three broadsheets before it was forced to close because of lack of funds brought about by pressure from the state.

The Nationalist government was very unforgiving in its attitude towards dissident writers.

In 1978, I was offered a study period at the International Writers' Program of the University of Iowa. In 1979, I was invited to an international conference in Amsterdam arranged by Pen International.

On both instances I was refused a passport.

It took three bannings of selections of my writing (because of my persistence in highlighting the faults of the state in my poetry) and 23 years before I was again issued a passport to attend the Frankfurt Book Fair in 1980. The other two people invited were Sipho Sepamla and Peter Randall. The three of us were considered *persona non grata* by the state. To make sure that I would be penitent for the displeasure I had caused, the state made me endure another five years of deprivation by not allowing me to travel outside the borders of the country, refusing to renew my passport in 1985. With the winds of change, my passport was renewed in 1991.

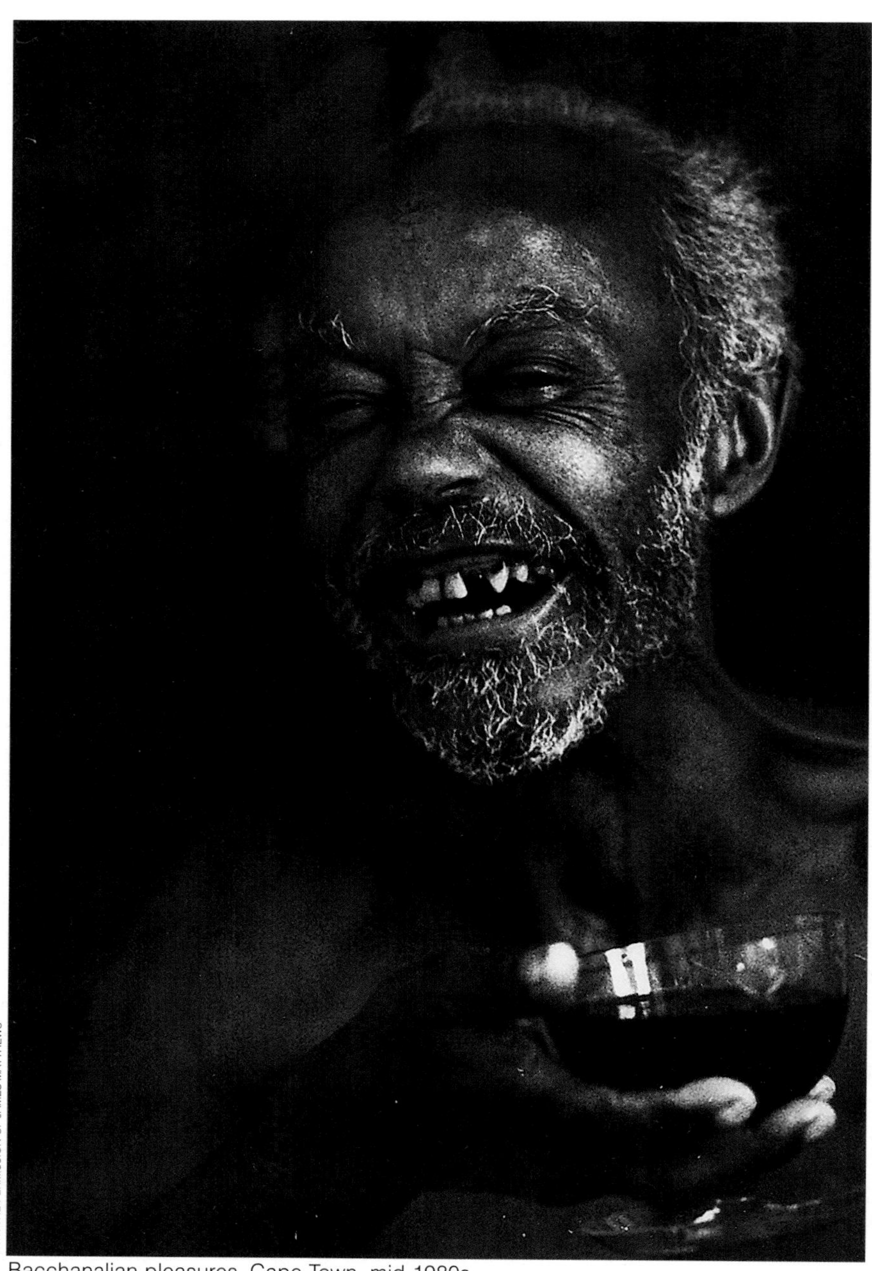

Bacchanalian pleasures. Cape Town, mid-1980s.

Azikwelwa

JAMES MATTHEWS

He did not have to walk. He looked over his shoulder at the hundreds coming along behind him, all walking, and in front of him hundreds more, walking. He was one of the few coloureds who walked along with the mass of Africans. They were old and young, big and small, foot-firm and limping, mothers and sons, fathers and daughters, grandparents and school children; some dressed in neat clothes with horn-rimmed glasses and attaché cases, and many in torn overalls and shoes with soles paper-thin, feeling each stone they trod on. They were all walking the long walk to Johannesburg.

Nights before the boycott was due, the location's fast-beating heart increased its pace. Wherever a man raised his voice, a group formed around him, and as the hours passed, there were many such groups until the location was one huge meeting place. There were the wild ones whose eyes only saw violence, and their cry was, 'Burn the buses!' Then there were those who whispered: 'Accept the terms.' But there were also the many who shouted defiantly, '*Azikwelwa!* We will not ride!'

When they started their walk the sky was still dark under the pulsating stars. He watched them from the inside of his room, and after a time went back to the warmth of his blankets. He had a bus to himself on the ride to the station. There were angry voices when he boarded the bus, but those who shouted the loudest were restrained by others with rosettes pinned to their

breasts. Then, when the bus passed the long, firm line of walkers, he heard their cry again. His return from work found them homeward bound, a song travelling their length. A stone hit the side of the bus and he peered through the rear window. Four men were shaking a youth by the shoulders and they all disappeared from view as the bus turned a bend in the road.

As if by a prearranged plan, the location's streets swarmed with people who embraced each other and sang at the tops of their voices. In the backyards of the shebeen queens, skokiaan flowed freely for those who had the money to pay for it. And even those who came with empty pockets were given something for their thirst. As they faced one another they cried, '*Azikwelwa*, my brother!'

Four days he watched them walk the long walk, and four nights he saw them dance and drink their aches away, and spirit of their pride filled him. Their word was as good as that of the white man. They said they would walk the many miles before paying the extra penny the bus demanded. There were many whites who scoffed at their determination, and this was their answer – the line of empty buses. He joined them on the fifth morning, when the first wave of walkers passed his door. From side streets poured rushes of walkers, and the mass of people flowed through the gates of the location.

On his left walked an old man who used a stick to help him along and in

front of him waddled a fat woman with a bundle of washing balanced on her head. He looked around him. There were many such women, and some of them had babies strapped to their backs, the backs, the heads of the babies jogging with the motion of mothers' hips.

It was still early, the first mile not done, and they were in a holiday mood. Bicycles carried two passengers. The location's ancient cars, which always threatened to fall apart, were loaded to capacity and wheezed their way forward. One man, his boots tied around his neck, joked with his friend and said that it made for easier walking. All joined in the laughter. They were walking the long walk, and they were proud.

The miles passed and the road was long: there was less laughter, but still they walked. The old, the sick, the weak, dropped behind. The front of the column was wide but behind it tapered off to a thin line of stragglers.

Then suddenly there were the police and the cars standing in rows, the people inside pulled out and forced to the side of the road. The owners protested that the cars were not used as taxis, but they were still charged with overloading. There were harsh demands for passes, and the fear as they waited for the vans to take them away. Then the next block of police, waiting with outstretched hands and ready batons for those who had not the slips of paper which gave them the right to move. There were many who slipped down side streets to escape, for the police wanted them to ride and not walk, so that they should be without a voice.

'Pass! Waar is dit?' he was asked. The owner of the voice did not bother to look at him. Only when he did not reply, did he turn his eyes.

'I don't carry a pass.'

'Then what are you doing here?'

'I'm walking!'

'Are you a kaffir or are you a communist?'

'I am walking!'

He walked past the policeman who had already grasped another victim by the shirtfront, demanding his pass.

A large car pulled to a halt in front of him, behind the wheel a young white woman. She opened the doors on each side and called out, 'Come on. Women and old people.' No one moved. Then a woman with a child on her back and a suitcase in one hand shyly approached the car and got into the back. Others followed. The old man shook his head saying that he was not too old to finish the long walk. More cars stopped. Their drivers were white and they took those who wanted to ride.

One of them asked the young policeman by whose orders he had stopped a car and demanded the removal of the passengers. The policeman stood undecided and the car pulled away. The policeman rushed towards the nearest man and screamed, '*Julle kaffirs dink julle is slim!*'

Messages were passed from those arrested, to assure an employer that an employee would come back to him, to tell children not to worry and to help each other.

And those who walked were still many, and their hearts were heavy, but they walked. Then the long walk was at an end, for below them was the city. The people of the city looked at them with disbelief and their shoulders straightened and their heads lifted and they smiled. They had walked the long walk, one more day.

It was late when he entered the chemist shop where he worked as a messenger.

'Jonathan, why are you late?'

'I walked.'

'All the way?'

The white man looked at him with surprise.

'All the way!'

'But why? You're not one of them.'

He could not tell the white man of the feeling inside him, that when he was with them he knew it was good.

He joined them on the Square at midday. They sat with mugs of coffee and still-hot fat cakes bought from the portable coffee stalls of the vendors. Some sat around draught boards, using bottle caps as counters, but most were clustered around those with newspapers. There were pictures on the front page showing the many walkers. The reports stated that the boycott would soon be over and that the leaders of the boycott had come to an agreement. There were angry murmurs among them, and some said aloud that they did not believe it. One man said what they all had on their minds. 'Why is it that we were not approached? Are we not the people who walk? Does the bus company think that because it has spoken to a few men, we, like sheep, will now meekly ride instead of walk?'

The last question was directed at one who wrote the colours of the boycott organisation on his breast in the location.

He was a short, wiry man and his eyes blinked owlishly behind the thick-lensed glasses he wore. He took them off, wiped the lenses nervously with his handkerchief, and replaced the glasses on the bridge of his wide, flat nose. He cleared his throat before speaking and then, in a surprisingly loud voice, said: 'Do not believe it, my brothers. It is not for our leaders to say we walk or ride before asking the will of the people of the location. The men of the bus company must think our leaders are but children to be so easily swayed by their words. Pay no heed to what is written in the newspapers because it is the word of the white man.'

His words reassured them but there were a few, already tired of the long walk, who said that it was a good thing. 'The white man has seen that the black man is also a man of his word.' Now they would ride.

Jonathan was filled with doubt. Always he was with those who suffered without protest. Always he was with those who had to bear the many pains. Always he was with those who were unwanted, and always they lost.

He had thought that the boycott would last only the first day. Then the people of the location, with their tired limbs, would once more ride the buses and their purpose would die. But when it entered the second day, the third day, and the day after that, his hopes mounted. Now, he began to hope that this would be the one time they would prove themselves men. It had become a symbol to him. As long as they walked, his life would not be altogether meaningless. He would be able to say with pride that he too was one of those who had walked the long walk when they proved to the bus company that they had a will of their own, and were not to be silenced into obedience by words.

Jonathan was depressed during his delivery round. When he read the newspapers his despair swamped him, and he felt cold in the afternoon sun. He felt betrayed. The paper stated that an agreement had been reached and that following morning the buses would be filled. The boycott would be over.

To forget, he busied himself with his work and was relieved when he was given a stack of deliveries that would keep him occupied for the rest of the afternoon.

Work done, he joined the line of walkers ascending the first incline out of the city. They were a silent lot, and when someone asked if it was to be the last day of the long walk, they answered him with shrugged shoulders and heads shaken in bewilderment. The lines merged into one long column of heavy hearts and dragging feet. There were no jokes, no laugther. Only doubts and uncertainty. The ringing footsteps turned into drumbeats of defeat.

The walk was long and the road without end. The cars stopped and they looked without interest at those who climbed inside. They passed with apprehension the first group of grinning policemen. Their betrayal seemed complete when they were not stopped.

A youth raised his voice.

'*Azikwelwa*, my brothers and sisters.'

Those who had heard the youth's outburst turned their heads and stared at him and they buzzed with curiosity.

'Has news been heard?' 'Do we walk the long walk tomorrow?' 'What has happened?' they shouted, but there was no answer.

Then a voice cried, 'We will hear tonight in the location', and it was taken up and passed along the ranks. The stride of the walkers seemed to lengthen, and Jonathan's heart kept pace with their footsteps.

They passed further blocks of policemen. No one was stopped or asked for a pass. The cars loaded with people passed unchallenged. The miles slipped behind them as they hurried to the location.

After supper, Jonathan walked with the others to the football field where the boycott organisation held its meetings and pushed himself to the front. The field filled. When he turned his head, he could no longer see where the field ended and the street began.

A speaker mounted an upended crate, hands held aloft. It was the same man who had spoken on the Square during the afternoon. His voice roared.

'The bus company has taken it upon itself, after speaking to those who could never speak for us, to have it printed in the papers of the white man that the boycott is ended! Is done with! That we have, like little children, agreed to their talks and will board the buses tomorrow. But they are wrong! This is our answer. *Azikwelwa*! *Azikwelwa*! ...' The rest of the speech was lost in the clamour pouring from the open throats. And when other speakers tried to speak they met with the same result.

Again the backyards of the shebeen queens were flooded and skokiaan was to be had for the asking.

Jonathan sat on the bench with a mug of skokiaan untouched, a bemused smile on his face. A drinker opposite was slumped against the wall and his wife looked boldly at Jonathan.

Looking at her, and the people swarming around him, Jonathan felt a surge of love sweeping through his body and he raised his mug to the woman.

'*Azikwelwa*, my sister!'

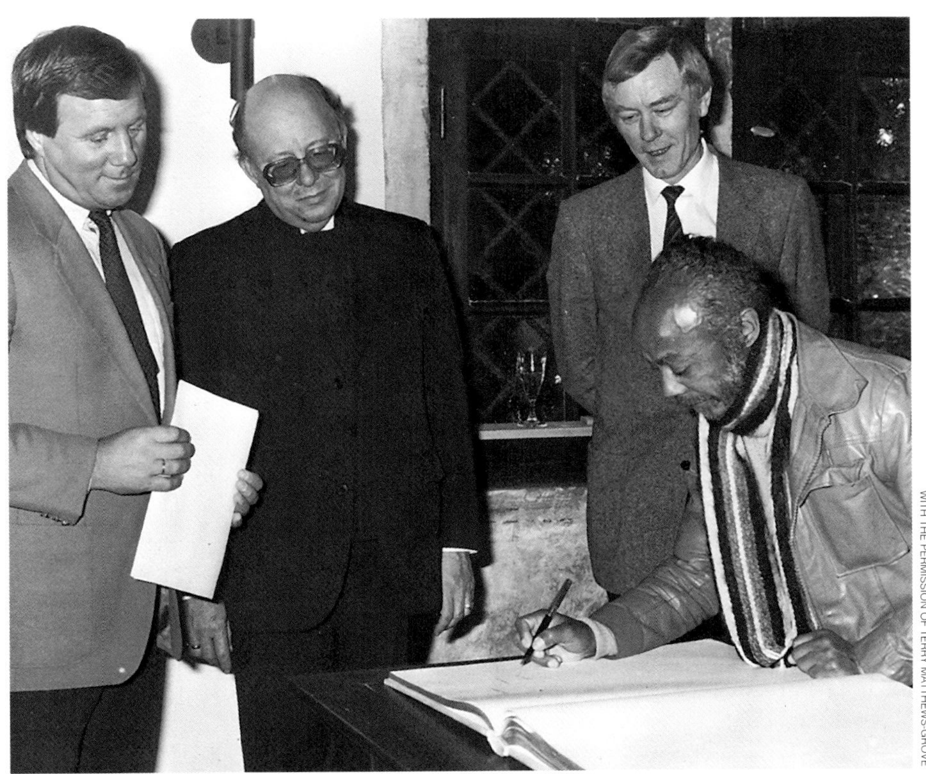

Matthews receiving the Freedom of Nürnberg. 1984.

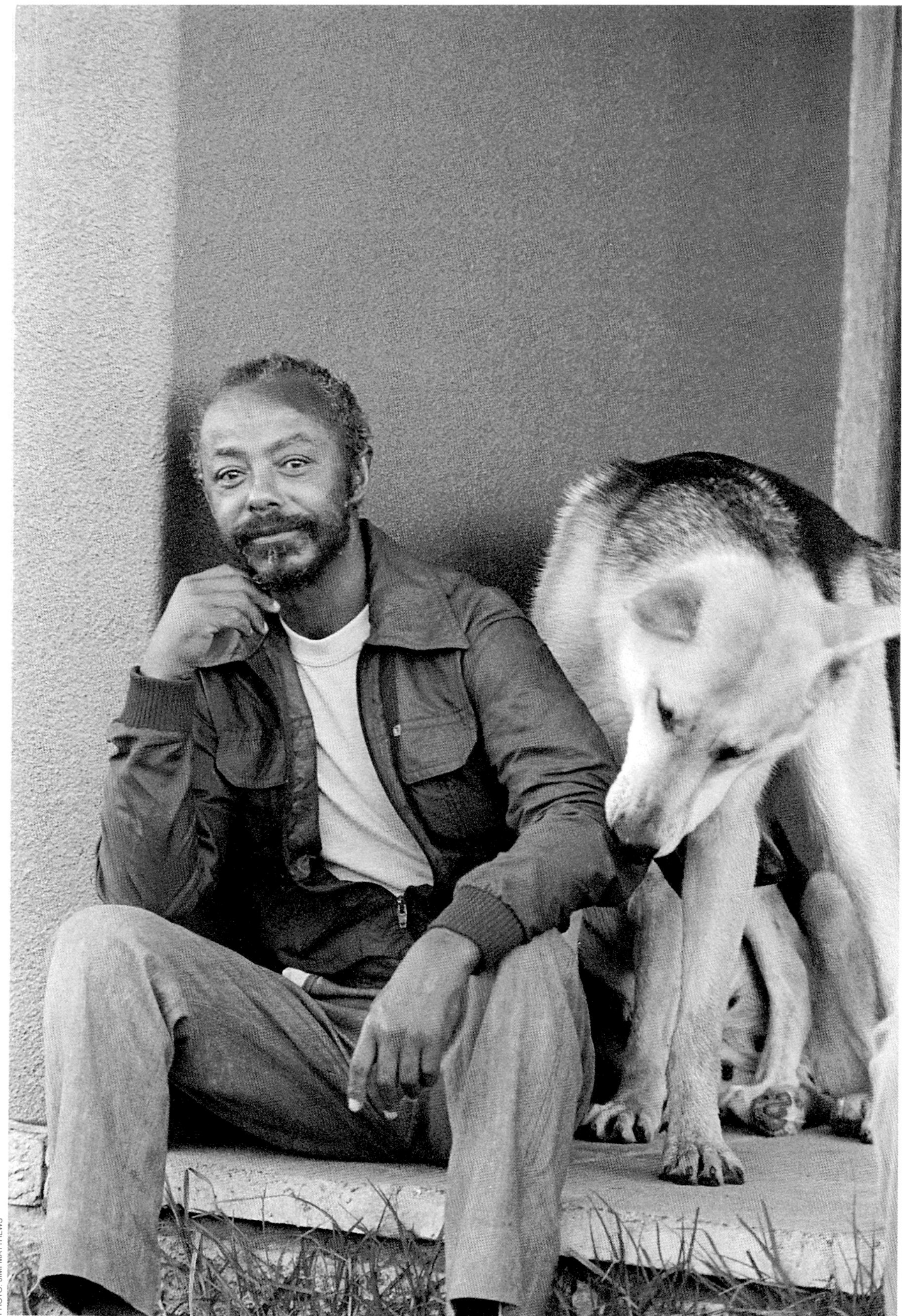

The poet and the licking dog. Matthews had to control his fear of dogs on this occasion. Lotus River, Cape Town, 1978.

'Being coloured is a state of mind'
or the complexities of identity, selfhood, and freedom in the writing of James Matthews

KAYZURAN JAFFER

It was the heady, frenetic eighties, a time of mass rallies, the walls throbbing with the rhythmic mantras of 'Boesak, Boesak!' and the hoarse, spine-tingling 'koezhoem, koezhoem!' of the toyi-toyi. I was pressed back against the wall near the entrance of the Samaj Centre in Athlone on the Cape Flats, wondering how to do my marshalling when I could not move in the crowd. I noticed a short, wizened figure next to me. Who could fail to recognise the black jeans and leather jacket and matching biker boots, and, of course, the trademark black beret jammed onto the head. He seemed oblivious to the noisy heat of the packed hall. I watched as he tapped someone close by: 'Yas, my bra, briek af 'n stuk van daai poster vir my' (Hey brother, break off a piece of that poster for me). He was pointing at a discarded placard lying on the floor. Whatever did he want that for? I was rather intrigued. Ignoring everyone around him, he started scribbling. Then he started pushing his way through the crowd to the front. I watched as he whispered into the ear of someone at the side of the stage.

And then there he stood, in the middle of the stage, struggling with the mike, trying to adjust it to his height. The audience went a bit quieter, not completely, though; there was still a group of students restlessly buzzing on the side of the hall. But it was quiet enough to hear his words. I do not remember the details of the poem, but that does not matter. The short poem captured the mood of the crowd and sent it reverberating through the hall in passionate and powerful images. His poem encapsulated the anger and pain of apartheid oppression, the rage and hatred that sustain people in the struggle for survival and endurance, and spoke not just of endurance, but of triumph and victory as well. His words exhorted the crowd to militant action. Almost two generations removed from the man on

stage, the student mass that packed the hall roared its approval of his powerful words.

At the time, of course, very few young people would have had extensive knowledge of James Matthews's work. His work had been banned for many years, and so would definitely not have been prescribed for school curricula. He was not a leading member of any of the political or community organisations that made up the United Democratic Front (UDF). He was renowned for his anti-social behaviour, and at best, was regarded as an eccentric. It was generally accepted, however, that his work had an undeniably profound impact on people, especially in the seventies when Black Consciousness politics inspired people. His passionate and angry poetry which expressed black pride, solidarity and outrage at apartheid oppression, still resonated with the call for a communal responsibility to oppose apartheid in the eighties and emphasised the need for a collective identification with the black majority. But the eighties were characterised by sectoral and structured organisations, of alliances across class, religious, community and interest lines. As someone who insisted on his independence, who resisted being put in a niche, he was also regarded as a maverick, as a loose cannon.

In 1990, the same year that the African National Congress (ANC) was unbanned, and people's organisations came out of the closet and openly declared their allegiance to the ANC, Matthews declared:

> freedom owns the poet's soul
> he shall not be garbed
> in a cloak of ideology
> his voice not laced by
> legislation[1]

Yet his reputation as the 'Godfather of BC writing'[2] still lives on. His poetry spoke directly to the hearts and minds of people and spoke of things they could identify with. His poetry is rooted in the time and reflects the process of history which it helped shape.

Matthews's work as writer and publisher spans more than five decades: short stories in the forties, fifties and sixties; poetry in the seventies and eighties; and the South African publication of his first novel in the late nineties. He has truly endured, and so has his work. He has been involved in almost every phase or stage of the development of South African literature, at least as far as black writing in South Africa is concerned. Mongane Wally Serote refers to him as the writer 'who set the standard of how we were going to deal with the things around us'.[3] Jacques Alvarez-Pereyre calls him 'a true teacher in the field of protest'.[4] Ursula Barnett lists him as one of the 'most prominent among the poets who started a new wave in black poetry in South Africa'.[5] Piniel Shava regards his poetry as 'among the most informative about the condition of blacks'.[6] Jane Watts registers his work in her comprehensive critical work *Black Writers from South Africa*.[7] What is clear from the range of critical works on South African literature, from university curricula and literary anthologies, is that James Matthews is one of the main black writers of our time.[8]

South African literary scholars have argued that the late forties and the fifties mark the first coherent upsurge of black writing in South African literature. The work of writers such as Can Themba, Casey Motsisi, Nat Nakasa, Lewis Nkosi, Todd Matshikiza, Ezekiel Mphahlele and Bloke Modisane appeared regularly in *Drum* magazine, started by Anthony Sampson in 1951. Their short stories, autobiographical sketches and reports focused on urban township life based mainly in Orlando, Sophiatown and other Witwatersrand townships. In Cape Town a number of coloured writers were making their mark as well: Dennis Brutus, Alex La Guma, Peter Clarke, Richard Rive, as well as James Matthews. Much of their work focused on the people of District Six and described how a range of individuals from this community confronts daily life. Their writings are considered 'black' in the same way as that of the 'Drum writers', in that they arose from, and were rooted in, the milieu in which they lived.

Although writing from different perspectives and describing different communities, these writers are considered to have common basis: they have given literary expression to the realities of black life as it confronted the early years of apartheid in South Africa. Their work described the numerous injustices, humiliations and abuses to which the black majority was subjected in all spheres of social, economic, political and psychological life. In brief, then, all these writers are said to have expressed the totality of the South African 'black experience'. Furthermore, when tracing the development of what has come to be 'black writing', scholars have noted that the Black Consciousness politics of the late seventies and early eighties mark a major shift in the focus of the work of writers of this period. Instead of merely describing the effects of apartheid life, their work was characterised by anger, militancy and pride.

What is striking is how many scholars have categorised and represented this corpus of 'black writing' in a largely unexplained way, a way which does not take into account the fluid, unfixed, often contradictory nature of identities, especially within the South African context. I would like to question such easy generalisations about 'black writing', which seem to be based on unproblematised notions of what 'black' in South Africa means. Many scholars fail to examine and explain the heterogeneity of the black experience, and, therefore, the heterogeneity of literary expressions of these experiences.

In her introduction Watts refers to 'their typical products'[9] when referring to a group of writers she categorises as being representative of the fifties, as well as repeated references to 'the history of black writing' and descriptions of the 'journey [of self-discovery] of black South African writers who write in English' when talking about writers such as Alex La Guma, Mongane Serote and Miriam Tlali. Shava categorises Matthews amongst the protest poets of the seventies. He singles out Matthews as the odd man out among Serote, Njabulo Ndebele, Mandla Langa and Mafika Gwala, but because of his anger, not because of his different 'black' experience.[10]

The failure to examine the heterogeneity of the black experience is especially pertinent when examining the work of Matthews. At first a short story writer, he began writing poetry in the seventies and is considered one of the angriest of the Black Consciousness poets. Unlike his stories, which focused mainly on personal experiences, his poetry is defiant and angry exclamations of black solidarity. He expresses the principles of Black Consciousness

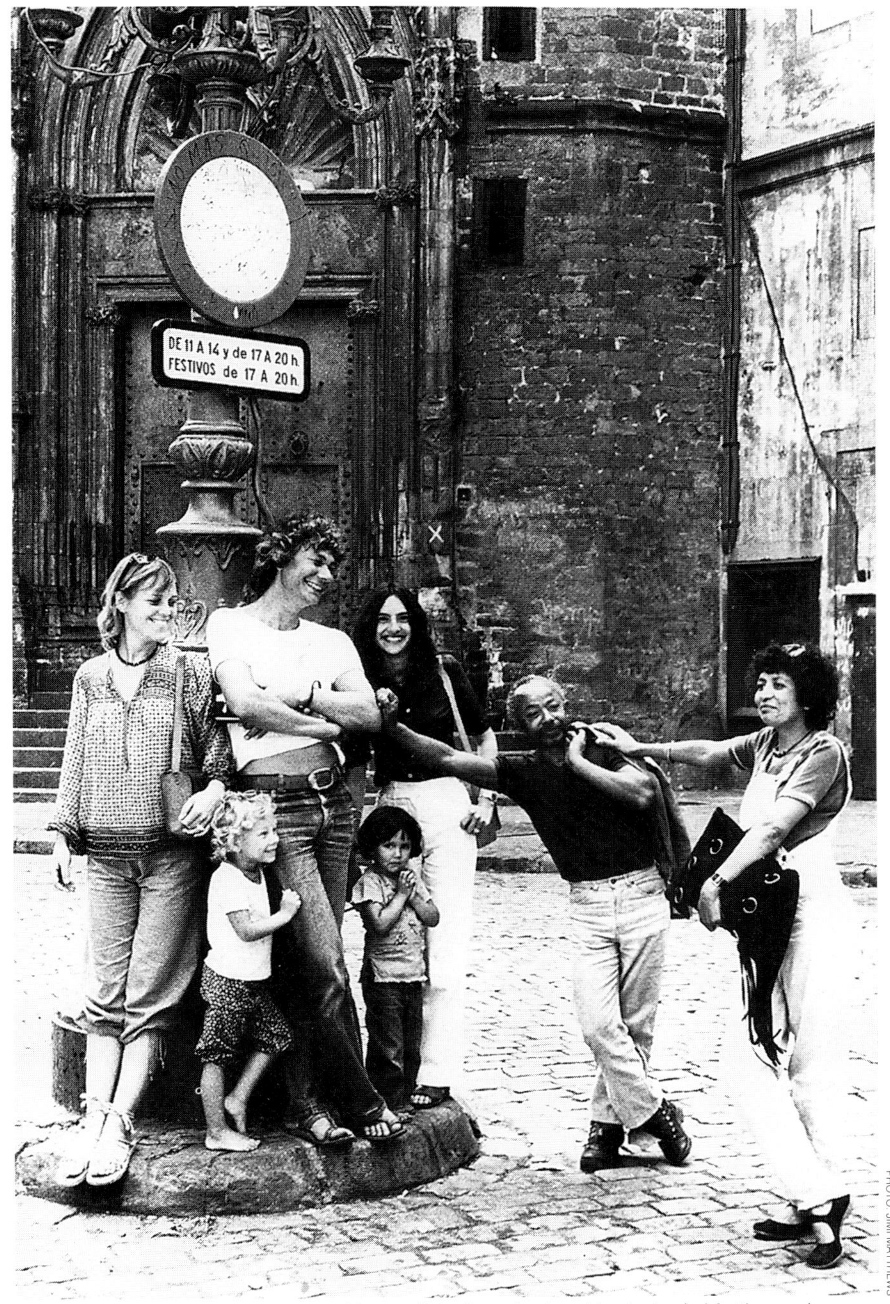

Lilli Hallett, George Hallett, Norah Moerat (Matthews's daughter-in-law), Matthews, Lorna de Smidt; in front are Mymoena Hallett and Leila de Smidt. Barcelona, 1980.

through his poetry, which he sees as 'the affirmativeness of [his] "blackness" and its inherent dignity'.[11] It is his poetry, which seems to embody certain assumed and predictable characteristics of 'black' poetry, that has received much more scholarly attention than have his prose works. However, what is evident from a closer look at his work is that Matthews's conventionalised Black Consciousness stance defined by generalised racial dualisms often wavers, unravelling the logic of generalised assumptions of 'black'

identity. These inconsistencies are not contradictory. They reveal the complexities of assertions of black identity in South Africa.

Matthews is classified coloured, a distinct category between black and white, according to the apartheid racial hierarchy. He focuses on this community as the subject of his early writing. His stories capture the rich detail of life in the coloured community in Cape Town. His characters speak in the language and accents of the people of District Six and Bo-Kaap.

115

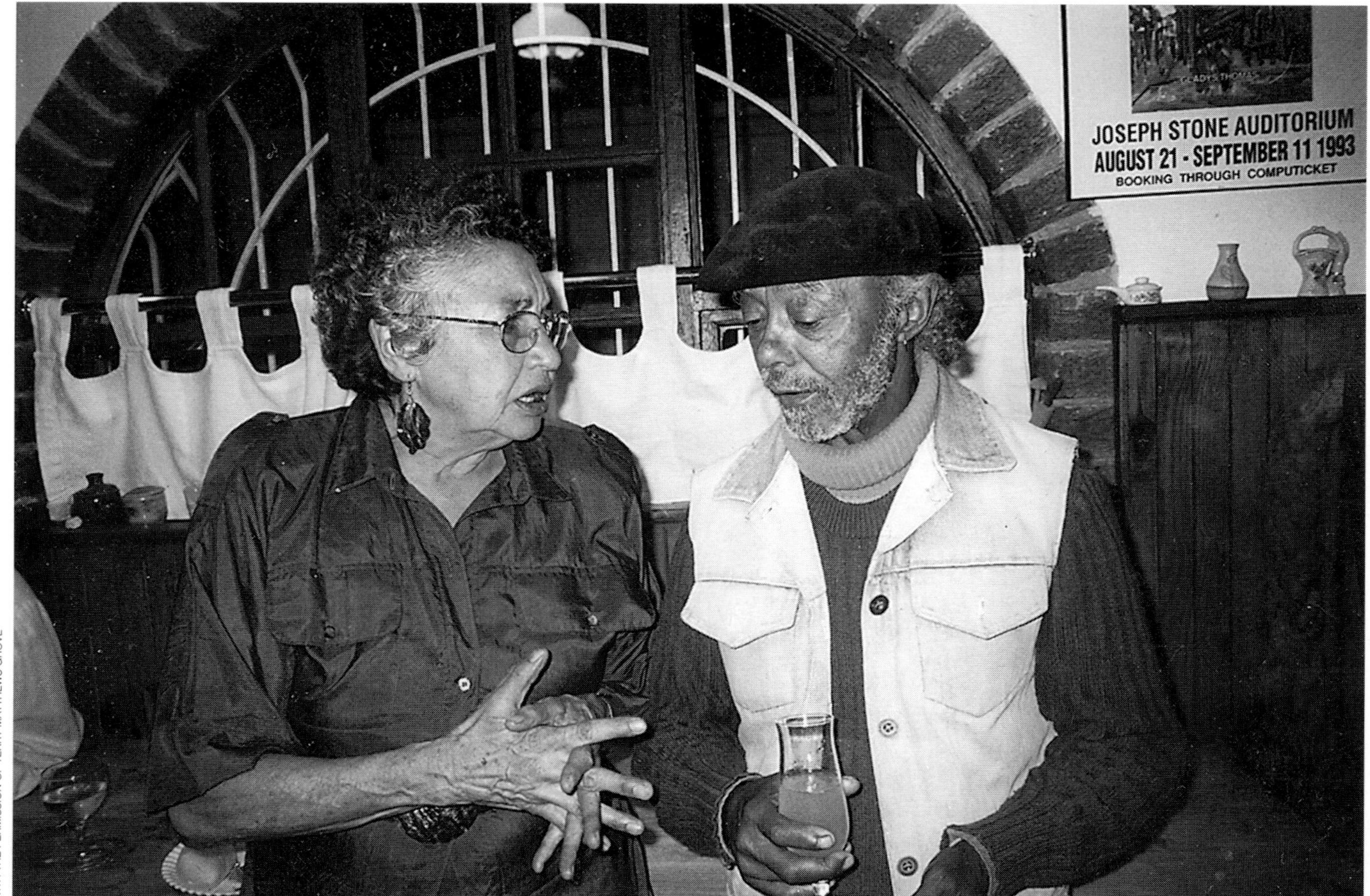

Matthews with Gladys Thomas, the co-contributor to *Cry Rage!*. In 1972 it was the first book to be banned by the apartheid government. Cape Town, 1997.

The experiences he describes are the experiences these people face daily under the oppressive apartheid system. There is poverty and degradation, humiliation and indignities, but also humour, humanity and hope.

Although the label 'coloured' was one which was designated by the white government, it found general acceptance in the community because it set them apart from the black group as a more favoured group. The distinctiveness of this group was further entrenched through legislation such as the Population Registration Act, the Group Areas Act and, in the Western Cape, the Coloured Labour Preference policy. This group was encouraged to think of themselves as superior to the black majority classified 'African', yet very definitely subordinate to the white minority. However, apartheid policies and laws were not the only means of fixing racial categories and collective identities. Physical features and popular myths relating to the culture, history, religious and social attitudes also developed as markers of the

collective identity of this group. Some coloureds were able to escape their racial destiny by passing as white if they were fair-skinned; others accepted their lot, placated by the scant comfort that they were better off than the 'blacks'. Therefore when Matthews's characters in his stories refer to 'black', they are referring to Africans, the black majority. In his novel *The Party is Over* he explains to a potential white patron that he is not a 'Black African writer' as he does not come from 'a tribal background' nor does he speak 'an indigenous language'.[12] Perhaps he would describe himself as a Black Coloured writer, and see no contradiction in the term.

Matthews began writing short stories during the forties, fifties and early sixties. He had his first short story published by *The Sun* newspaper when he was seventeen years old. His stories were published regularly in *Drum, Flamingo, Staffrider* and *Wietie* magazines, and apart from *The Sun,* in other newspapers like *Golden City Post, Cape Times* and *Cape Argus. Quartet,* a short story collection that included stories by Matthews, Alex La Guma, Richard Rive and Alf Wannenburgh, was the first such collection to achieve international recognition for these writers.[13]

For Matthews one of the greatest moments of his career as a writer was when he received a copy of his short story collection *Azikwelwa*, which was translated and published in Sweden in 1963.[14] Thereafter two novels were published in Swedish and German, *Schattentage* (1985) and *Die Träume des David Patterson* (1986). None of these novels appeared in South Africa during this time. Only in 1997 was one, *Die Träume des David Patterson,* reworked and published in Cape Town as *The Party is Over*. His second novel, *Schattentage* – 'Darkened Windows, Darkened Rooms' – has yet to be published in South Africa, in the language in which it was written.

In the seventies Matthews started writing poetry. He published *Cry Rage!* (1973*), Pass Me a Meatball, Jones* (1977), *no time for dreams* (1981*), Poisoned Wells and Other Delights* (1990) and he edited *Black Voices Shout!* (1974).[15] He also contributed accompanying poems to a book of photography, *Images*, by George Hallett.[16] The collection *Cry Rage!*, which includes poetry by Gladys Thomas, has the dubious honour of being the first book of poetry banned in South Africa, a fate that also awaited his subsequent poetry collections. During the uprisings of 1976 he was detained for four months at Victor Verster prison, during which time he wrote the poems published in the collection *Pass Me a Meatball, Jones*. More recently, Matthews has been writing love poetry, the kind of writing the South African reality has long prevented him from exploring. A collection of Matthews's love poetry is due to be published soon.

The banning of his work, as well as the unwillingness of local publishing houses to publish his work, forced Matthews to either publish himself or publish abroad. It is abroad, therefore, that Matthews had his largest audience and where his work received greatest acclaim. In Germany, for example, he was awarded the freedom of the towns Lehrte and Nürnburg in 1984. Although invited abroad several times, he was consistently refused a passport for most of his writing career, and was forced, therefore, to turn down countless invitations to conferences, conventions, book fairs and other international gatherings. It was only through the intervention of the West German government in 1980 that he received a passport for the first time.[17]

When the apartheid government started clamping down on writers and their work in the late sixties, Matthews stopped writing short stories, more to avoid self-censorship than out of fear of the authorities. However, a collection of his stories did appear in South Africa in 1974. He published this collection himself through his BLAC (Black Literature, Arts and Culture) publishing house. The collection, *The Park and Other Stories*, included stories that had been published abroad.[18] This collection is Matthews's only pre-1990 work to escape banning.

An expanded collection, also entitled *The Park and Other Stories*, was published in 1983.[19] The twenty-four stories in the collection capture the entire range of life of those who were classified 'coloured' in South Africa. His characters are gangsters and drunks, housewives, students and priests; middle-class, working-class, rural and urban people. He describes the lives and experiences of farm labourers, artists and intellectuals.

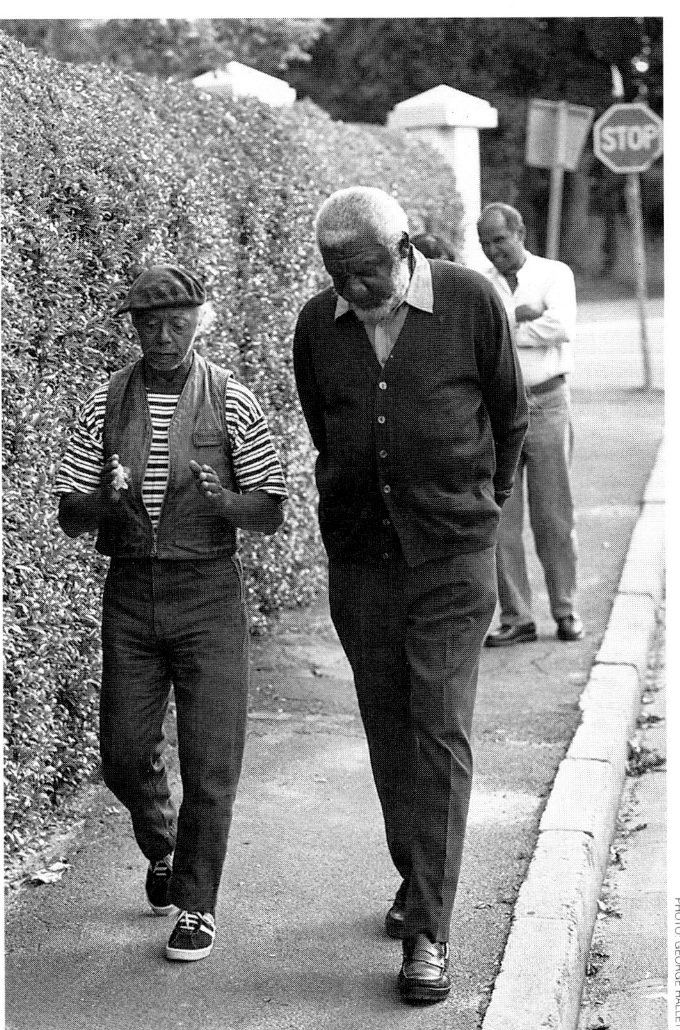

Matthews with the Gambian writer, Lenrie Peters; in the background is the Somalian novelist, Nuruddin Farah. Cape Town, 1999.

117

Matthews describes how people are confronted with the oppressive apartheid laws at every turn.[20] He is fascinated by how people respond to their circumstances: some acquiesce humbly as a means of survival; some simmer silently with impotent rage; some refuse to submit and fight the system; others are awakened from their apathy and ignorance by particular experiences.

In 'The portable radio' the main character is a young man who has given up on life. He finds comfort only in drink, and his story ends, predictably, in tragic violence. In 'Caesar's law' the young pregnant girl in despair runs away from the priest who refuses to allow her to marry her white boyfriend. Other stories describe the humiliation and powerlessness of the characters in the face of apartheid. In 'The park' a little boy defiantly returns to play on the swing in the park he was barred from because of his skin colour. The park attendant is torn between his duty to uphold the law and the desire to defy it; in the end fear of the white boss decides his actions: All his feelings urged him to leave the boy alone, to let him continue to enjoy himself, but the fear that someone might see him hardened him.

'Get off! Go home!' he screamed, his voice harsh, his anger directed at the system that drove him against his own.[21]

In 'A case of guilt' a respectable middle-class man is falsely arrested for the non-payment of tax and gets a taste of the humiliation and debasement of prison experience. The apartheid system has dehumanised the men he meets there, reducing them to beasts, not the dumb beast of burden like Herman in 'The awakening', but predators preying on the vulnerable and weak. In the apartheid jail, as in apartheid society outside, 'abnormality was the norm'.[22]

In several of the stories there is the dawning awareness of the main character to the injustices of the apartheid system and the commitment to doing something about it. In 'The awakening' the farm labourer, Herman, becomes aware of his oppression after reading a pamphlet which a student hands to him on a trip to Cape Town. In 'Tribute to a humble man' a young man from a small village is so impressed by what he hears of Imam Haron's life and death that he decides that 'whatever the nature of his [future] studies, they would lead in the same direction Imam Haron had taken'.[23] In 'Azikwelwa' Jonathan joins what he at first considers to be exclusively the

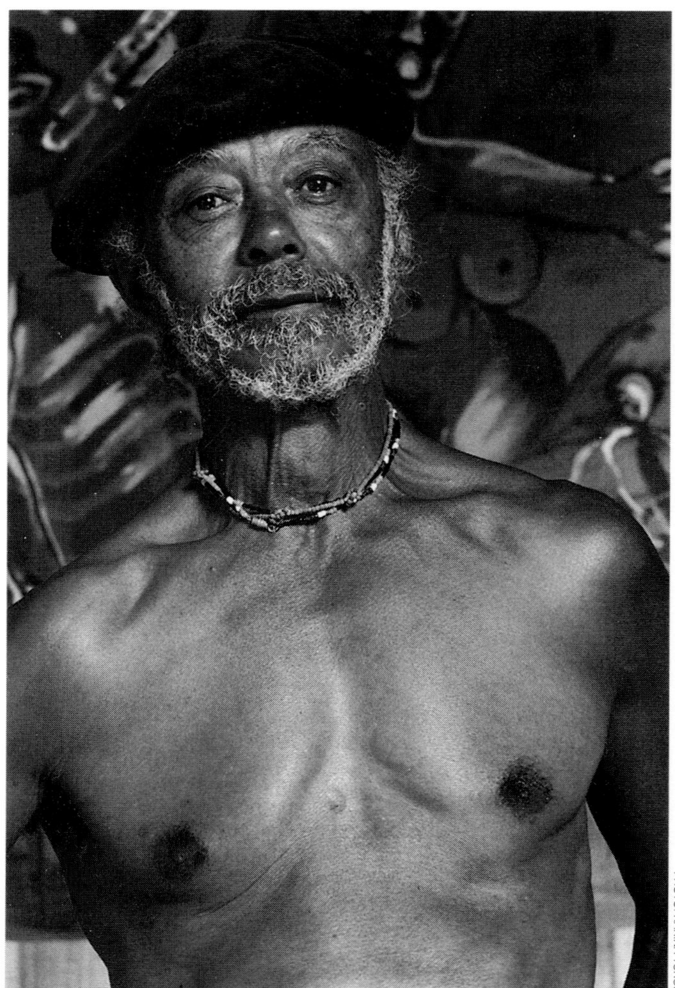

Throughout his life Matthews kept up his daily workout. In 1997, at the age of 68, he took out a ten-year contract at his local gymnasium. Cape Town, 1998.

Africans' fight. Standing back and observing the bus boycotters, their commitment so impresses him that 'the spirit of their pride filled him'.[24] He joins in the boycott and walks to work with the people from the location, in common cause with the Africans.

In 'Whites only', on the other hand, we see skilfully drawn the growing anger and frustration with apartheid's petty laws, as well as of the white-racist attitudes accompanying the racist system. As the main character travels into the city by train to shop and see to business, he faces humiliations and indignities wherever he goes. As he goes about his business his anger grows in intensity until the point of explosion:

The hall, the girl, the attendant, everybody and everything else disappeared in the anger that consumed him. His body was on fire and he had to blink hard to keep the tears back. He could not think coherently.

118

*His mind was filled with obscenities which were
repeated over and over until it became a blank screen
with the obscenities flashing on it in multicoloured
letters.*[25]

But the anger which a moment ago had threatened
to overwhelm him fizzles into futility and impotence
as he 'meekly followed [the white attendant], his
body strangely dead and heavy'.[26] The character in
this story has not quite reached the stage of resistance where he is able to be defiant in the face of those
who oppress him. Descriptions of the daily humiliations of apartheid and the conditions of life are
reflected back to the readers, bringing the awareness
into their consciousness. In this way they are urged
to overcome these debased self-images and commit
themselves to overcoming the system. The deep anger
and rage at what the 'white man's law has done'[27]
expressed in Matthews's work reflect the same emotions experienced by countless others like him.

It was the Black Consciousness politics of seventies that were the context for the development of his
writing to an emphasis on militancy and revolutionary
didacticism. It was a shift that Matthews, and many
other writers of this period, seems to have been com-
pelled to make. He is unable to play the role of the
detached observer. He is part of his community and
as such he cannot remain aloof. He remains acutely
aware of the constraints and pressures he is subjected
to as a writer in apartheid South Africa.

Richard Rive says in a personal essay: 'I would
have preferred to have written about being a writer
anywhere without ethnic or geographical limitations.'[28] This is a statement that Matthews certainly
would endorse. In *The Party is Over* the main character, David Patterson, chafes with frustration at not
being able just to write about 'slices of life' as they
play themselves out in the environment in which he
lived. Instead the black writer was pressurised to
'rant and rave about the [political] system itself with
the people becoming props'.[29] Black writers were
forced into the role as political writers and typecast
by publishers and readership alike within ethnic and
racial categories. In one of his poems, written at the
beginning of the eighties, Matthews laments:

i wish i could write a
poem
record the beginning of
dawn

the opening of a flower
at the approach of a bee
describe a bird's first flight
then i look at people
maimed, shackled, jailed,
the knowing is now clear
i will never be able to write
a poem about dawn, a bird or a
bee[30]

Instead his sensibilities and experiences forced him
to write about:

Soweto skies aflame with anger
wind carrying the wails of the slain[31]

Another factor which impacted on Matthews's role as
a black writer, was his readership or audience. The
fact that he was writing for people other than those
he was writing about was a source of frustration as
well. The people he would have preferred as his
readership were mostly semi-literate or illiterate.
Neither could they afford to buy books, or even the
newspapers like *Cape Times* and *Cape Argus*, in
which his early stories were published. In addition,
as we see from the character Yvonne in *The Party is
Over*, black and coloured people had so been cowed
by apartheid education and social reality that even
when able to read, preferred to escape into the
worlds of pulp fiction and picture stories.

This of course meant that the readers who had
access to his work were either those from the educated
black and coloured middle class, a tiny minority, or
liberal whites who were curious about township life.
Like many others writing the 'protest' literature of
the sixties Matthews directed his work at a mainly
white and foreign readership at first, in an attempt to
force them into an awareness of the injustices experienced by the black South African majority. He soon
became aware of the futility of this, though. His frustration and anger at playing the role of the 'black
writer' is described in the short story 'The party'[32]
which he later integrated into his novel. The novel
has many scenes where the main character rages at
the condescension of white liberal 'arty' types, who
add black artists to their collection. Rive also testifies
to conferences and occasions where black artists are
invited 'in order that a white audience might find a
vicarious delight in listening to a black who is not
only articulate but can also write poetry'.[33]

With the advent of Black Consciousness, though, there was another purpose for the black writer:

Its essence is the realisation by the black man of the need to rally together with his brothers around the cause of their oppression – the blackness of their skin – and to operate as a group to rid themselves of the shackles that bind them to perpetual servitude. The philosophy of Black Consciousness therefore expresses group pride and the determination of the black to rise and attain the envisaged self.[34]

Black Consciousness, with its emphasis on black pride and militancy, had a profound influence on Matthews's work, especially his poetry:

I am Black
my Blackness fills me to the brim
like a beaker of well-seasoned wine
that sends my senses reeling with pride[35]

This Black Consciousness period gave him the opportunity to explore a different medium – poetry. It also resolved to some extent the feelings of isolation and alienation he experienced through being forced to publish abroad. Switching to poetry gave him a chance to reach the people he really wanted to. His poetry found a ready audience at public meetings and rallies. The concepts of black self-reliance and pride which were basic tenets of Black Consciousness politics also led to the establishment of his own BLAC publishing house, which meant he no longer had to rely on the beneficence of white-owned publishing companies. The anger and pain of his short stories were a continued characteristic of his poetry, but the rage was more intense, and had lost the satirical edge of the stories he wrote before. As Shava puts it:

Among the poets who wrote before the 1976 Soweto uprising, James Matthews is probably the angriest. His anger goes far beyond that of poets like Wally Serote in that Matthews is not content just to be angry against a system that oppresses blacks – he openly advocates hatred.[36]

The French critic, Alvarez-Pereyre, although mostly positive in his criticism, has described Matthews's work as 'protest didacticism', his poetic style as 'simplistic' and his poetry as 'a catalogue of the evils currently due to apartheid'.[37] *He has been criticised for posturing and declaiming, his poetry but 'a public address system for the declarations of a muzzled prose writer'.*[38]

Matthews himself has consistently in his work rejected the title of poet:

To label my utterings poetry
and myself a poet
would be as self-deluding
as the planners of parallel development
I record the anguish of the persecuted
whose words are whimpers of the woe
wrung from them by bestial laws[39]

In the poem which opens the collection *Cry Rage!* he writes:

It is said
that poets write of beauty
of form, of flowers and of love
but the words I write
are of pain and rage

I am no minstrel
who sings songs of joy
mine a lament

I wail of a land
hideous with open graves
waiting for the slaughtered ones

balladeers strum their lutes and sing of happy times
I cannot join in their merriment
my heart drowned in bitterness
with the agony of what the white man's law has done[40]

In poems like these, however, Matthews is more than just disclaiming the role of poet. He is also expressing an awareness that writers were doing more than presenting a different content. There was a growing awareness of the need to break away from the old forms of literature, so long the preserves of the white minority. Using the language of the people and so directly addressing them, he rejects the old cultural models.

He goes beyond merely describing the suffering and humiliations of apartheid. The poetry in *Cry Rage!* is directed at two kinds of readers – he informs white readers about his disgust and anger, and he tries to make his black readers aware of their oppression

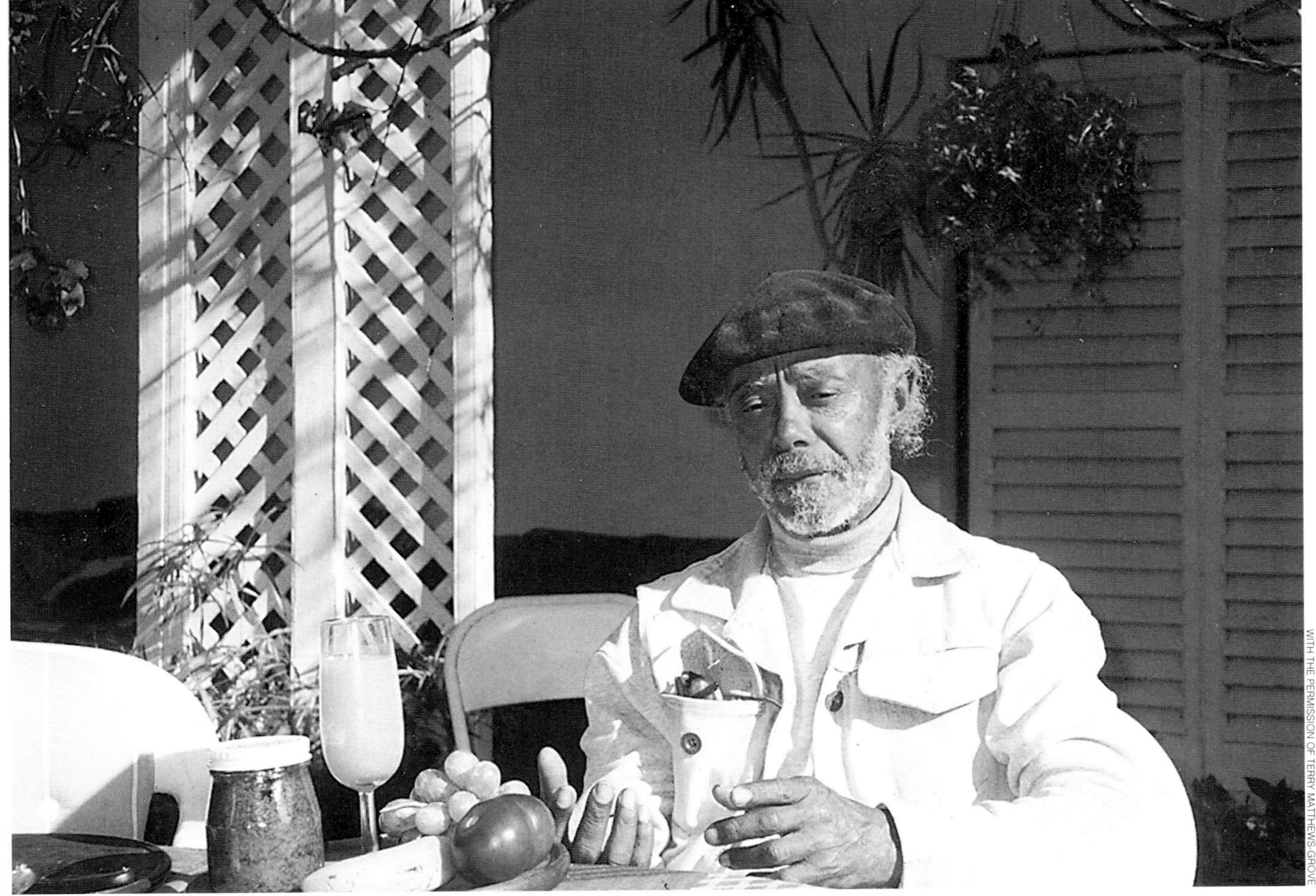

Age brought sobriety and clean living. Saldanha, 1998.

and to instill in them the courage to act. His poems often end in warnings of the consequences of the refusal of whites to change. The anger expressed in the poems is a declaration of war, his words a call to action:

> The time is now
> too long in our ears
> we have heard the rattle
> cough of dying children[41]

And

> our blood will not be
> the colour of our shame
> for each death we die
> each death we die
> flowers of hatred will blossom[42]

Later in the same poem, we hear the familiar clarion call of the period's protest poetry:

> the horrors inflicted upon us
> will be returned in growing numbers
> the land must be washed in blood
> so that a new crop of us will sprout[43]

However, even in his Black Consciousness-influenced poetry, we see that he problematises easy generalisations about racial dualisms. He does not present a Manichaean framework of clearly defined evil and good distinctions, in which whites are always simplistically presented as evil oppressors and everyone else the black victims. While targeting those whites who are either responsible for apartheid or indifferent to the way blacks are made to suffer, he acknowledges the role of whites who have spoken out against apartheid:

> then there was that priest upon the hill
> who fasted for freedom
> he said his prayers in a tomb
> of a man not of his faith

the flesh fell from the face
of this man of God
as he did penance for the death
of a man whose sermon was one of peace[44]

He targets, too, those blacks who have betrayed their people and who have allowed themselves to be co-opted as allies of the apartheid regime:

we watch through the window
as they sit feasting
at a table loaded with equality
and grow frantic at its flavour[45]

Matthews's work expresses a radicalism which at the time seemed essential for the awakening and liberation of the black man in South Africa. What then of the black woman? His portrayal of women in his work wavers between proclaiming the superior beauty of the black woman over the white woman[46] and ridiculing some black women's attempts to adhere to white standards of beauty.[47]

In his short stories, especially, his descriptions of female characters are not sympathetic ones. In 'The portable radio' the aunt is described as a screeching harridan, with a 'mean voice'.[48] She is said to have a 'sharp tongue'[49] and spitefully switches off the light so that the main character has no access to the radio. Her mean-spiritedness ends in violence, with of course, the inevitable tragic end for the main character as well. Other female characters are described in a no more sympathetic light. Women are either long-suffering but silent wives and mothers, fighting for survival, or they are flesh, described as 'busty', 'saucy', the '"property" of men'.[50]

In the story 'Colour blind' all the characters are women, reminiscing about life before the Group Areas Act forcibly removed them from the areas in which they were living. Stephanie finds herself in Manenberg, a desolate housing estate on the Cape Flats. Her only comfort in her life of poverty is the respectability and civility of her life 'before' – as well as her white forebears and the knowledge that some of her family members had managed to escape by passing for white. What the story portrays, however, is the ambivalence of her situation. Although she clings to the pride in those who have managed to escape the economic and social drudgery of apartheid, there is also a feeling of desolation and betrayal at being left behind.

Interestingly, though, there is a slight departure from the usual depiction of women in the story 'The awakening', a story of a farm worker's growing awareness of his oppressed life. Unlike Herman, his wife Maria can read. It is she who reads and explains the pamphlet Herman receives from students in town. However, the final decision to leave is Herman's to make. It seems as if Matthews presents Maria as the educated one in order to emphasise the depth of Herman's oppression. As a farm worker he has had no access to education. It was deemed unnecessary for black workers to have education as they were meant to be labourers. Thus Herman is presented as the stereotypical labourer who has that much longer a journey to make before awakening to the reality of his oppression.

The Party is Over is Matthews's only full-length novel to be published in South Africa. Written and set in the sixties, it was published abroad in the eighties. It is a bit of an anomaly, therefore, and comes across as dated and anachronistic. However, its interest lies in the strong autobiographical undercurrent and illustrates something of a personal credo on the part of Matthews. It tells the poignant story of David Patterson, who battles to overcome the frustration of being a coloured artist and the personal despair of a failed marriage. Aimlessly stumbling from one drinking spree to another, he battles to overcome the torment of an artistic dry spell. Gradually he alienates everyone, friends, wife, fellow artists, as well as those who want to sponsor and support his work. It is an intensely focused personal story, which Matthews admitted has strong autobiographical elements. Matthews's descriptions of the network of relationships offer a picture of the social and political settings of Cape Town in the heydays of apartheid, a picture familiar to the reader of his short stories.

David Patterson struggles against being forced into the part of political writer and being categorised according to his colour:

'I've had some stories published without any strings of colour attached. I'd like to keep it that way. If I'm going to succeed, I want to make it because my writing is good, not because the market is hungry for Black writers from Africa. In any case, I can't really be classified as a Black African writer.'
'Why not?' Zelda was perplexed.
'Let me put it this way: I don't come from a tribal background, neither do I speak an indigenous

122

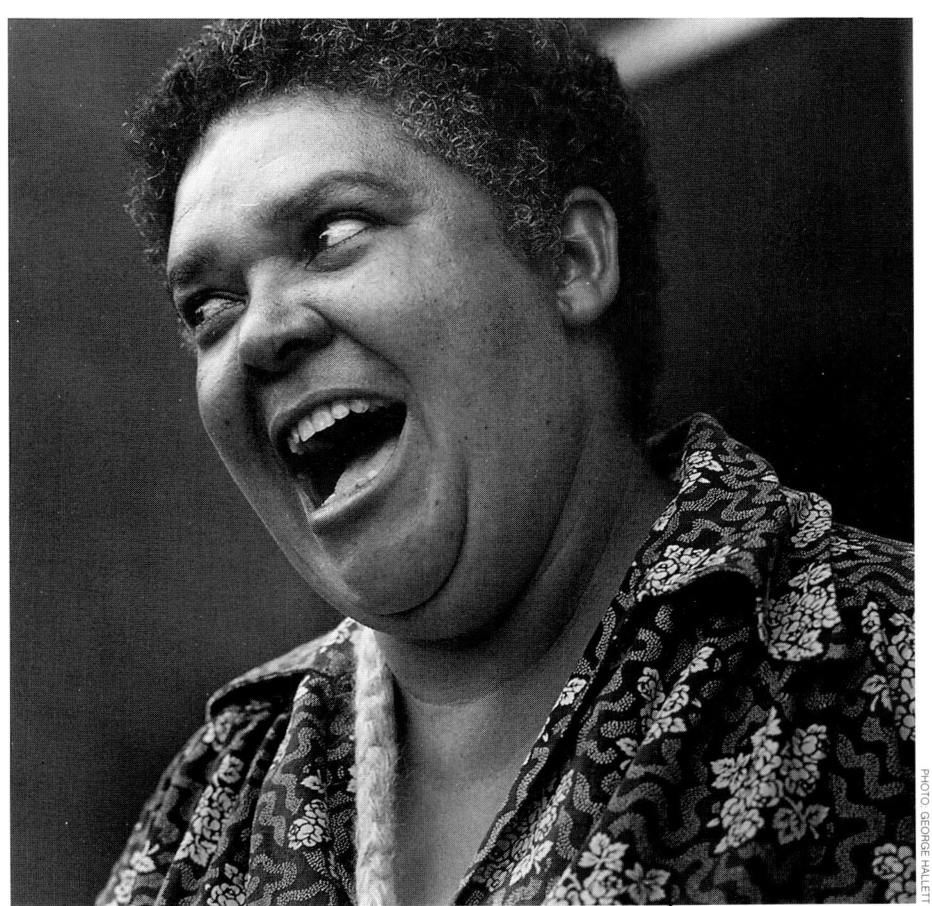

Bessie Head and Matthews struck up an enduring friendship during her brief stay in Cape Town in the early sixties. While writing *A Question of Power*, she wrote more than forty letters to Matthews, expressing her anxieties.

language. I'm not white, but I am not African either.' David fell silent. It would be a waste of time to explain to these misguided people that he sometimes felt that the Coloureds had become the new lost tribe of Israel.[51]

Patterson's struggle to regain his creative energy as a writer is a struggle for selfhood, for a sense of belonging that seems always to elude him. He is caught in a continual state of tension between a range of complex and conflicting identities. Living in Athlone and working as a messenger, his work as a writer nonetheless admits him to white circles. It is in these circles he is able to discuss literature, theatre and music in a way he cannot at home. It is in these social gatherings, too, that he is likely to find people willing to publish his work and so advance his writing career. And so he attends the art exhibitions and parties arranged by whites. He envies the ease with which Ron Brink seems to move around, able to 'bridge the divide as if there was none at all',[52] hoping that he would also be able to 'acquire a similar smoothness of manner and forever be rid of the unease he felt'.[53] He soon realises that he is on show as that anomaly, 'the artistically-inclined coloured',[54] and that he would not have been invited otherwise. Ron Brink was 'their pimp, without compunction procuring virgin after virgin for their inspection'.[55] On these occasions, his pent-up anger explodes into abusive and anti-social behaviour, as if reverting to type, the uncivilised, drunken coloured. He returns time and time again to these circles, however, impressed by their gracious living and cultured conversation, escaping the social drudgery of his job and domestic circumstances, yet resenting the terms under which he gains his escape.

His relationship with his wife is similarly complex and problematic. He has an affair with one of their friends, Paula, yet is devastated when his wife Yvonne leaves him. Yvonne is not interested in books or her husband's ambition to be a writer. She is unable to understand the anguish he is going through as a writer, nor she can understand his desire to write about their surroundings and the people they know.

She brags about him to the neighbours without
having an inkling of what drives him artistically.
Dawn, on the other hand, encourages him. She is a
well-read librarian, educated and middle class, totally
unlike his wife. Although committed to his wife, he
thinks 'it's a pity her mind doesn't match her shape'.[56]
His love for Yvonne seems to be based on the physical:
he describes her physical characteristics, her body, her
breasts. The relationship with Dawn is a platonic one,
a relationship of the mind, not the body. Yet when he
discovers that Yvonne is having an affair with his
friend, Melvyn, he is devastated. He discovers that his
romantic notions of love are totally different to his
wife's ideas of love and marriage. David Patterson discovers the role of the writer as detached outsider has
painful consequences, one being his alienation from
all those who are close to him. At the end of the novel
he seems to accept this, finding his solace in drink.

Like the lost tribe of Israel to which Matthews
compares coloureds, David Patterson is caught
between two worlds, yet comfortable in none. There
are consistent emphases on his interest in western
European culture. He and his friends have long discussions on the merits and demerits of American
conductors, Fellini's films, French novelists. Their
talk 'never dwelled on the rape-and-robbery cases
which filled pages of the *Post*; they never concerned
themselves with the sports-roundup'.[57] Thus while on
one level Matthews focuses on markers of race to
indicate his characters' discomfort in arty circles, on
another he distances himself from stereotypical subject positions which he ascribes to the character of
Yvonne and her neighbours. Popular notions of the
coloured as mixed, the tainted, in-between group,
have often revolved around notions of cultural and
moral imperfections. In the novel these notions are
articulated as depictions of certain characters, with
Matthews's emphatic rebuttal of stereotyped
coloured culturelessness.

Although Matthews proclaims his assertion of
Black Consciousness principles in his work, he is
unable to consistently retain its dualistic and essen-
tialising logic, as I have tried to show above. On the
contrary, from the perspective of the logic of the
nature of identity formation, the 'inconsistencies' are
not contradictory. He acknowledges that different
and often conflicting identities have emerged within
the coloured community. In a newspaper article in
which he reflects on the psyche, the history and the
aspirations of the coloured community, he gives an
overview of the complexities of identity formation:

*For some, there is no problem being identified as
coloured, as for them it holds no stigma. It is a term
that was acceptable to their grandparents and parents,
and they do not find it offensive to be addressed as
coloured. They show their admiration for a black person as head of state, but show displeasure if labelled
'black', although they do not express antagonism
towards blacks. [...] Anti-black racism has developed
among some coloureds, and is on the increase among
those who feel their position is threatened by what they
see as the government's favourable treatment of blacks.
[...] For those who have absorbed the policy of Black
Consciousness, the acceptance of being coloured and
black is not as contradictory as it might appear,
because being black does not mean rejecting being
coloured. Being black is part of their political stance –
a stance they still feel necessary now – and does not
exclude them their place in coloured ranks.*[58]

Matthews's poetry and prose give literary expression
to the complexities of South African assertions of
black identity. The quest for selfhood and a sense of
belonging, for freedom, is not found in unified and
fixed identities, in the binarism of ethnic compart-
ments:

Freedom is not the colour of my   black skin
my blackness a cloak to flaunt
proclaiming that only I am free
because of the bondage suffered
freedom coloured by blackness   is a dream
there is no time for dreams[59]

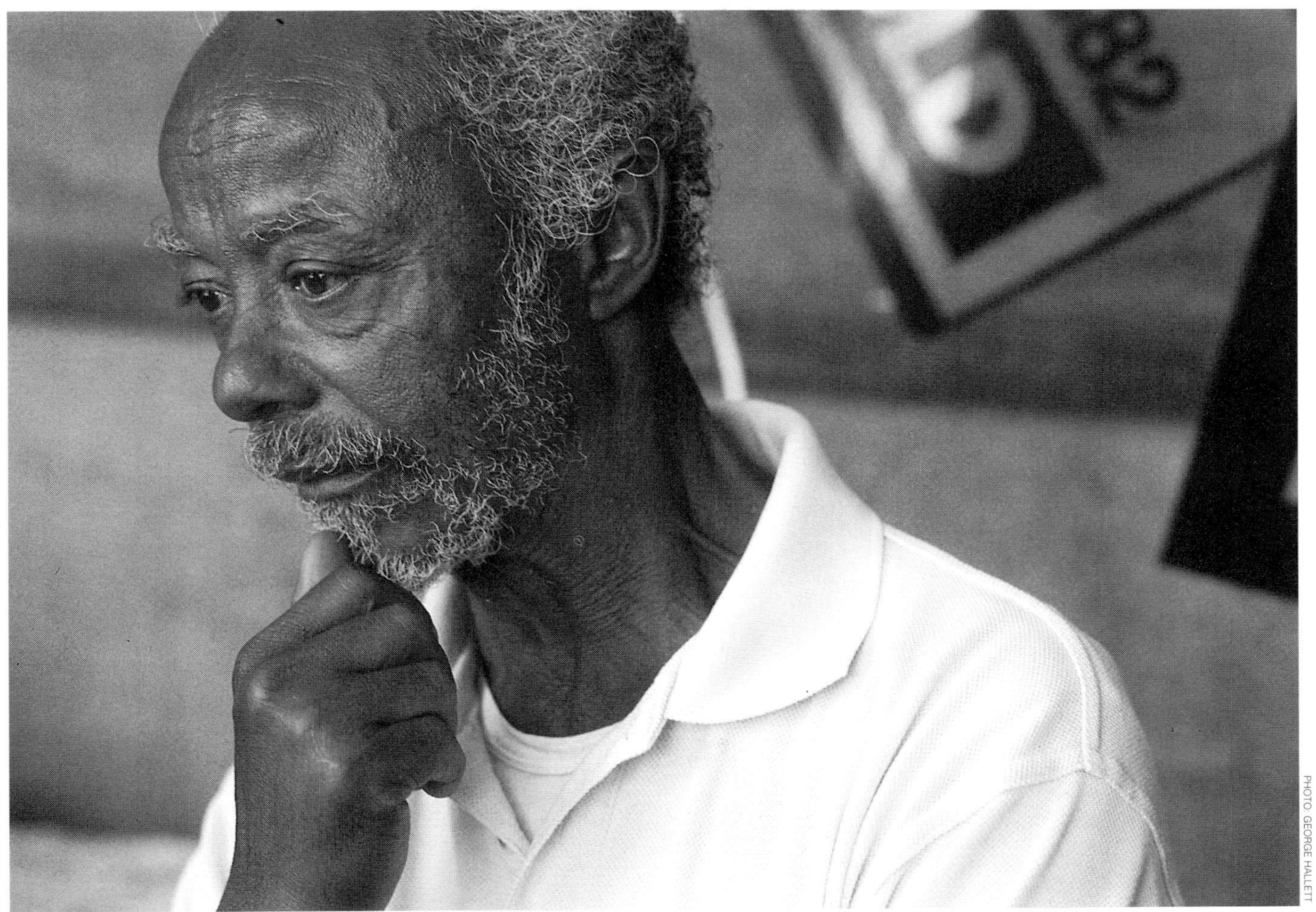

Matthews listening attentively to a conversation. Cape Town, 1992.

References

MORE THAN BROTHERS: PETER CLARKE AND JAMES MATTHEWS AT SEVENTY

1 J. Matthews, *The Party is Over*, (Cape Town, 1997), 48.
2 Ibid., 113.
3 See 42.
4 P. Clarke, *Plain Furniture*, (Plumstead, 1991), 32.
5 Ibid., 30.
6 E. Miles, *Land and Lives: A Story of Early Black Artists*, (Cape Town, 1997), 149–150.
7 See 42.
8 Clarke, *Plain Furniture*, 71–72.
9 P. Clarke, 'Photo Album', (1959), 17.
10 H. Wyngaard, 'Die skaapwagter en die kunstenaar', *De Kat*, July 1998, 65.
11 R. Rive, *Advance Retreat*, (Cape Town, 1983), 38–48.
12 P. Hardy (ed.), *Peter E. Clarke: The Hand is the Tool of the Soul*, (Cape Town, 1992), 8.
13 Miles, 153.
14 E. *Berman, Berman's Art & Artists of South Africa*, (Halfway House, 1983), 98.
15 M. Martin, 'Foreword', in P. Hardy (ed.), *Peter E. Clarke: The Hand is the Tool of the Soul*, (Cape Town, 1992), 1.
16 Hardy, 5.
17 Ibid.
18 Ibid., 10.
19 Miles, 150–151.
20 J. Matthews, personal communication, 23.8.99.
21 R. Rive, *Writing Black*, (Cape Town, 1981), 11.
22 Matthews, 168.
23 See 41.
24 Matthews, 159.
25 See 105–106.
26 See 106.
27 See 40.
28 M. Gwala, 'Towards a National Culture', interviewed by T. Ngwenya, *Staffrider*, 8 (1) (1989), 70.
29 See 117.
30 Undated personal communication.
31 Rive, *Writing Black*, 6.
32 H. Willemse, 'James Matthews beur steeds stroom-op', *Die Suid-Afrikaan*, 36 (1992), 36–37.
33 Rive, *Writing Black*, 18.
34 A. Odendaal and R. Field (eds), *Liberation Chabalala: The World of Alex La Guma*, (Bellville, 1993), xxiv.
35 A. Paton, 'Four Splendid Voices', in R. Rive (ed.), *Quartet: New Voices from South Africa*, (New York, 1963), 14.

SOCIAL CONDITIONS, CULTURAL AND POLITICAL LIFE IN WORKING-CLASS CAPE TOWN, 1950 TO 1990

1 E.P. Thompson, *The Making of the English Working Class*, (Harmondsworth, 1977), 209.
2 See D. Coplan, *In Township Tonight! South Africa's Black City Music and Theatre*, (Johannesburg, 1985).
3 See N. Barnett, 'Race, Housing and Town Planning in Cape Town, c.1920–1940', (MA thesis, University of Cape Town, 1993).
4 V. Bickford-Smith, E. van Heyningen, and N. Worden, *Cape Town in the Twentieth Century*, (Cape Town, 1993), 149.
5 Ibid., 152.
6 Ibid., see S. Jeppie, 'Popular Culture and Carnival in Cape Town: the 1940s and 1950s', in S. Jeppie and C. Soudien (eds), *The Struggle for District Six: Past and Present*, (Cape Town, 1990).
7 M. Wilson and A. Mafeje, *Langa: A Study of Social Groups in an African Township*, (Cape Town, 1963).
8 Jeppie, 'Popular Culture and Carnival in Cape Town: the 1940s and 1950s', 36.
9 Ibid., 83.
10 Bickford-Smith et al., 146.
11 D. Pinnock, 'Ideology and Urban Planning: Blueprints of a Garrison City', in W. James and M. Simons, *The Angry Divide: Social and Economic History of the Western Cape*, (Cape Town, 1989), 164.
12 J. Valentine, interview with C. Soudien (Cape Town), 17.6.1999.
13 Bickford-Smith et al., 213.
14 Ibid., 222.
15 Ibid., 135 on the 'golden age' of the fifties.
16 Ibid., 136–137.
17 C. Soudien, 'The Uses of District Six in the Non-Racial Discussion', in Z. Erasmus and E. Pieterse (eds), *Coloured by Place, Coloured by History*, (Cape Town, forthcoming).
18 R. Rive, 'District Six: Fact and Fiction', in S. Jeppie and C. Soudien (eds), *The Struggle for District Six: Past and Present*, (Cape Town, 1990), 112.
19 L. Fortune, *The House on Tyne Street: Childhood Memories of District Six*, (Cape Town, 1996), 6.
20 Deborah Hart, 'Political Manipulation of Urban Space: The Razing of District Six, Cape Town', in S. Jeppie and C. Soudien (eds), *The Struggle For District Six: Past and Present*, (Cape Town, 1990), 123.
21 Ibid.
22 Fortune, 6.
23 J. Bailey and A. Seftel, *Shebeens Take a Bow: A Celebration of South Africa's Shebeen Lifestyle*, (Johannesburg, 1994), 113.
24 Ibid., 116.
25 *New Age*, 7.11.1957, 8.
26 R. Humphries, 'Administrative Politics and the Coloured Labour Preference Policy During the 1960s', in W. James and M. Simons, *The*

Angry Divide: Social and Economic History of the Western Cape, (Cape Town, 1989), 173.

27 Botto, R. 'Some Aspects of the Leisure Occupations of the African Population in Cape Town', (MSocSc thesis, University of Cape Town, 1954), 131.

28 Bickford-Smith et al., 182.

29 Pinnock, 163.

30 Fortune; N. Ngcelwane, *Sala Kahle District Six,* (Cape Town, 1998).

31 Soudien, 'The Uses of District Six in the Non-Racial Discussion'.

32 Bickford-Smith et al., 136.

33 *Mail and Guardian,* 2–8 July, 1999, 6; see also a graphic story of a convicted rapist about how he went about raping a young girl in *Cape Times,* 5.7.1999, 7.

34 *Mail and Guardian,* 2–8 July, 1999, 6.

35 G. Moloi, *My Life,* (Johannesburg, 1987).

36 A. Tabisher, interview with C. Soudien (Cape Town), 7.6.1999.

37 C. McBride, undated personal communication.

38 Valentine, interview.

39 *New Age,* 3.10.1957, 4.

40 Ibid., 27.6.1957, 6.

41 K. Kondlo, 'The Culture and Religion of the People of Langa during the period ca. 1938–ca. 1958', (BA Honours, University of Cape Town, 1990), 46.

42 *New Age,* 27.6.1957, 6.

43 Kondlo, 39; R. Molapo, 'Popular Culture in Langa', in *Papers of Cape Town History Workshop,* (Cape Town, 1991).

44 Kondlo, 45.

45 See S. Jeppie, 'Aspects of Popular Culture and Class Expression in Inner Cape Town, circa 1939–1959', (MA thesis, University of Cape Town, 1990), 38.

46 Ibid., 79.

47 Ibid., 42.

48 Ibid.

49 Bickford-Smith et al., 191.

50 V. Layne, 'A History of Dance and Jazz Band Performance in the Western Cape in the Post-45 Era', (MA thesis, University of Cape Town, 1995).

51 Tabisher, interview.

52 N. Alexander, 'Non-Collaboration in the Western Cape', in W. James and M. Simons (eds), *The Angry Divide: Social and Economic History of the Western Cape* (Cape Town, 1989), 183.

53 Ibid., 184.

54 Ibid., 188.

55 L. Chisholm, 'Making the Pedagogical More Political and the Political More Pedagogical: Education Traditions and Legacies of the Non-European Unity Movement, 1943–1985', in W. Flanagan, C. Hemson, J. Muller and N. Taylor (compilers), *Vintage Kenton: A Kenton Education Association Commemoration',* (Cape Town, 1994).

56 N. Alexander, interview with C. Soudien, (Cape Town), 9.6.1999.

57 V. Kolbe, interview with C. Soudien, (Cape Town), 25.5.1999.

58 Ibid.

59 Tabisher, interview.

60 Ibid.

61 Ibid.

62 E. Salo, personal communication, 25.9.1998.

TRIPTYCH

1 P.E. Clarke, 'Peertjiesdorp carpenter', *Plain Furniture,* (Plumstead, 1991), 46.

2 Anonymous, 'Eager students at art classes for coloureds', *Cape Argus,* 8.10.1947.

3 S.V. Petersen, *Die enkeling,* (Cape Town, 1944), *Die stil kind,* (Cape Town, 1948), *As die son ondergaan,* (Cape Town, 1945).

4 L. Maurice, letter to Solly Disner, 2.12.1959.

5 L. Maurice, letter to Peter Clarke, 24.3.1953.

6 Ibid.

7 O.Kokoschka, taped 'Introduction', (Villeneuve, Switzerland), August 1959.

8 F.L. Alexander, *Art in South Africa since 1900,* (Cape Town, 1962), 23.

9 P. Hardy, *The Hand is the Tool of the Soul,* (Cape Town, 1992), 3.

10 R.E. Shikes, *The Indignant Eye,* (Boston, 1969), 374.

11 E.Kai, 'Meet six of the Cape', *Cape Times,* 4.6.1966.

12 Cited in L. Herzberg, 'Once a Labourer always an Artist', *Personality,* 21.5.1970.

13 Clarke, 'Family enlargements', *Plain Furniture,* 45.

14 See L. Davis, 'Peter Clarke's Work' (BAFA III essay, University of Cape Town, 1993).

15 P.E. Clarke, 'Eleven o'clock the Wagons the Shore: a story', *The New African,* October 1962.

16 Ibid.

17 Clarke, 'The boat from the minesweeper', *Plain Furniture,* 12.

18 P.E. Clarke, interview with Nic Maritz and Elza Miles, (Kalk Bay), 28.8.1998.

19 P.E. Clarke, 'We Shall Appear Like Strolling Players', (unpublished manuscript, 1985).

20 Clarke, interview with Nic Maritz and Elza Miles.

21 Clarke, 'D.J. Ancestor', *Plain Furniture,* 32.

22 D.C. Driskell, *Soul Motion III – Peter Clarke South African Artist-Poet,* (Nashville, 1973).

23 Cited in Hardy, 7.

24 H. Wyngaard, 'Die skaapwagter en die kunstenaar', *De Kat,* July 1998, 64.

25 W. Haftmann, *Painting in the Twentieth Century,* Volume I, (London, 1968), 28.

26 Ibid.

27 Clarke, 'Making discoveries', *Plain Furniture,* 15.

28 *Cape Times,* 11.7.1958.

29 Clarke, 'Shepherd at the Crossroads'.

30 Clarke, 'We shall appear like strolling players'.

31 D. Lautenbach, 'A truly haunting triptych', *Cape Argus,* 26.11.1985.

32 Clarke, *Plain Furniture,* 78.

33 P.E. Clarke, interview with Nic Maritz, (Hillside, Fish Hoek), 29.5.1992.

34 Ibid.

35 Ibid.

36 Clarke, 'We shall sppear like strolling players'.

37 Ibid.

'BEING COLOURED IS A STATE OF MIND' OR THE COMPLEXITIES OF IDENTITY, SELFHOOD, AND FREEDOM IN THE WRITING OF JAMES MATTHEWS

1 J. Matthews, *Poisoned Wells and Other Delights,* (Athlone, 1990), 1.

2 H. Wyngaard, 'Struggle-skrywers het nog iets te sê', *De Kat,* February 1998, 67.

3 Cited in M. Van Wyk Smith, *Grounds of Contest,* (Cape Town, 1990), 101.

4 J. Alvarez-Pereyre, *The Black Poetry of Commitment in South Africa,* (London, 1984), 208.

5 U. Barnett, *A Vision of Order,* (Cape Town, 1983), 70.

6 P. Shava, *A People's Voice,* (London, 1989), 91.

7 J. Watts, *Black Writers from South Africa,* (London, 1989).

8 See R. Attridge and R. Jolly (eds), *Writing South Africa,* (Cambridge, 1998) and M. Chapman, *Southern African Literatures,* (New York, 1996).

9 Watts, 2.

10 Shava, 3.

11 J. Matthews, 'Being Coloured is a State of Mind', *Cape Argus,* 16.2.1998, 8.

12 J. Matthews, *The Party is Over,* (Cape Town, 1997), 62.

13 R. Rive (ed.), *Quartet: New Voices from South Africa,* (New York, 1963).

14 See H. Willemse, 'James Matthews beur steeds stroom op', *Die Suid-Afrikaan,* 36 (January 1992), 36.

15 J. Matthews and G. Thomas, *Cry Rage!* (Johannesburg, 1973); J. Matthews (ed.), *Black Voices Shout!,* (Athlone, 1974); J. Matthews, *Pass Me a Meatball, Jones,* (Athlone, 1977); J. Matthews, *no time for dreams,* (Athlone, 1981); J. Matthews, *Poisoned Wells and Other Delights,* (Athlone, 1990).

16 G. Hallett and J. Matthews, *Images,* (Athlone, 1979).

17 M. Wessels, 'Matthews se put: vergiftiging of vergiffenis?', *Vrye Weekblad*, Book Supplement, (Summer 1990), 16.

18 J. Matthews, *The Park and Other Stories,* (Athlone, 1974).

19 J. Matthews, *The Park and Other Stories,* (Johannesburg, 1983).

20 See Anon., 'Short and good, but seldom sweet', *Frontline*, (April 1984), 14–15.

21 Matthews, *The Park and Other Stories*, (1983), 211.

22 Ibid., 164.

23 Ibid., 57.

24 Ibid., 147.

25 Ibid., 59.

26 Ibid.

27 Matthews and Thomas, 1.

28 R. Rive 'On being a Black Writer in South Africa', E. Mphahlele and T. Couzens (eds), *The Voice of the Black Writer in South Africa,* (Johannesburg, 1980), 21.

29 Matthews, *The Party is Over*, 62.

30 Matthews, *no time for dreams*, 1.

31 Ibid., 14.

32 Matthews, *The Park and Other Stories,* (1983), 177–188.

33 Rive, 22.

34 Ibid., 25.

35 Matthews, *Black Voices Shout!,* 64.

36 Shava, 86

37 Alvarez-Pereyre, 207–208.

38 Cited in Barnett, 69.

39 Matthews and Thomas, 70.

40 Ibid., 1.

41 Matthews, *no time for dreams*, 22.

42 Ibid., 23.

43 Ibid.

44 Matthews and Thomas, 31.

45 Ibid., 4.

46 Ibid., 69.

47 Ibid., 48.

48 Matthews, *The Park and Other Stories*, (1983), 1.

49 Ibid., 4.

50 Ibid., 45.

51 Matthews, *The Party is Over*, 62.

52 Ibid., 49.

53 Ibid.

54 Ibid., 45.

55 Ibid., 49.

56 Ibid., 43.

57 Ibid., 104.

58 Matthews, 'Being Coloured is a State of Mind'.

59 Matthews, *no time for dreams*, 62.

Bibliography

COMPILED BY ANDREW MARTIN
AND HEIN WILLEMSE

PETER E. CLARKE

Awards
Drum International Short-story Award, 1955.
C. P. Hoogenhout Book-illustration Award for *Snoet-alleen* (Freda Linde), 1965.
Accademico Onorario (Accademia Florentina delle Arti del Disegno, Florence, Italy), 1965.
Honorary Fellow in Writing (University of Iowa, Iowa City, USA), 1975.
Diploma of Merit, Literature (Universita delle Arti, Salso Maggiore Terme Pr. Italy), 1982.
Book-illustration Award for *A Message in the Wind* (Chris van Wyk), 1982.
Diploma of Merit, Art (Universita delle Arti, Salso Maggiore Terme Pr. Italy), 1982.
Honorary Doctor of Literature (World Academy of Arts & Culture, Taipei, Taiwan), 1984.
Honorary life member (Museum of African American Art, Los Angeles, California, USA), 1984.

Major one man exhibitions
Golden City Post exhibition, Cape Town, 1957.
Mbari Cultural Centre, Ibadan, Nigeria, 1965.
Chem-Chemi Cultural Centre, Nairobi, Kenya, 1965.
Edrich Gallery, Stellenbosch, 1970.
Shell Harbour Art Centre, Shell Harbour, NSW, Australia, 1973.
Fisk University, Nashville, Tennessee, USA, 1973–1974.
Kuumba workshop, Southside, Chicago, USA, 1976.
'Our world is a ghetto', South African Association of Arts, Cape Town, 1977.
Community Arts Project, Mowbray, Cape Town, 1977.
Public Library, Grassy Park, Cape Town, 1977–1978.
'Illusions & Other Realities', Atlantic Art Gallery, Cape Town, 1981.
Sandvika Kino Vestibyle, Sandvika, Norway, 1978–1979.
Jerusalem Artists House, Jerusalem, Israel, 1984.
'The hand is the tool of the soul' (Retrospective exhibition), Natale Labia Museum, Muizenberg, Cape Town, 1992.
Drawings of Tesselaarsdal, Caledon Museum, 1996.
'Vital Expressions', Association of Arts Gallery, Bellville, 1998.
'Vital Expressions', Technikon Natal Art Gallery, Durban, 1999.
'A Personal View', Lipschitz Gallery, Cape Town, 1999.
Bertolt Brecht House, Berlin, Germany, 2000

Major international group exhibitions
South African Graphic Art, Yugoslavia, 1960.
South African Graphic Art, Galerie Schoninger, Munich, Germany, 1961.
South African Graphic Art, Sao Paulo, 1961.
5th International Graphic Art Biennale, Ljubljana, Yugoslavia, 1963.
International Graphic Art, Albertine Museum, Vienna, Austria, 1963.
XXXII Biennale, Venice, Italy, 1964.
6th International Graphic Art Biennale, Ljubljana, Yugoslavia, 1965.
1st Exhibition of International Graphics, Palazzo Strozzo, Florence, Italy, 1968.
2nd Exhibition of International Graphics, Palazzo Strozzo, Florence, Italy, 1969.
South African Graphics Touring, Western Europe, 1971.
Benefit exhibition of Graphics, Pratt Graphics Center, New York, USA, 1973.
Tercera Bienniale Internacional del Grabado de Buenos Aires, Argentine, 1972.
Norway Series of Graphic Art, Atelier Nord, Oslo, Norway, 1979–1982.
Botswana Art Festival, Gaborone, Botswana, 1982.
International Exhibition of Prints, Kanagawa, Japan, 1983–1984.
Norwegian International Print Bienniale, Frederikstad, Norway, 1984.
10 Internationale Triennale für Originale Grafik, Grenchen, Switzerland, 1985.
Botschaften aus Südafrika, Museum für Völkerkunde, Frankfurt am Main, West Germany, 1986.
'Freedom Now', Namibian independence exhibition, Windhoek, Namibia, 1990.
'Zeitzeichen – Art from Contemporary Africa', Museum für Völkerkunde, Frankfurt am Main, Germany, 1992.
St Virgil Bildungshaus, Salzburg, Austria, 1992.
3rd Triennale World Exhibition of Prints, Auvergne, France, 1994.
Troisiéme Triennale Mondiale Déstampes – Chamalieres, France 1994.
18th International Exhibition of Prints, Kanagawa, Japan, 1995.

Major representation in private and public collections
Arnold Becher Museum, Steinkopf, South Africa.
Baerum Kommune, Sandvika, Norway.
Caledon Muncipal Museum, Caledon, South Africa.
Cape Town City Library, Cape Town, South Africa.
Community Arts Project, Cape Town, South Africa.
Dennis W. Koles, Kiama, NSW, Australia.
District Six Museum, Cape Town, South Africa.
Durban Art Museum, Durban, South Africa.
Fisk University, Nashville, Tennessee, USA.
Fuba Collection, Johannesburg, South Africa.
Hymie and Jean Berndt, Kenilworth, South Africa.
Johnson Publishing Company, Chicago, Ill., USA.
King George VI Art Gallery, Port Elizabeth, South Africa.
Kunsthalle der Stadt, Bielefeld, Germany.
Library of Congress, Washington DC, USA.
Livingstone High School, Claremont, Cape Town, South Africa.
Municipal Collection, Fish Hoek, South Africa.
Municipal Museum, Simon's Town, South Africa.
Museum of Contemporary Art, Skopje, Yugoslavia.

Nasou Publishing Company, Cape Town, South Africa.
National Art Gallery, Gaborone, Botswana.
Peninsula Technikon, Bellville, South Africa.
Pretoria Art Museum, Pretoria, South Africa.
SA Fine Worsted Co. Factory, Cape Town, South Africa.
Sasol Collection, Stellenbosch, South Africa.
South African National Gallery, Cape Town, South Africa.
Stichting Afrika Museum, Berg en Dal, The Netherlands.
University of Fort Hare, Alice, South Africa.
University of the North-West, Mmabatho, South Africa.
University of Stellenbosch, Stellenbosch, South Africa.
University of the Western Cape, Bellville, South Africa.
University of Zululand, KwaDlangezwa, South Africa.
William Humphreys Art Gallery, Kimberley, South Africa.

Exhibition catalogues

1985. *10th International Triennial of Original Graphic Prints*, Grenchen: Kunstgesellschaft.

1987. *Botschaften aus Südafrika: Kunst und Künstlerische Produktion Schwarzer Künstler*, Frankfurt am Main; Museum für Völkerkunde.

1987. *Schwarze Kunst: John Muafangejo und Peter Clarke,* Bonn: Das Institut für Auslandbeziehungen.

1988. *Contemporary Fine Art on Ceramic,* Cape Town: SA Red Cross Society.

1990. *16th International Independent Exhibition of Prints in Kanagawa 90*, Kanagawa: Committee of International Independent Exhibition of Prints.

1990. *Intergrafik 90: 9 Internationale Triennale Engagierter Grafik in der Deutschen Demokratischen Republik*, Berlin: Verband Bildender Künstler der DDR.

Cover designs and book and magazine illustrations

Agthe, J. and Mundt, C. 1991. *Signs of the time*, Frankfurt am Main: Museum für Völkerkunde.

Clarke, P. 1987. *Peter Clarke – South African Artist*, Information Brochure.

Clarke, P. 1991. *Plain Furniture,* Plumstead: Snailpress.

Contrast 66. 1988. Cape Town: SA literary journal.

Cook, P.A.W. 1958. *Kwane: An African Saga*, Cape Town: Maskew Miller.

Gabral, A. 1980. *Unity and Struggle*, London: Heinemann.

Gravett, E. 1991. *Ten Poems*, Plumstead: Snailpress.

Jabavu, D.D.T. 1958. *Izidungulwana*, Cape Town: Maskew Miller.

Karibuni Afrika. 1989. *Karibuni Afrika*, Frankfurt am Main: Dritte Welt Haus.

La Guma, A.1962. *A Walk in the Night*, Ibadan: Mbari Publications.

Lewis, G. 1987. *Between the Wire and the Wall,* Cape Town: David Philip.

Linde, F. 1964. *Snoet-alleen*, Cape Town: John Malherbe.

Linde, F. 1964. *Ken jy die kierangbos?*, Cape Town: John Malherbe.

Mbiti, J. 1963. in *Der Wanderer von Land zu Land* 5, Zürich: Schwizerischen Evangelischen Missionrat.

Matthews. J. 1962. *Azikwelwa*, Malmö-Lund: Bo Cavefors Bokförlag.

Matthews, J. 1983. *The Park and Other Stories*, Johannesburg: Ravan Press.

Mphahlele, E. 1961. *The Living and The Dead and Other Stories*, Ibadan: Ministry of Education.

Mzamane, M. 1980. *Mzala: The Stories of Mbulelo Mzamane,* Johannesburg: Ravan.

Paton, A. 1960. *Aber das Wort sagte Ich nicht*, Gutersloh: I.M. Bertelsmann Lesring.

Research in African Literatures 9 (1–3). 1978. Austin: University of Texas Press.

Van Wyk, C. 1982. *A Message in the Wind*, Cape Town: Maskew Miller.

Short stories and other prose publications

1954. Muscle man's girl, in: *Drum*, Dec: 52–54.

1955. The departure, in: *Drum,* Apr: 50–56.

1956. Willy-Boy! The delinquent, in: *Drum*, Apr: 50–55.

1960. [Peter Kumalo (pseud.)], Death in the sun, in: Hughes, Langston (select.), *An African Treasury: Articles, Essays, Stories, Poems by Black Africans*, New York: Crown, 118–120.

1962. Eleven o'clock: the wagons, the shore: a story, in: *The New African*, 1(10): 8–9.

1963. In a far country – travel notes, in: *The New African*, 2(7): 132–133.

1964. Winter shepherding, in: *Contrast*, 3(2): 40–48.

1970. Figures and settings, in: *Contrast*, 6(4): 81–90.

1972. Pastorale, in: *Izwi*, 1(6): 28–33.

1974. Pastorale, in: Gray, Stephen (ed.), *On the Edge of the World: Southern African Stories of the Seventies*, Johannesburg: Ad. Donker, 34–38.

1980. Some very strange souls, in: *The Voice*, Jun 18–24: 11.

1985. Thoughts in the dark, in: *Stet*, 3(2): 22–25.

1988. A season of changes, in: Engle, Paul and Nieh, Hauling (eds), *The World comes to Iowa*, (Iowa City), 150–152.

1988. Reflections on hunger, in: *New Observations*, 56: 4–5.

1991. *Plain Furniture*, Plumstead: Snailpress.

1991. Missionaire au vin, in: Ladan, E and Doyle, J. (eds), *Artists' Palate: A Collection of Artists' Recipes,* Wynberg: Ladan & Doyle, 104–105.

1995. The changing of the season, in: Oliphant, Andries Walter (ed.), *The Change of Seasons and Other Stories*, Johannesburg: National Arts Coalition, Bartel Arts Trust and Cosaw Publishing, 175–188.

Poetry

1960. [Peter Kumalo (pseud.)], Play song, in: Hughes, Langston (select.), *An African Treasury: Articles, Essays, Stories, Poems by Black Africans*, New York: Crown, 188.

1973. The looking glass, in: *Contrast, 32*, 8(4): 21–29.

1971/72. Crash victim, Beneath her blouse, in: *Poetry South*, Summer: [6], [19].

1972. Winter journey, in: *South African Outlook*, 102: 153.

1973. Blind boy, Dam in the veld, in: *South African Outlook*, 103: 136.

1973. Part conscience, in: *New Nation*, 6(10): 11.

1973. Railway bridge; Steenberg, in: *Contrast, 32*, 8(4): 29–30.

1973. Young shepherd bathing his feet; Winter journey; The dam in the veld; Spring funeral; Woltemade; The well; Evening cycle ride; Blind boy; Public elevator; Pick-pocket; Party conscience; Waiting for the Silver Town bus; Monday-morning blues; The snake in the bedroom; Still-life with artificial eye; Population explosion; Small stoep; country dorp: two views; Shepherd at the crossroads; Railway foreman; The showpiece; Terror stalks the townships; Going to Siberia; Young man on a dirt truck; Woman with a wig; Greenshade; Heatwave; Objet d'art; Approaching autumn; Summer; Caledon country; Dead tree: wind-blown; Beneath her blouse, in: Driskell, David C, (ed.), *Peter Clarke: South African Artist-Poet*, Nashville, Tenn.: Division of Cultural Research, The Department of Art, Fisk University, 19–36.

1976. At Effigy Mounds National Monument, Iowa, in: *Contrast 40*, 10(4): 45–46.

1976. For Karl, a farm labourer; Questioning eyes; Buying FLs in a small white town, in: *Black World*, Mar: 48.

1976. Distant thunder; The notice on the wall, in: *Mundus Artium*, 9(2): 48, 49.

1976. Two proverbs, in: *Ba Shiru*, 7(2): 55.

1977. The untouchable, in: *Ba Shiru*, 8(1): 30.

1977. Distant thunder; The notice on the wall, in: *The Gar*, 31(31): 21.

1978. A winter night, in: *Ba Shiru*, 9(1/2): 72.

1982. In air, in: Couzens, Tim and Patel, Essop, (eds), *The Return of the Amasi Bird: Black South African Poetry 1891–1981*, Johannesburg: Ravan Press, 274.

1986. Bread and cake, in: *Ekapa*, 1: 2.

1986. Ancient graves in the Namib; Hyena; for the mother of a child shot dead during the riots; Bloodhounds; David and Goliath; Phulaphulani; Poem vir Don B: small town pianist; Boodskap vir Boetatjie, in: Clarke, Peter; Hollmann, Rudien; Matthews, James; Willemse, Hein [comp.], *Vakalisa Poetry 2*, Landsdowne: Vakalisa, 2–11.

1986. Play song, in: Turner, Dulcie May (collect.), *Chosen for you: A Book of Poems for South African Children*, Pretoria: Van Schaik, 89.

1987. Late afternoon; Botswana, in: *Contrast 63*, 16(3): 22.

1988. 1; Bread and cake; Hard times; 4; About Hansel and Gretel; In Oslo one winter's night; 7; Visiting day at the orphanage; Corner shop; Ein Kerem: Israel; 10; and 11 – (Reflections on hunger), in: *New Observations*, (56): 4–5.

1989. What about laughter?, in: Coetzee, Ampie and Willemse, Hein (eds), *iQabane Labantu: Poetry in the Emergency*, Bramley: Taurus, 38.

1991 Walking between reeds; Phulaphulani; Bloodhounds, in: *Kunapipi*, 13(1/2): 110–111, 112–113, 114.

1991. To learn, in: *Slug newsletter*, 15(13): 17.

1991. The letter to Halfon, in: Villani, J. and Leslie, N. (eds), *The Epistolary Form and the Letter as Artefact,* Youngstown, 55.

1992. Being elderly; The lady in the fish & chips shop, in: *Slug newsletter,* 16: 16.

1993. Dining table; Registering for school, 1936, in: Malan, Robin (comp.), *New Outridings*, Cape Town: Oxford University Press, 44–45, 54.

1993. Fantasia: A poem inspired by a painting by Eris Silke, in: *Slug newsletter*, 23: 1

1993. Kakkapiella: the caterpillar, in: *Slug newsletter*, 25: 4.

1993. Bread and words, in: *The Cape Librarian*, 37(9): 37.

1989. The departure, in: Chapman, Michael, (ed.), *The Drum Decade: Stories from the 1950s*, Pietermaritzburg: University of Natal Press, 79–86.

1996. Wine from Carmel; Corner shop; Ein Kerem; Showing me her pictures: a kibbutz child, in: *Die Plain Ding*, 17 Dec: 7, 11.

1996. Registering for school, 1936; Oupa's chair; Bookshelf; Small bench; Beachcombing; Young shepherd bathing his feet, in: Malan, Robin (comp.), *My African World: Poems for Younger Readers*, Cape Town: David Philip, 4, 14, 15, 15, 65, 83.

Criticism and interviews

Anon. 1954. Drum authors, *Drum,* Dec: 55.

Anon. 1955. Contest winner, *Drum,* Apr: 55.

Anon. 1957. Peter Clarke's exhibition, *New Age,* 14 Feb: 2.

Anon. 1958. Peter Clarke's exhibition, *New Age,* 13 Feb: 3.

Anon. 1958. Coloured artists hold Jo'burg exhibition, *New Age,* 10 Feb: 8.

Anon. 1961. Peter Clarke: Coloured Artist, *South African Panorama*, Nov: 6–7.

Anon. 1976. Iowa Art – in Triplicate, *Des Moines Sunday Register*, 18 Jan: 10–11.

Anon. 1978. Peter Clarke on exploration trip, *The Voice*, 23 Sept: 13.

Anon. 1991. *Plain Furniture* launch, *Slug newsletter,* (11), (reprinted from *False Bay Echo*).

Anon. 1992. Focus on Peter Clarke, *New Nation*, 20–26 Nov: 21.

Bennun, Mervyn.1957. Art must help solve life's problems say coloured artist, *New Age*, 7 Mar: 6.

Best, Cynthia.1993. Peter Clarke: Godfather of community art, *ADA Magazine,* 35.

Cassiere, Diane. 1997. Forgotten folk of Simon's Town, *Cape Times*, 3 Nov: 11.

Davis, L.1993. Peter Clarke's Work, BA Fine Arts III Essay, Cape Town: University of Cape Town.

De Roubaix, Elizabeth. 1991. Review, *The Cape Librarian* 36 (9): 32.

Dikeni, Sandile. 1998. Who's laughing now: Where's comedy at in SA?, *Top of the Times* [suppl. to the *Cape Times*], 18 Dec: 1, 3.

Driskell, David C. ed., 1973. *Peter Clarke: South African Artist-Poet*, Nashville, Tenn.: Division of Cultural Research, The Department of Art, Fisk University.

Green, Molly. 1991. Clarke at best when home, *Cape Times*, 20 Jun: 8.

Green, Molly. 1991. Clarke at best when home, *Slug newsletter* (11): 9.

Klima, Vladimir. 1971. Prose writing and society in South Africa, in: Klima, Vladimir, (ed.), *South African Prose Writing in English (Dissertationes Orientales: 32),* Prague: Oriental Institute, 149–160.

Shapiro, Leonard. 1999. Salute to a man of words and images: Insight into the work of poet and visual artist Peter Clarke, *Top of the Times* [suppl. to the *Cape Times*], 4 Jun: 3.

Telkins, S.1976. International acclaim for South Africa's Clarke, *Topic* 101: 21–23.

Tonight reporter.1999. Book art exhibition, *Cape Times,* 20 Aug: 2.

Wyngaard, Heindrich. 1998. Die skaapwagter en die kunstenaar, *De Kat,* Jul: 64–66.

Wyngaard, Heindrich. 1999. Ontdekkings by die herlees van dagboekaantekeninge, *Die Burger*, 18 May: 7.

JAMES MATTHEWS

Awards

Freedom of the City of Lehrte, West Germany, 1984.

Freedom of the City of Nürnberg, West Germany, 1984.

Honorary Fellow in Writing (University of Iowa, Iowa City, USA), 1984.

Short stories and other prose publications

1953. The years behind, in: *Weekend magazine* [suppl. to *Cape Times*], 25 Dec, 8.

1953. The day that was different, in: *Weekend magazine* [suppl. to *Cape Times*], 15 Aug, 6.

1954. The champ! in: *Drum*, Jan: 32–34.

1954. Dead end! in: *Drum*, Sept: 34–37.

1954. [Matt, S. (pseud.)] Vengeance trail, in: *Hi-Note* [suppl. to *Zonk*], Nov: 13, 22, 28, 49.

1955. [Matt, S. (pseud.)] Island lovers, in: *Hi-Note* [suppl. to *Zonk*], Feb: 14–15, 46, 47.

1956. Willy-Boy! The downfall, in: *Drum*, Apr: 50–56.

1956. Penny for the guy, in: *Drum*, Nov: 46ff.

1957. Third class, in: *Weekend magazine* [suppl. to *Cape Times*], 2 Mar: 8.

1958. Azikwelwa!, in: *Africa South*, 3(1): 118–123.

1962. The park, in: *Presence Africaine*, 16(44): 95–105.

1962. [Pelle, Fritz-Crone (trans.)] *Azikwelwa*, Malmö-Lund: Bo Cavefors.

1963. Incident, in: *The New African*, 2(1): 16–17.

1963. The mistake, in: *The New African*, 2(5): 88–89.

1963. The party, in: *Transition*, 4(10): 9–12.

1963. Azikwelwa, The party; The park; Incident, in: Rive, Richard (ed.), *Quartet: New Voices from South Africa*, New York: Crown, 35–44, 147–161, 191–208.

1964, 1978. The park, in: Rive, Richard (comp. and ed.), *Modern African Prose: An Anthology*, London: Heinemann, 160–174.

1964, 1977. The second coming, in: Komey, Ellis Ayitey and Mphahlele, Ezekiel, (eds), *Modern African Stories*, London: Faber and Faber, 113–123.

1970. The second coming, in: *Lotus: Afro-Asian Writings*, 2(6): 36–46.

1971. The park, in: Moore, Jane Ann (ed.), *Cry Sorrow, Cry Joy! Selections from Contemporary African Writers*, New York: Friendship Press, 170–185.

[1973?] Azikwelwa; No exit, in: *Blac*, 1(1): 2–4, 2–3.

1973. The 11.41 to Simonstown, in: *Drum*, 8: 43–45.

1974. The 11.41 to Simonstown, in: Gray, Stephen (ed.), *On the Edge of the World: Southern African Stories of the Seventies*, Johannesburg: Ad. Donker, 149–154.

1974. *The Park and Other Stories*, Athlone: Blac.

1975. Whites only, in: *Fireweed*, (3), 55–60.

1977, 1979. [Rutkies, Annaliese (trans.)] *So ist das nun mal Baby! Der Alltag der Schwarzen in Südafrika: Erzählungen*, Wuppertal: Hammer.

1978. The park, in: Marquard, Jean, (ed.), *A Century of South African Short Stories*, Johannesburg: Ad Donker, 317–326.

1980. No Exit, in: *Geneva-Africa*, 18(2): 96–99.

[1980]. A case of guilt, in: *Wietie* 1:36–37, 39, 41.

1980, Azikwelwa, in: Mutloatse, Mothobi (ed.), *Forced Landing: Africa South – Contemporary Writings*, Johannesburg: Ravan, 35–40.

1980, 1981. Azikwelwa, in: Mutloatse, Mothobi (ed.), *Africa South Contemporary Writings*, London: Heinemann.

1980, 1983. The 11.41 to Simonstown, in: Gray, Stephen (ed.), *Modern South African Stories: Revised and Expanded Edition of On the Edge of the World.* Johannesburg: Ad. Donker, 149, 154.

1981. The park, in: Gardner, John, (ed.), *Between the Thunder and the Sun: An Anthology of Short Stories,* Cape Town: OUP, 30–40.

1983. Azikwelwa, in: Davis, Geoffrey and Senior, Michael, (eds) *South Africa – The Privileged and the Dispossessed,* Paderborn: Ferdinand Schoningh, 94–100.

1983. *The Park and Other Stories,* Johannesburg: Ravan.

1985. Up the Mississipi, in: *Stet,* 3(2): 10–11.

1985. [Wolter, Jürgen (trans.)] *Schattentage,* Dortmund: Weltkreis.

1986. [Utz, Iise (trans.)] *Die Träume des David Patterson,* Dortmund: Weltkreis.

1986. 11.41 naar Simonstown, in: Dorsman, Robert and February, Vernie (eds), *Een kwestie van identiteit: Verhalen van zwarte Zuidafrikaanse schrijvers,* Amsterdam: SUA, 92–100.

1986. The park, in: Mzamane, Mbulelo Vizikhungo, (ed.), *Hungry Flames and Other Black South African Short Stories,* Harlow: Longman, 35–44.

1988. The visit, in: Davis, Geoffrey V; Manaka, Matsemela and Jansen, Jurgen, (eds), Towards liberation: culture and resistance in South Africa, *Matatu,* 3/4(2): 65–73.

1989. Dead end!, in: Chapman, Michael, (ed.), *The Drum Decade: Stories from the 1950s,* Pietermaritzburg: University of Natal Press, 60–65.

1989. The day that was different, in: *Akal,* 1(2): 34–35.

1989. The park, in: Ferguson, Ian; King, Melissa; Ryan, Pamela; Scherzinger, Karen and Williams, Michael, (eds), *Cross-Currents: An Anthology of Short Stories,* Pretoria: Acacia, 307–316.

1989. *The Park and Other Stories,* Harlow: Longman.

1990. No regrets, in: *Tribute,* Nov: 118–121.

1990. A tattoo, in: *Akal,* 2(2): 13–15.

1991. Tent town, in: *Tribute,* Oct: 126–128,130.

1991. 11.41 to Simonstown, in: Turner, Anne, (ed.), *The Best of South African Short Stories: Over Seventy Illustrated Stories of Our Land and its People,* Cape Town: The Readers Digest Association South Africa, 279–282.

1992. Taxi to town, in: *Staffrider,* 10(3): 43–47.

1993. The park, in: Trump, Martin and Marquard, Jean, (eds), *A Century of South African Short Stories,* Parklands: Ad Donker, 167–176.

1993. The park, in: Mosieleng, Percy and Mhambi, Temba, (eds), *Contending Voices in South African Fiction,* Johannesburg: Lexicon, 72–82.

1994. The park, in: Zander, Horst, (comp.), *Contemporary South African Short Stories,* Stuttgart: Reclam, 73–94.

1995. To town, in: *Tribute,* Sept: 136–138.

1995. The park, in: Adams, Anthony and Durham, Ken, (eds), *Writing from South Africa (Figures in a Landscape),* Cambridge: Cambridge University Press, 49–58.

1995. Credit card Christmas gifts, in: *Tribute,* Dec: 136–139.

1996. That was the day, in: *Tribute,* May: 136–138.

1997. *The Party is Over,* Cape Town: Kwela Books.

1997. The party is over, in: *Tribute,* Jun: 104–105,107.

1997. The passing of Sarah, in: *Tribute,* Sept, 104–105, 107.

1998. Suffer little children, in: *Tribute,* Feb: 107–109.

1999. The piano, in: Oliphant, Andries Walter (ed.), *At the Rendezvous of Victory and Other Stories,* Cape Town: Kwela Books, 147–151.

Poetry

1970. Alienation, in: *Cape Times,* 8 Aug: 29.

1972. (with Thomas, Gladys), *Cry Rage!,* Johannesburg: Spro-cas.

1973. Untitled, in: *Reality,* 5(2): 9–10, 12.

1973. Rage Aigue Comme Unelane..., in: *L'Afrique litteraire et artistique,* 28: 15.

[1973?] confused whitey asks...; Black voices shout...; I weep for the fruit of my womb..., in: *Blac,* 1(1): 1, 5, 7. [1973?] Tribute to martyrs; soweto skies are aflame with anger...; we do not have dreams..., in: *Blac,* 1(3): I, 1, 2.

1974. *Black Voices Shout!,* Athlone: Blac.

1975. how do you...; women of dimbaza and ilinge...; living in our land is a political action..., in: *Fireweed,* (3):46–47, 50, 52–53..

1975. *Black Voices Shout!: An Anthology of Poetry,* Athlone: Blac; Austin, Texas: Troubadour.

1976. We do not have dreams, in: *Bandwagon,* Sept: 15.

1976. Tribute to martyrs, in: *Anti-Apartheid News,* Nov: 7.

1980. (with Thomas, Gladys) [Rutkies, Annaliese (trans.)], *Schrei deinen Zorn hinaus, Kind der Freiheit,* Erlangen: Ev. Luth. Mission.

1977. We Do Not Have Dreams ...; White man ...; Freedom's child ...; Suffer little children ...; Student protest; Liberal student crap!, Can the white man speak for me?, in: *The Gar* 31, Mar: 19, 22.

1977. Poem, in: *Cape Times,* 23 Mar, 10.

1977. Steve Biko, in: *Muslim News,* 23 Sept, 8.

1977. *Pass Me a Meatball, Jones,* Athlone: Blac.

1977, 1981. [Rutkies, Annaliese (trans.)] *Flügel kann man stutzen, Gedanken im Gefängnis,* Erlangen: Ev. Luth. Mission.

1978. At the first offer ...; I delighted ...; The day i was taken from my office was as ...; The voices of ..., in: *Staffrider,* 1(4): 8.

1978. Poems of Prison and Release, in: *The Gar* 32: 8–9, 12.

1979. Tribute to martyrs, in: *The Greenfield Review:* 2.

1979. Nina. *Staffrider,* 2(4): 29.

1979. (with Hallett, George) *Images,* Blac; Athlone.

1980. Trip to Botswana, in: *Staffrider,* 3(4): 20.

1980. Tribute to martyrs, in: *Geneva-Africa,* 18(2): 104.

1981. *no time for dreams,* Athlone: Blac.

1982. I share the pain of my black brother; The echoes of breaking; It is night, in: Plumpp, Sterling (ed.), *Somehow We Survive: An Anthology of South African Writing,* New York: Thunders Mouth Press, 40, 81, 94.

1982. Prison sequence; Trip to Botswana, in: Couzens, Tim and Patel, Essop (eds), *The Return of the Amasi Bird: Black South African Poetry 1891–1981,* Johannesburg: Ravan, 319–322, 365–366.

1983. Freedom's child, in: Davis, Geoffrey and Senior, Michael, (eds), *South Africa – The Privileged and the Dispossessed,* Paderborn: Ferdinand Schoningh, 143.

1984. The day I was taken from my office; At the first offer; Nina; They say, in: Gray, Stephen, (ed.), *Modern South African Poetry: Revised and Expanded Edition of A World of Their Own,* Johannesburg: Ad Donker, 147–148, 148, 148–149, 149.

1985. Freedom's Child, in: Leveson, Marcia and Paton, Jonathan (eds), *Voices of the Land: An Anthology of South African Poems,* Craighall: Ad Donker, 35.

1985. There are poets who parade, in: *Writers' Forum,* Jun: 9.

1986. Living in our land is a political action; They say, in: Chapman, Michael (ed.), *The Paperbook of South African English Poetry,* Craighall: Ad Donker, 162, 162.

1986. The face of my mother takes the shape; Trip to Botswana, in: Malan, Robin (comp.), *New Inscapes: A Collection of Verse,* Cape Town: Oxford University Press, 261, 261–262.

1986. it is said ...; The day I was taken from my office, in: Ndaba, Sisa (ed.), *One Day in June: Poetry and Prose from Troubled Times,* Johannesburg: Ad. Donker (Paper Books), 19, 52–53.

1986. Asvat, Farouk, *Exiles Within,* Johannesburg: Writers' Forum.

1986. They say, in: Chapman, Michael and Voss, Tony (eds), *Accents: An Anthology of Poetry from the English-speaking World,* Craighall: Ad Donker, 199.

1986. it is not beirut; i hear the sound of people; children of the new dawn; should i play the poet changing words; death wears a multi-coloured mask; zeguiner (sic) brother and sister; ode to parlour patriots; she would allow the censors to silence her words; time will dawn when we shall sing; of what use am I, in: Clarke, Peter, Hollmann, Rudien; Matthews, James and Willemse, Hein (comps), *Vakalisa Poetry 2,* Landsdowne: Vakalisa.

1988. [Ingrid Rein (trans.)] *Vergiftete Brunnen und andere freuden: Gedichte,* Cologne: Weltkreis.

1988. The face of my mother takes the shape; Trip to Botswana, in: Malan,

Robin (comp.), *Explorings: A Collection of Poems for the Young People of Southern Africa*, Cape Town: David Philip, 122, 152.

1988. The day I was taken, in: Oliphant, Andries Walter and Vladislavic, Ivan (eds), *Ten Years of Staffrider: 1978–1988*, Johannesburg: Ravan, 199–200.

1998. [Untitled]; Learning to laugh, in: *Tribute*, Jan: 93, 94.

1989. no time for dreams; Poisoned wells and other delights, in: *Nouvelles du Sud, Afrique Australe: Les Situations et Ses Representations en Litterature*, Silex: Cerpana, 12, 8–11.

1989. The day I was taken, in: *Illuminations*, (8): 13–14.

1989. am i a fly entwined; there will be many crosses planted in our land; your eyes are thundering stars demanding sanctuary; the agony of colour, in: Coetzee, Ampie and Willemse, Hein (eds), *iQabane labantu: Poetry in the Emergency*, Bramley: Taurus, 118–121.

[1990?]. All my life I have been ...; from the house of cripples ...; you shall find many corners ..., in: Johnstone, Abduraghiem (ed.), *Rhythms in the Flame*, Cape Town: COSAW, 13, 22, 25.

1990. it is said ..., in: Paton, Jonathan (ed.), *The Land and People of South Africa*, London: Harper Collins, 38.

1990. *Poisoned Wells and Other Delights*, Athlone: Blac.

1991. i shed myself of clothes ..., in: *New Observations*, (83): 21.

1992. it is said..., in: Gray, Stephen and Finn, Rosemary (eds), *Broken Strings: The Politics of Poetry in South Africa*, Cape Town: Maskew Miller Longman, 52–53.

1993. Living in our land is a political action, in: Ullyatt, A.G. (comp.), *The Lonely Art: An anthology of poems*, Pretoria: Academica, 15–16.

1994. Dedication: dedicated to Imam Abdullah Haron; Then there was that priest upon the hill..., in: [Centre for Development Analysis], *Remembrance of a Martyr: Imam Abdullah Haron*, Cape Town: Silk Road International, 49, 50.

1995. The face of my mother takes the shape, in: Malan, Robin (comp.), *Poetry Works 1: A Workbook Anthology for Students & Teachers*, Cape Town: David Philip, 69.

1996. I know fear, in: Hendry, J. O. (select.), *Rainbow Voices: An Anthology of Poetry*, Johannesburg: Hodder & Stoughton, 147.

1997. do I offer bouquets of reconciliation as I ..., in: *Tribute*, Jul: 108.

1997. The face of my mother takes the shape, in: Malan, Robin (comp.), *Worldscapes: A Collection of Verse*, Cape Town: Oxford University Press, 121.

1997. Steve Biko: The spirit lives on, in: *Cape Times*, 9 Sept: 4.

1998. Death of Dr. Moerat: a poet's reflection, in: *Cape Times,* 29 Jan: 11.

1998. has freedom's fruit turned into a bitter crop ..., in: *Tribute*, Jun: 111.

1998. [Untitled], in: *Tribute*, Mar: 110.

[1999]. last night ..., in: *Carapace*, (23): 16.

1999. When I think of a place called home ..., in: *Cape Times*, 22 Feb:18.

1999. Red, red rose; Bouquets; Freedom's fruit, in: Harpur, C. A. L. and Kirsten, L. R. (eds), *Mindscapes VI: South African Anthology of Poetry and Prose*, Glosderry: Mallard.

2000. *Flames and Flowers*, Cape Town: Kwagga.

Criticism, interviews and newspaper reports

Abrahams, Cecil A. n.d. The context of aesthetics in South African literature, n.d: n.p.

Abrahams, Cecil. 1983. A variety of literature: new books from black South Africa. *Canadian Journal of African Studies* 17 (1): 107–110.

Alvarez-Pereyre, Jacques. 1980. Huis-clos ou impasse? Quelques remarques sur "No Exit". *Geneva-Africa*, 18 (2): 106–108.

Alvarez-Pereyre, Jacques. 1983. Les guetteurs de laube: poesie et apartheid. *Canadian Journal of African Studies*, 14 (2): 353–354.

Alvarez-Pereyre, Jacques. 1984. [C. Wake (trans.)] *The Poetry of Commitment in South Africa*, London: Heinemann.

Amosu, Margaret. 1966. Review [Quartet], *Black Orpheus* (20): 63.

Anon. 1954. Drum authors, *Drum,* Jan.

Anon. 1972. Black protest poetry to be read, *Rand Daily Mail,* 8 Dec: 1.

Anon. 1972. Black emotions to set off racial sparks, *Pretoria News,* 12 Dec: 28.

Anon. 1972. Protest poems attack white Christians, *Cape Times,* 16 Dec: 4.

Anon. 1973. La creation poetique en Afrique du Sud, *L'Afrique Litteraire et Artistique* (28): 8–15.

Anon. 1973. A coloured cry of rage stifled, *The Star*, 10 Mar: 3.

Anon. 1976. Hundreds of black leaders gaoled under new security law, *Anti-Apartheid News*, (Nov): 6.

Anon. 1978. Easy to be wrong, *Weekend Argus*, 2 Sept: 8.

Anon. 1978. PEN writers harassed, *The Star*, 4 Sept: 2.

Anon. 1978. Jim Matthews cannot travel, *The Voice*, 9 Sept: 4.

Anon. 1980. Black images, *South*, Nov: 45.

Anon. 1984. Ein 'Kulturarbeiter' las Gedichte, *Braunschweiger Zeitung*, 25 Feb.

Anon. 1984. 'Schrei denien Zorn hinaus, Kind der Freiheit', *Wolfenbüttler Zeitung*, 25/26 Feb.

Anon. 1984. 'Nicht länger Flüsse der Frucht weinen, *Vaihinger Kreiszeitung*, 13 Mar.

Anon. 1984. Short and good, but seldom sweet, *Frontline*, Apr: 12–16.

Anon. 1984. Athlone poet sobs at German Book Fair, *Cape Herald*, 18 Oct: 1.

Anon. 1991. Local Writers Honoured, *The Cape Librarian*, 36 (1): 43–44.

Anon. 1996. The Face of my mother; They say, in: *College of Careers. A guide to studying 'New Inscapes'*, Cape Town: MJI Study Aids, 30–31,40–41.

Anon. 1997. They say, in: *Guidelines, 'Accents', KwaZulu-Natal English first language, grade 12 (standard 10)*, Bramley: Guidelines, 59–60.

Anon. 1997. They say; The face of my mother, in: *Guidelines. Poetry – Gauteng, English first language, standard 10, 1997: 'New Inscapes', Poetry Spectrum, The Wind at Dawn: A Study Guide.* Bramley: Guidelines, 70, 74.

Anon. 1998. Poet sues Mufamadi over seized works, *The Sunday Independent*, 9 Aug: 2.

A.R. 1975. You know this intimately, *Cape Herald*, 27 Sept: 41.

Balogun, F Odun. 1991. The structure of irony in African short stories, in: Balogun, F. Odun, (ed.), *African Literatures in the 20th Century* [A guide based on the *Encyclopedia of World Literature in the 20th century*], New York: Greenwood, 37–53.

B.R.: 1972. Heart of the black man, *Sunday Tribune*, 24 Dec: 14.

Cartey, Wilfred. 1969. Alienation and flight: apartheid, *Whispers from a Continent: The Literature of Contemporary Black Africa*. New York: Random House, 1969: 106–142.

Caulker, Elaine, 1974. Transcript of radio interview with J. Mattthews, M. Dues and O. Mtshali on their poetry which includes comments by N. Gordimer and J. Polley. Transcript includes readings of poems by S. Sepamla and W. Serote, BBC Arts and Africa, (10): 1–4.

Cornwell, Gareth. 1982. James Matthews "protest songs": the problem of evaluation, in: Chapman, Michael (ed.), *Soweto Poetry*, Johannesburg: McGraw-Hill, 184–190.

Chapman, Michael. 1984. The fiction-maker: the short story in literary education, AUETSA Conference papers; volume I. Johannesburg: Rand Afrikaans University, 41–63.

Chapman, Michael. 1989. More than telling a story: "Drum" and its significance in black South African writing, in: Chapman, Michael (ed.), *The Drum Decade: Stories from the 1950s*. Pietermaritzburg: University of Natal Press, 183–232.

[Court reporter]. 1986. Banned literature: SA author in court, *Cape Times*, 17 Jul: 3.

Davis, Geoffrey; Klink, Christel; Haas, Hildegard and Mathius, Andrea (eds), 1982. Interview with the South African writer Gladys Thomas, *Baobab: Schriften zur Afrikanischen Literatur und Politik*, (2): 76–91.

Davis, Geoffrey. 1983. James Matthews: "Azikwelwa", in: Davis, Geoffrey and Senior, Michael (eds), *South Africa: The Privileged and the Dispossessed: Interpretations and Suggestions for Teaching: Teachers' Book*. Paderborn, Germany: Schoningh, 311–324.

[De Klerk, Linda]. 1999. '*New Inscapes': Western Cape: English Second Language, Grade 12, 1999: A Study Aid (Guidelines Study Aids: The Blue Book Series).* Bramley: Guidelines Study Aids, 25–26.

De Klerk, W.A. 1973. The writer as politician, *New Nation*, Apr.

De Vries, Abraham H. An interview with Richard Rive, *Current Writing*, 1(1): 45–55.

Dikeni, Sandile, 1992. Drinking deep from the poet's poisoned wells ..., *Cape Times*, 7 Nov: 17. [Also published in *ADA Magazine*, 1993, 83.]

Dorsey, David. 1977. Review [*Black Voices Shout!*] *World Literature Today*, 51(2): 322–323.

Dunton, Chris. "Wheyting be dat?" The treatment of homosexuality in African literature, *Research in African Literatures* 20 (3), 422–448.

Edmunds, Marion. 1997. Poet sues the police, *Mail & Guardian*, 17–23 Jan: 8.

Egner, Hanno. Gleiche rechte und moglichkeiten nicht nur auf dem papier, sondern auch in der realität, *Südafrika/Namibia* (60), 2–7.

Egner, Hanno. 1995. *Genrewechsel: Zum Einfluss der Produktions–, Distributions– und Rezeptionsbedingungen auf die Schwarze Südafrikanische Literatur der apartheid-ara*, Frankfurt am Main: Lang.

Ehmeir, Walter. 1994. Writing in history: South African literature in English and the political change in the 1960s, Ph.D thesis, University of Vienna.

Fonkoua, Romuald-Blaise.1995. Poetique et politique = Poetry and Politics, *Notre Librairie* (122): 98–115.

Gardner, Colin, 1991. Negotiating poetry: a new poetry for a new South Africa, *Theoria* (77): 1–14.

Gordimer, Nadine. 1973. *The Black Interpreters: Notes on African Writing.* Johannesburg: Spro-cas/Ravan.

Gordimer, Nadine. 1976. Writers in South Africa: The New Black Poets, in: Smith, Rowland (ed.), *Exile and Tradition: Studies in African and Caribbean Literature,* London: Longman & Dalhousie University Press, 132–151.

Greig, Robert. 1984. Liberal fiction of the 60s has not worn well, *Cape Times,* 1 Jan: 8.

Gumede, Mervyn William T. 1997. Cry rage at the WaBenzis: an angry poet raises his pen, *The Sunday Independent,* 26 Oct: 19.

Gumede, Mervyn William T. 1998. The party finally begins for the enfant terrible of protest writers, *The Sunday Independent*, 22 Mar: 20.

Handley, Patricia. 1994. James David Matthews: South African short–story writer, novelist and poet, in: Benson, Eugene and Conolly, L.W. (eds), *Encyclopaedia of Post-colonial Literatures in English (2),* London: Routledge, 1002–1003.

Haresnape, Geoffrey. 1996. Literature and revolution: some samples of South African English poetry as a discourse leading towards revolution, unpublished paper, Third International Poetry Festival (Jerusalem).

Hotz, Pavel. 1974. Cultural Schizophrenia, *Contrast* 35, 9(3): 59–61.

Hove, Chenjerai. 1984. Review – Matthews, James: The Park and Other Stories, *The African Book Publishing Record,* 10(3): 156.

Isaacs, Sharkey. 1996. James Matthews: writes his way into international consciousness, *Cape Argus,* 4 Oct: 13.

Isermann, Gerhard and Meyer-Roscher, Walter, 1981. Besuch aus Südafrika in der EZ, *EZ-Information*, 38, 20 Sept, 9.

Johnson, Alex C. 1998. Review [*The Party is Over*], *The African Book Publishing Record*, 24: 282.

Knipp, Thomas. 1993. English-language poetry, *A History of Twentieth Century African Literatures,* Lincoln: University of Nebraska Press: 105–137.

Laurence, Patrick. 1972. Worn out with his own rage, *The Star,* 18 Dec: 26.

Laurence, Patrick. 1973. A cry is strangled, *The Star*, 19 Mar: 22

[*Learn and Teach*]. 1992. Angry young poet now an enraged old man, *The Star,* 18 Mar: 19.

Levy, Moira. 1986. Crying rage from Belgravia Road, *Weekly Mail*, 27 Feb: 18.

Ligny, Michel. 1965. "Modern African stories" [Review], *Presence Africaine* (56): 163–170.

Lindfors, Bernth. 1966. Post-war literature in English by African writers from South Africa: a study of the effects of environment upon literature, *Phylon* 27 (1): 50–62.

Lindfors, Bernth (ed.), 1976, 1985. *Contemporary Black South African Literature: A Symposium,* Washington DC: African Literature Association; Three Continents Press, 55–77.

Lindfors, Bernth. 1977. Popular Literature in English in Black South Africa, *Journal of Southern African Affairs*, 11(1): 121–129.

Lubinsky, R. 1988. Too narrow a view of race in South Africa, *Rand Daily Mail,* 20 Feb: 20.

Lursen, Neil. 1980. Bitter-sweet memories, *The Argus*, 30 Jan: 9.

Magasa, Amidu. 1978. Tribune libre: l'apartheid et l'hypocrisie de gauche en France, *Peuples Noirs Peuples Africains* (2): 183–187.

Manganyi, N Chabani. 1982. The censored imagination, in: Chapman, Michael (ed.), *Soweto Poetry*, Johannesburg: McGraw-Hill, 146–149.

Matthews, James. 1982. Is black poetry valid? [Unpublished paper presented at Symposium on Culture and Resistance, Gaborone.]

Matthews, James. 1982. Foreword to Essop Patel's *They Came at Dawn,* Chapman, Michael (ed.), *Soweto poetry*, Johannesburg: McGraw-Hill, 88.

Matthews, James. 1956. Jazz your way to heaven!, *Drum,* (Jun): 43–45.

Matthews, James. 1956. Dr Francis Herman Gow (Masterpiece in bronze), *Drum,* (Jul): 27.

Matthews, James. 1959. What price snobbery, *Drum,* May: 13.

Matthews, James. 1982. Introduction to "Cry Rage!", in: Chapman, Michael (ed.), *Soweto Poetry,* Johannesburg: McGraw-Hill, 98.

Matthews, James. 1984. [How I evaluate myself as a writer ...] in: Daymond, M.J., Jacobs, J.U., and Lenta, M. (eds) *Momentum: On recent South African writing*. Pietermaritzburg: University of Natal Press, 72–74.

Matthews, James. 1989. [Translation of letter sent to Jean Sevry, Director of Cerpana] Nouvelles du Sud (12), *Afrique Australe: Les Situations et Ses Representations en Litterature.* s.l.: Silex/Cerpana, 8.

Matthews, James. 1993. Germany after the Wall: A South African's despair and shame in Frankfurt, *Die Suid-Afrikaan* (44): 26.

Matthews, James. 1977. [Letter from James Matthews to Wayne Kamin, 20 Jan], *The Gar* 31, Mar: 19.

Matthews, James. 1996. Read the tired writers from the apartheid era and discover the merit in their work [Letter], *The Sunday Independent,* 21 Jul: 11.

Matthews, James. 1998. Being coloured is a state of mind: caught between two worlds, different identities evolve within the community, *Cape Argus,* 16 Feb: 8.

Matthews, James. 1998. A black voice shouts, [Interview by Charles Molele], *Tribute,* Feb: 60–63.

Matthews, James. 1998. Manenberg: where the living is hard, *Tribute,* May: 70–71.

Matthews, James. 1999. Shrieks of anguish rend our city, *Cape Argus* 9 Nov: 13.

McCormack, Richard. 1992. Political protest through the literary medium: the short stories of James Matthews as expressions of protest in the context of oppression of the individual within apartheid South Africa, BA Honours thesis, Rand Afrikaans University.

Meihuizen, Nicholas. 1993. Yeats, Revolution and South Africa, *Theoria,* 81 (2): 155–164.

Menge, Lin. 1972. Cry rage – black protest in poetry, *Rand Daily Mail,* 8 Dec: 23.

Molakeng, Saint. 1997. Book gives closer look at artists lives, *Sowetan,* 24 Dec: 12.

Mzamane, Mbulelo Vizikhungo. 1986. Introduction, in: Mzamane, Mbulelo Vizikhungo, (ed.), *Hungry Flames and Other Black South African Short Stories,* Harlow: Longman, ix–xxvi.

Nicol, Mike. 1999. Windprints, *Lifestyle* [suppl. to the *Sunday Times*], 31 Nov: 12–13.

Nkwanywa, Derrick. 1988. Gripping tales of the ghetto, *New Nation*, 21–27 Jan: 17.

Obe, Adobe. 1980. Books and a boycott, *The Guardian*, 15 Oct: 8.

Oelker, Petra. 1984. Mit Bildern gegen die Apartheid, *Hamburger Rundschau*, 26 Apr, 15.

Okurut, A. Omare. 1985. Azania Shall Be Free: A Profile of James Matthews, *ALA Bulletin*, 11 (3):19–20.

Pakendorf, Gunther. 1998. Eerste roman vir protesdigter, *Die Burger,* 21 Jan: 6.

Paton, Alan. 1963. Four splendid voices, in: Rive, Richard (ed.), *Quartet: New Voices from South Africa,* New York: Crown, 11–14.

Paton, Allan [sic]. 1993. Writing in Africa Today, *A Collection of Solomon T.*

Plaatje Memorial Lectures: 1981–1992, [Mmabatho]: Institute of African Studies, University of Bophuthatswana, 1993: 95–106.

Povey, John F. 1993. English-language fiction from South Africa, in: Owomoyela, Oyekan. *A History of Twentieth Century African Literatures,* Lincoln: University of Nebraska Press, 85–104.

Pretorius, William, 1978. [The ripples of change on the river of tradition], *Rapport*, 14 May: 18.

Rabkin, David, 1975. *Drum* Magazine 1951–1961, and the works of black South African writers associated with it, Ph.D thesis, University of Leeds.

Renault, Mary; Gordon, Gerald and Naudé, Adele, 1978. Clamp that jars, *Rand Daily Mail*, 11 Sept: 14.

Rothfuchs, Steve. 1997. Still raging after all these years, *Mail & Guardian*, 14–20 Nov: 43.

Sevry, Jean. 1985. 25 Questions sur la litterature de l'Afrique du Sud, *L'Afrique Litteraire et Artistique,* (75): 15–43.

Sheckels, Theodore F. 1996. *The Lion on the Freeway: A Thematic Introduction to Contemporary South African Literature in English,* New York: Peter Lang.

Schütt, Peter. 1984. Ich versuche, im Lande zu bleiben, *Deutsche Volkszeitung,* 22, 1 Jun, 12.

Stafford, Faith. 1979. Profile: James Matthews, *Index on Censorship,* 8 (6): 54–55.

Tetteh-Lartey, Alex. 1982. Transcript of radio interview at the "Symposium on Culture and Resistance in South Africa" in Gabarone. On culture and politics, BBC Arts and Africa, 450G: 1–5.

Trump, Martin. 1990. Part of the struggle: Black writing and the South African liberation movement, in: Trump, Martin (ed.), *Rendering Things Visible: Essays on South African Literary Culture,* Johannesburg: Ravan, 161–185.

Tucker, D.E. 1995. The face of my mother takes the shape, *"New Inscapes",* compiled by Robin Malan: Western Cape 1996, English second language, standard 10: a study guide, Bramley: Guidelines, 62–63.

Van Vuuren, Helize. 1990. South African prison poetry and Breyten Breytenbach, AUETSA 1990: Conference papers (I) : African and South African themes, [Stellenbosch: University of Stellenbosch].

Venter, Sahm. 1990. Free spirit, *Tribute,* Feb: 22–25.

Vivan, Itala. 1995. Black poets of South Africa: witnesses of suppressed and/or forgotten history, in: Thumboo, Edwin; Kandiah, Thiru (eds), *The Writer as Historical Witness: Studies in Commonwealth Literature.* Singapore: UniPress, 504–518.

Wessels, Mari. 1990. Matthews se put: vergifting of vergiffenis? *Vrye Weekblad,* 14 Dec: 16.

Willemse, Hein. 1991/1992. James Matthews beur steeds stroom-op, *Die Suid-Afrikaan,* 36: 36–38.

Williams, Merle A. 1997. Shelley and the Soweto poets: projects of resistance, visions of freedom, *English Studies in Africa,* 40 (2): 77–87.

Woodson, Dorothy C. 1988. in: Henige, David (ed.), *Drum: an index to 'Africa's leading magazine' 1951–1965,* Madison: University of Wisconsin-Madison.

Wyngaard, Heindrich. 1998. Struggle-skrywers hét nog iets te sê, *De Kat,* Feb: 66–68.

Index of Awards, Persons, Publications and Works of Art

Contributors

At school GEORGE HALLETT was interested in painting and photography. Richard Rive, his English teacher, showed his paintings and photographs to Peter Clarke. After perusing his work, Clarke expressed the view that Hallett was a better photographer than a painter. At the age of twenty he began a correspondence course in photography with City and Guilds of London. Like Rive and Clarke, James Matthews was also influential in Hallett's political and cultural development. Having no success at finding a job as a photographer, he left for Europe in 1970. Prior to his departure Matthews persuaded Hallett to photograph District Six before it was razed to the ground. In London he freelanced for *The Times* and designed book covers for Heinemann Publishers. He subsequently lived and exhibited in France and the Netherlands. His photographs were exhibited in the USA, Norway, Germany, Sweden and South Africa, among other countries. He returned to South Africa in 1995, the same year in which he received a Golden Eye Award from World Press Photo. He was also awarded the Hasselblad Award for Outstanding Contribution to Photography and the 1999 *Cape Times* Award for Excellence in Photo Journalism.

KAYZURAN JAFFER has lectured extensively on media and popular culture in South Africa. Her previous publications include articles on South African theatre and popular culture. She is particularly interested in representations of identities. Until recently she taught English Literature at the University of the Western Cape. At present she is the Deputy Head of Public Affairs at the same institution.

JIMI MATTHEWS is a graduate of the London Film School. He started his professional career as a stills photographer, and has exhibited in Cape Town, Johannesburg, London, Stockholm, Amsterdam, Copenhagen and Frankfurt. He has directed documentary films and designed book and record covers. His film documentaries have been shown at festivals in London, Berlin, Amsterdam, Tokyo, Perugia and San Paolo. As a TV News cameraman he covered most of the major conflicts in Africa over the last decade. He has also travelled extensively throughout Africa, Europe and Middle East. He was formerly the Head of Reuters Television for Southern Africa. Presently he is Head of News and Current Affairs at e.tv, an independent South African television station.

ELZA MILES studied Fine Arts at the University of Pretoria and obtained a Masters of Fine Arts degree in 1964. In 1983 she completed her D.Litt et Phil. degree on the art of Maggie Laubscher. She taught Art History at the Rand Afrikaans University, and simultaneously worked as a printmaker. Her publications include *Lifeline out of Africa: The art of Ernest Mancoba; Current of Africa: the art of Selby Mvusi* and *The world of Jean Welz.* Her book on Mancoba won the Old Mutual Literary Award in 1996. Currently she is a researcher at the Johannesburg Art Gallery.

CRAIN SOUDIEN was born in Johannesburg. He was educated at the Universities of Cape Town and South Africa and holds a Ph.D. from the State University of New York at Buffalo (USA). He is the co-editor of two books on District Six, Cape Town. His research interests include race, culture and identity, school and socialisation, youth, school effectiveness and urban history. Apart from his academic work, he is actively involved in a number of social and educational projects, including the District Six Museum, which he and colleagues established in 1989. He is an Associate Professor in the School of Education, University of Cape Town and teaches in the fields of Sociology and History of Education.

HEIN WILLEMSE holds a doctorate in Literature from the University of the Western Cape. He previously taught at the University of the Western Cape and served as a freelance journalist on the editorial boards of several publications. In the past he edited or co-edited books on Afrikaans literature, inter alia *Swart Afrikaanse skrywers*, *Die reis na Paternoster* and more recently *Die stukke wat ons sny* (Kwela, 1999). He presently manages OLM Communications, a company directed at the development of rural adult education and communications.

Acknowledgements

Making a book is always a collaborative venture. My appreciation goes to:

Annari van der Merwe whose enthusiasm for this book convinced me that it was possible and above all necessary;
Nazli Jacobs who worked long, frustrating hours to make it a reality;
Kayzuran Jaffer, Elza Miles and Crain Soudien for their in-depth contributions, for keeping to their deadlines and supporting the idea without reservation;
George Hallett without whose vast, precious collection of photographs this book would probably have been impossible;
Andrew Martin at the National English Literary Museum for his valuable assistance with the bibliography;
Jimi Matthews for going the extra mile and hunting down rare photographs between moving house and a demanding job;
Terry Matthews-Grove for being the custodian of their family's pictures;
Heindrich Wyngaard and Elza Miles for persuading Peter Clarke to share his dear photographs;
Julie-Anne Justus for taking a final, critical look at the manuscript;
Clive Hanekom and Erika Oosthuysen for stopping the gaps and keeping up the contact between all the different parties;
Carol-Ann Mohamed for coping with the intrusions in our household, for sharing my passion and for suggesting the title of this book;
The Tessa Sayle Agency and David Philip Publishers for permission to use the stories of Alex La Guma and Richard Rive; Naspers, the successors in right, for permission to reproduce 'Willy-Boy!' from *Drum*;
Our sponsors, the Arts & Culture Trust of the President and the National Arts Council, for keeping the cover price as affordable as possible.

The following pieces were published elsewhere:
'De man die zijn haar kort liet knippen' (in: *Stet* 3(2): 22-25);
'Winter shepherding' (in: *Plain Furniture*, 1991),
'Riva' (in: *Advance Retreat,* 1983);
'Nocturne' (in: *Quartet*, 1963);
'Willy-Boy!' (in: *Drum*, April 1954: 50-54);
'Azikwelwa' (in: *The Park and Other Stories*, 1983).

HEIN WILLEMSE
Somerset West
December 1999

1 — The Fall of Icarus
2 — Beyond the boundaries of human sight
3 — Between Earth & Moon
4 — In that dark house
5 — Their backyard
6 — Riddle
7 — Something quite startling
8 — The blind musician
9 — Reaching out
10 — He won't bite
11 — They lived there a long time ago
12 — The wanderers
13 — A barren place
14 — Woodgatherers
15 — Carrying water
16 — Burning grass
17 — Food for thought
18 — Give us this day
19 — Our daily bread
20 — Misunderstood
21 — Thirst conquers all
22 — Tryst
23 — Life goes on
24 — Sick humour
25 — We are the Roman soldiers
26 — Confidences
27 — Spitting flames
28 — Mending nets
29 — A simple meal
30 — Mask
31 — We're not afraid
32 — But why don't we get married?
33 — The eavesdropper
34 — I didn't mean it that way
35 — Lovers' quarrel
36 — Mine is the silent face
37 — A handful of thorns
38 — Nocturne
39 — Night flight
40 — The moon, passing, sees nothing
41 — Dij alweer tyd om op te staan
42 — The sun also rises
43 — Walking between reeds
44 — A small backyard
45 — Lines of flight
46 — The other side of the wall
47 — Today
48 — The window is open
49 — Ambition
50 — Someday I'm going to try to fly high
51 — Hold fast to dreams

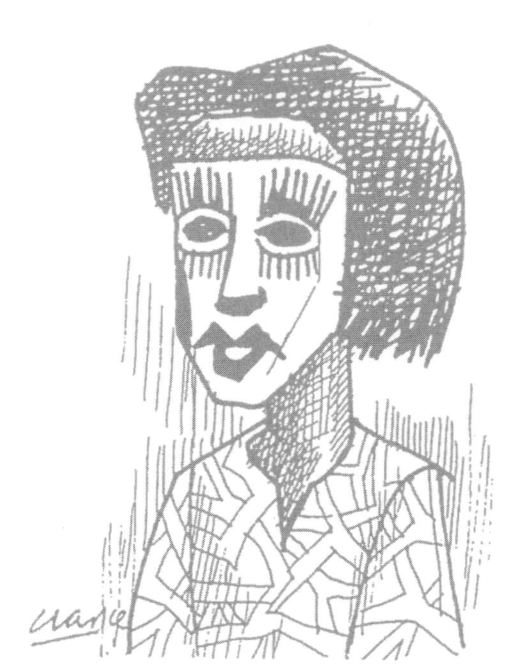

It's funny — in a way — how immediately behind a mask you've become transformed into another person. You are no longer who you used to be. For a moment you ask yourself who you are if you aren't who you are. The whole world, of which you were a part, now exists only on the outside of the mask. You, on the inside, behind the mask, have taken on the external face of another character.

You could play games with people & with yourself. You can go on questioning yourself about your true existence disguised as someone else — until in the end the whole thing becomes so complicated that you find yourself wondering why a stranger's mind & thoughts inhabit the face behind the mask.